Get the eBook FREE!

(PDF, ePub, Kindle, and liveBook all included)

We believe that once you buy a book from us, you should be able to read it in any format we have available. To get electronic versions of this book at no additional cost to you, purchase and then register this book at the Manning website.

Go to https://www.manning.com/freebook and follow the instructions to complete your pBook registration.

That's it!
Thanks from Manning!

Quantum
Computing in Action

JOHAN VOS

MANNING

SHELTER ISLAND

For online information and ordering of this and other Manning books, please visit
www.manning.com. The publisher offers discounts on this book when ordered in quantity.
For more information, please contact

  Special Sales Department
  Manning Publications Co.
  20 Baldwin Road
  PO Box 761
  Shelter Island, NY 11964
  Email: orders@manning.com

©2022 by Manning Publications Co. All rights reserved.

No part of this publication may be reproduced, stored in a retrieval system, or transmitted, in
any form or by means electronic, mechanical, photocopying, or otherwise, without prior written
permission of the publisher.

Many of the designations used by manufacturers and sellers to distinguish their products are
claimed as trademarks. Where those designations appear in the book, and Manning Publications
was aware of a trademark claim, the designations have been printed in initial caps or all caps.

⊖ Recognizing the importance of preserving what has been written, it is Manning's policy to have
the books we publish printed on acid-free paper, and we exert our best efforts to that end.
Recognizing also our responsibility to conserve the resources of our planet, Manning books
are printed on paper that is at least 15 percent recycled and processed without the use of
elemental chlorine.

The author and publisher have made every effort to ensure that the information in this book
was correct at press time. The author and publisher do not assume and hereby disclaim any
liability to any party for any loss, damage, or disruption caused by errors or omissions, whether
such errors or omissions result from negligence, accident, or any other cause, or from any usage
of the information herein.

Development editor:	Dustin Archibald
Technical development editors:	Jan Goyvaerts, Alain Couniot
Review editors:	Ivan Martinović, Adriana Sabo
Production editor:	Andy Marinkovich
Copy editor:	Tiffany Taylor
Proofreader:	Melody Dolab
Technical proofreader:	Nick Watts
Typesetter:	Dennis Dalinnik
Cover designer:	Marija Tudor

Ⅿ Manning Publications Co.
20 Baldwin Road
PO Box 761
Shelter Island, NY 11964

ISBN: 9781617296321
Printed and bound by CPI Group (UK) Ltd, Croydon, CR0 4YY

brief contents

contents

I started working on my PhD thesis in 1995 at Delft University of Technology in the Netherlands. My work was mainly focused on the acoustic wave equation, and I needed to combine theoretical models with experimental data, which, of course, required data processing and visualization. Around that same time, a new programming language named Java was unveiled. Several things made Java attractive for scientific work, including its portability to different platforms, which made it easy to create applications with a user interface and execute them on the various platforms I was working on.

However, it occurred to me that there was a large gap between the scientific world and the IT world. While researchers in science are typically trying to find answers to difficult questions, ITers are working on implementing the results of science and dealing with scalability, failover, code reuse, and functional or object-oriented development. Often, ideas and models created by scientists need to be implemented by ITers. Scientists should not worry about unit tests, while ITers should not have knowledge of the Standard Model of physics; but somehow, the handover between the two areas should be smooth.

I was privileged to be a frequent co-speaker with James Weaver, a long-time Java expert who became interested in quantum computing. Because of my background in science, he asked me to co-present on quantum computing.

If you need to do a presentation about something, it often helps if you know at least something about the subject. Even though I had worked on the acoustic wave equation, quantum computing was something different. Hence, I was forced to learn about quantum computing. The best way to learn something is to work with it; so, to understand quantum computing, I created a simulator of a quantum computer in Java, named Strange. Step by step, I added functionality to Strange, and by implementing it, I got a better idea of what quantum computing means for developers.

My general observation that scientists face different issues than developers turned out to be true for quantum computing. I believe that one of the significant challenges in quantum computing is finding ways for existing developers to use quantum computing without requiring them to understand the physics behind it. But it also works the other way: great algorithms that may lead to improvements in various areas often require a good understanding of modern IT development before they can be successful.

It is my belief that quantum computing can lead to major breakthroughs in several domains, including healthcare and security. With this book, I hope to explain to developers how you can benefit from quantum computing without having to become experts in quantum physics.

acknowledgments

Thank you to my family for their constant support and patience, which has provided me the opportunity to write this book.

I'd like to thank my colleagues at Gluon for their support, especially in many technical ways. Likewise, the continuous support and encouragement from the Java and JavaFX communities has motivated me to make this a book that is useful to developers.

Many thanks to the entire Manning team who helped me realize this book. In particular, I'd like to thank Mike Stephens, Andrew Waldron, Dustin Archibald, Alain Couniot, Jan Goyvaerts, and Candace Gillhoolley for your knowledge and guidance along the way. Thanks also to Tiffany Taylor, Keir Simpson, Melody Dolab, Meredith Mix, and Andy Marinkovich for guiding the book through production and for your commitment to making the book the best it can be.

For obvious reasons, the past couple of years have been intense. We are certainly living in a strange time in which scientific work has become more relevant than ever. Studying quantum computing forced me to dive deep into the mysteries of nature. I am very grateful to all the scientists who are working to understand and explain the fundamental concepts of nature, so that hardware and software developers can work on concrete benefits based on those new insights.

To all the reviewers: Aleksandr Erofeev, Alessandro Campeis, Antonio Magnaghi, Ariel Gamino, Carlos Aya-Moreno, David Lindelof, Evan Wallace, Flavio Diez, Girish Ahankari, Greg Wright, Gustavo Filipe Ramos Gomes, Harro Lissenberg, Jean-François Morin, Jens Christian Bredahl Madsen, Kelum Prabath Senanayake, Ken W. Alger,

Marcel van den Brink, Michael Wall, Nathan B Crocker, Patrick Regan, Potito Coluccelli, Rich Ward, Roberto Casadei, Satej Kumar Sahu, Vasile Boris, Vlad Navitski, William E. Wheeler, and William W. Fly; your suggestions helped make this a better book.

about this book

Most available resources about quantum computing are about either the mind-boggling physics that is used to enable quantum computing or the high-level consequences that can be expected when quantum computing becomes mainstream. In this book, we address the questions many developers ask: How will quantum computing affect my daily development, and how can I benefit from it? To answer this, we look at quantum computing from the perspective of a developer: we assume that hardware is or will be available (via native hardware or simulators), and we write code that is agnostic to marketing hype.

Who should read this book?

This book is written for developers who are interested in knowing whether and how they can benefit from quantum computing, now or in the future, or in general, what impact will quantum computing have on their work. The reader is not expected to know anything about quantum physics. The book explains the areas where quantum computing might lead to improvements and how developers can use it similarly to how they use modern hardware (such as GPUs) without knowing the internal details.

How this book is organized: a roadmap

This book contains three parts. Part 1 gives some basic information about quantum computing. Part 2 introduces the fundamental concepts that make quantum computing different from classical computing. Part 3 covers algorithms and code that are directly applicable to existing developers, and that use quantum advantages.

Part 1 introduces quantum computing:

- Chapter 1 discusses the importance of quantum computing without using buzz-words or participating in the hype. Down-to-earth developers often say, "Show me the code," and that is what this book does.
- In chapter 2, we build our first Java application (the typical HelloWorld application) using the Java-based quantum simulator Strange. The Strange quantum simulator shields developers from the low-level details of quantum computing yet provides APIs that internally benefit from quantum concepts.
- Chapter 3 introduces the qubit as the fundamental building block in quantum computing, similar to the regular bit in classical computing.

Part 2 introduces the relevant concepts of quantum computing:

- Chapter 4 discusses superposition, one of the core principles of quantum physics. This chapter contains code that allows you to use quantum superposition in your Java applications.
- Chapter 5 explains how different qubits can stay connected via quantum entanglement and what that means for applications.
- Chapter 6 introduces quantum networking as a specific application of quantum computing.

Part 3 deals with code examples and gradually introduces more complex algorithms that are useful to developers. Although the focus is on explaining the use of the algorithms, some explanations of the internals of the algorithms are given, as well, to help you work on similar algorithms:

- Chapter 7 explains the HelloWorld application shown in chapter 2. This simple application has no direct benefits (similar to HelloWorld applications in general) but shows how quantum applications can be created.
- Chapter 8 builds on chapters 6 and 7 and shows how a Java application can be created that uses quantum networking and provides a secure communication channel between two parties.
- Chapter 9 explains the Deutsch-Jozsa algorithm. This algorithm is easy to implement in Java with Strange, and it familiarizes you with some of the typical patterns in quantum computing.
- Chapter 10 discusses one of the most famous quantum algorithms: Grover's search algorithm. This algorithm has real practical implications for developers.
- Chapter 11 is about Shor's algorithm, which is probably the most popular existing quantum algorithm. This algorithm requires a combination of classical and quantum computing, and is therefore a great topic to conclude the book.

About the code

Throughout this book, many examples and demo applications are shown and referenced. Those applications use the Strange quantum simulator. Because Strange is an evolving project, the applications in the book are expected to evolve as well.

The examples in the book depend on the latest public released version of Strange that was available at the time of this writing. This version is tagged and uploaded to well-known repositories (such as Maven Central). Because of this, the code in this book is expected to work in the future, even if the Strange APIs change. A snapshot of the code examples in this book at the time of publication is available at https://www.manning.com/books/quantum-computing-in-action. You can also get executable snippets of code from the liveBook (online) version of this book at https://livebook.manning.com/book/quantum-computing-in-action. The evolving code repository for the examples is available at https://github.com/johanvos/quantumjava.

This book contains many examples of source code, both in numbered listings and in line with normal text. In both cases, source code is formatted in a `fixed-width font` `like this` to separate it from ordinary text. In many cases, the original source code has been reformatted; we've added line breaks and reworked indentation to accommodate the available page space in the book. In rare cases, even this was not enough, and listings include line-continuation markers. Additionally, comments in the source code have often been removed from the listings when the code is described in the text. Code annotations accompany many of the listings, highlighting important concepts.

liveBook discussion forum

Purchase of *Quantum Computing in Action* includes free access to liveBook, Manning's online reading platform. Using liveBook's exclusive discussion features, you can attach comments to the book globally or to specific sections or paragraphs. It's a snap to make notes for yourself, ask and answer technical questions, and receive help from the author and other users. To access the forum, go to https://livebook.manning.com/#!/book/quantum-computing-in-action/discussion. You can also learn more about Manning's forums and the rules of conduct at https://livebook.manning.com/#!/discussion.

Manning's commitment to our readers is to provide a venue where a meaningful dialogue between individual readers and between readers and the author can take place. It is not a commitment to any specific amount of participation on the part of the author, whose contribution to the forum remains voluntary (and unpaid). We suggest you try asking the author some challenging questions lest his interest stray! The forum and the archives of previous discussions will be accessible from the publisher's website for as long as the book is in print.

about the author

Johan Vos is a Java Champion, active OpenJDK contributor, project lead for OpenJDK Mobile, and co-spec lead for Open-JFX. Johan holds a PhD in applied physics from Delft University of Technology. He is a co-author of *ProJava FX2/8/9* and of *The Definitive Guide to Modern Java Clients with JavaFX*.

Johan has been active in the development of open source software. He was part of the Blackdown team that ported Java to Linux systems. Apart from his lead role in OpenJFX, he also contributes to a number of Java and JavaFX related libraries, including Strange and StrangeFX, which are discussed in this book.

about the cover illustration

The figure on the cover of *Quantum Computing in Action* is captioned "Femme Dalécarlie," or Dalecarlian woman. The illustration is taken from a collection of dress costumes from various countries by Jacques Grasset de Saint-Sauveur (1757–1810), titled *Costumes de Différents Pays*, published in France in 1797. Each illustration is finely drawn and colored by hand. The rich variety of Grasset de Saint-Sauveur's collection reminds us vividly of how culturally apart the world's towns and regions were just 200 years ago. Isolated from each other, people spoke different dialects and languages. In the streets or in the countryside, it was easy to identify where they lived and what their trade or station in life was just by their dress.

The way we dress has changed since then and the diversity by region, so rich at the time, has faded away. It is now hard to tell apart the inhabitants of different continents, let alone different towns, regions, or countries. Perhaps we have traded cultural diversity for a more varied personal life—certainly for a more varied and fast-paced technological life.

At a time when it is hard to tell one computer book from another, Manning celebrates the inventiveness and initiative of the computer business with book covers based on the rich diversity of regional life of two centuries ago, brought back to life by Grasset de Saint-Sauveur's pictures.

Part 1

Quantum computing introduction

Chances are good that you heard about quantum computing before you started reading this book. The core components of quantum computing are rooted in a mind-boggling scientific discipline called *quantum physics*. The potential consequences of quantum computing are huge and will have a deep impact on our society, including the areas of security, finance, and science. As a consequence, you can read about quantum computing in specialized scientific papers as well as in popular lifestyle magazines.

But what does quantum computing mean for developers involved in computing today? This book talks about the potential impact of quantum computing on the life of developers.

In part 1, we briefly explain the concepts and consequences of quantum computing so that we can narrow it down to the parts that are relevant to developers. We first introduce the basic ideas; then, in chapter 2, you learn how to create a simple Java application that uses quantum computing. We introduce the Strange library, which allows you to keep programming in Java (or other high-level languages) and still use quantum concepts. Chapter 3 introduces a fundamental unit of quantum computing: the qubit.

Evolution, revolution, or hype?

This chapter covers

- Setting the expectations for quantum computing
- Understanding what kinds of problems are suited for quantum computers
- Options for Java developers to work with quantum computing

The number of books, articles, and blog posts about quantum computing is constantly increasing. Even if you read only basic information about quantum computing (QC), it is clear that this is not just an incremental enhancement of classical computing. The core concepts of QC are fundamentally different, and its application area is also different. In some areas, quantum computers are expected to be able to address problems that classical computers can't.

Furthermore, because QC is based on quantum physics, there is often some mystery associated with it. Quantum physics is not the simplest part of physics, and some aspects of quantum physics are extremely difficult to understand.

Thus QC is often pictured as a mysterious new way of working with data that will drastically change the world. The latter is true, at least based on what we know at this moment. Many analysts believe it will take between 5 and 10 years before real, useful QC is possible, and most believe the impact will be huge.

In this book, we try to stay close to reality. We want to explain to existing and new Java developers how you can use QC in your existing and new applications. As we will show, QC indeed has a huge impact on a number of important issues in the IT industry. We will also explain why it is essential to prepare for the arrival of real quantum computers and how you can do that using Java and your favorite toolset (such as your IDE and build tools). Although it is true that real quantum hardware is not yet available on a wide scale, developers should realize that building software using QC takes time as well. Thanks to quantum simulators and early prototypes, nothing is preventing you from starting to explore QC in your projects today. Doing so will increase the chances that your software will be ready by the time the hardware is available.

1.1 Expectation management

The potential impact of QC is enormous. Researchers are still trying to estimate the impact, but at least in theory, there might be significant consequences for the IT industry, security, healthcare, and scientific research and thus for mankind in general. Because of this substantial impact, a quantum computer is often incorrectly pictured as a huge classical computer. This is not true, and to be able to see the relevance of QC, one must understand why QC is so fundamentally different from classical computing. It has to be stressed that there are still many roadblocks that need to be addressed before the big ambitions can be realized.

> **Managing expectations**
> - Don't assume QC will fix everything.
> - QC is fundamentally different from classical computing.
> - QC is mainly suitable for complex problems.
> - QC and classical computers will have to work together.
> - The hardware is complex and not in our scope.
> - Although the hardware is not yet crystallized, we can already work on software, thanks to quantum simulators and early prototypes.

The potential success of QC depends on various factors that can be put into two categories:

- *Hardware*—New and complex hardware is needed.
- *Software*—To use the capabilities offered by quantum hardware, dedicated software needs to be developed.

1.1.1 Hardware

A number of uncertainties prevent wide-scale use of QC at this moment. In addition, it should be stressed that quantum computers will not fix every problem.

The hardware needed for QC is by no means ready for mass production. Creating quantum hardware in the form of a quantum computer or a quantum coprocessor is extremely challenging.

The core principles of QC, which we explain in this book, are based on the core principles of quantum mechanics. Quantum mechanics studies the fundamental particles of nature. It is generally considered to be one of the most challenging aspects of physics, and it is still evolving. Some of the world's brightest physicists, including Albert Einstein, Max Planck, and Ludwig Boltzmann, have worked on the theory of quantum mechanics. But a significant problem when doing research in quantum mechanics is that it is often extremely difficult to check whether the theory matches the reality. It is no less than amazing that theories were created predicting the existence of some particles that had not yet been observed. Observing the smallest elements of nature and their behavior requires special hardware.

It is already difficult to investigate and manipulate quantum effects in closed lab environments. Using those quantum effects in a controllable way in real-world situations is an even more significant challenge.

Many experimental quantum computers that exist today are based on the principles of superconducting and operate at a very low temperature (such as 10 millikelvin, or close to –273 degrees Celsius). This has some practical restrictions that are not encountered with classical computers operating at room temperature.

In this book, we make an abstraction of the hardware. As we discuss later, there is no reason for software developers to wait until the hardware is ready before they start thinking about software algorithms that should eventually run on quantum hardware. The principles of QC are understood and can be simulated via quantum computer simulators. It is expected that quantum software written for quantum computer simulators will also work on real quantum computers, provided the core quantum concepts are similar.

A few words about hardware

Clearly, the hardware problem isn't solved, and it is generally expected to be several years before hardware is available that can be used to solve problems that are currently impossible to solve with classical computing. The hardware solution needs to support a large number of reliable *qubits* (the fundamental concept of QC, discussed more later in the chapter) that are available for a reasonable amount of time and can be controlled by classical computers.

At the time of this writing, a number of early quantum computer prototypes exist. IBM has a 5-qubit quantum computer available for public use through a cloud interface and quantum computer, with more qubits in the research labs and for clients. Google has a quantum processor named Bristlecone that contains 72 qubits. Specialized companies like D-Wave and Rigetti have QC prototypes as well.

We need to mention that it is not trivial to compare different quantum computers. At first sight, the number of qubits may sound like the most important criterion, but it can be misleading. One of the significant difficulties when building quantum computers is keeping the quantum states as long as possible. The slightest disturbance can destroy the quantum states, and therefore quantum computers are subject to errors that need to be corrected.

1.1.2   Software

Although there are areas where QC could, in theory, lead to huge breakthroughs, it is generally agreed that quantum computers or quantum processors can take over some tasks from classical computers, but they won't replace classical computers. The problems that can be solved using QC do not differ from problems that today are tackled using classical computers. However, because QC uses a completely different underlying approach, the problems can be handled in a completely different way; and for a given set of problems, a dramatic increase in performance can be achieved using QC. As a consequence, quantum computers should be able to solve problems that today are not practically solvable because there are not enough computing resources to solve them—for example, to simulate chemical reactions, optimization problems, or integer factorization.

A few words on time complexity

The complexity of algorithms is often expressed as the *time complexity*. In general, algorithms take longer to complete when the amount of input data increases. Problems are often put into different categories that indicate *how much harder* the problem becomes when the input is larger. This is often expressed in terms of Big O notation (see https://web.mit.edu/16.070/www/lecture/big_o.pdf for a definition).

Let's assume that there are *n* items of input data. If each item requires a fixed number of steps, the total time for the algorithm to complete is linear with *n*. In this case, the algorithm is said to take *linear time*.

Many algorithms are more complex than this. When the number of input items increases, the total number of steps required may grow with the square of *n*, n^2, or even with the kth power of *n*, n^k, for a fixed value of *k*. In this case, the algorithm is said to take *polynomial time*.

Some algorithms are even harder to solve when the number of input items grows. If no known algorithm can solve a problem in polynomial time, we say the algorithm takes *nonpolynomial time*. Algorithms are said to take *exponential time* if they require exponentially more steps when *n* increases. When a problem requires 2^n steps, it is clear that the complexity increases drastically because *n* is in the exponent of the number of steps. In another example, which we discuss later, the number of required steps is $e^{\sqrt{(64/9)b(\log b)^2}}$ with *b* the number of bits, hence the problem is also said to be of exponential complexity.

It turns out that quantum computers will be most helpful for tackling problems that cannot be solved by classical computers in polynomial time but that *can* be solved by a quantum computer in polynomial time. A common example is integer factorization, which is a common operation in encryption (such as the widely used cryptosystem RSA), or *breaking* encryption, to be more precise. The basic idea in integer factorization is to decompose a number into prime numbers that, when multiplied together, yield the original number: for example, 15 = 3 × 5. Although this is easy to do without a computer, you can imagine that a computer is helpful when the numbers become bigger, as in $146963 = 281 \times 523$.

The larger the number we want to factor, the longer it will take to find the solution. This is the basis of many security algorithms. They use the idea that it is close to impossible to factor a number consisting of 1,024 bits. It can be shown that the time required to solve this problem is on the order of

$$e\sqrt{(64/9)b(\log b)^2}$$

Equation 1.1

where b is the number of bits in the original number. The e at the beginning of this equation is the important part: in short, it means that by making b larger, the time required to factor the number becomes exponentially larger. The diagram in figure 1.1 shows the time it takes to factor a number with b bits.

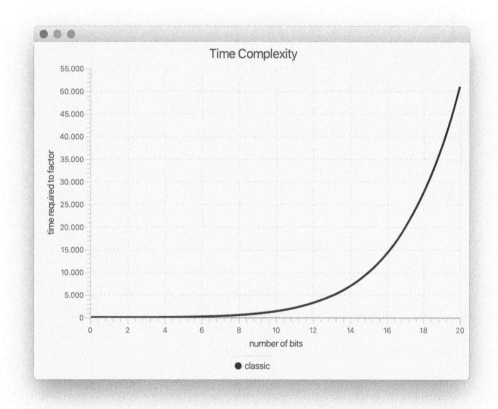

Figure 1.1   Time grows exponentially with the number of bits.

Note that the absolute time is not relevant. Even if the fastest existing computers are used, adding a single bit makes a huge difference.

This problem is said to be nonpolynomial, as no known classical algorithm can solve the problem in polynomial time. Hence, by increasing the number of bits, it is almost impossible for classical computers to find a solution to this problem.

However, this same problem can be handled by a quantum algorithm in polynomial time. As we will show in chapter 11, using Shor's algorithm, the time to solve this problem using a quantum computer is on the order of b^3.

To show what that means, we overlay the required time using a quantum algorithm on a quantum computer over the required time using a classical algorithm on a classical computer. This is illustrated in figure 1.2.

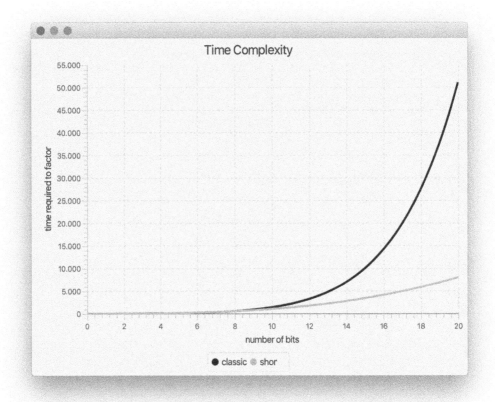

Figure 1.2   Polynomial time versus exponential time

Starting from a number of bits, the quantum computer will be much faster than the classical computer. Moreover, the greater the number of bits, the greater the difference. This is because the required time for solving the problem on a classical computer increases exponentially when the amount of bits grows, whereas the same increase in bits will cause only a polynomial increase for the quantum algorithm.

These kinds of problems are said to be *polynomial in quantum*. They are the ones that it makes the most sense for quantum computers to deal with.

NOTE Shor's algorithm is one of the most popular QC algorithms. There are a few reasons we discuss it only in chapter 11, though. First, to have a reasonable understanding of how the algorithm works, you must have a handle on the foundations of QC. Second, with the current state of the hardware, and even with fast innovations, most experts believe we are still many years from the moment when a quantum computer will be able to factor a reasonably sized key in a practical amount of time. You shouldn't wait to think about Shor's algorithm until it is too late, but on the other hand, we don't want to give you false expectations. Finally, although the impact of Shor's algorithm can be huge, there are other areas where QC can make an enormous difference, including healthcare, chemistry, and optimization problems.

1.1.3 Algorithms

Shor's algorithm is a great example of a computational problem that is hard to solve on a classical computer (nonpolynomial in time) and relatively easy to solve on a quantum computer (polynomial in time). Where does the difference come from? As we discuss in chapter 11, Shor's algorithm transforms the problem of integer factorization into the problem of finding the periodicity of a function, such as finding the value p for which the function evaluation $f(x + p) = f(x)$ for all possible values of x. This problem is still hard to solve on a classical computer, but it is relatively easy to resolve on a quantum computer.

Most algorithms that are known today to be suitable for quantum computers are based on the same principle: transform the original problem into a problem space that is easy to solve using quantum computers. The classic approach is shown in figure 1.3. The best known algorithm is applied to the problem, and the result is obtained.

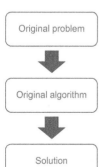

Figure 1.3 Typical approach: solving a problem on a classical computer

If we can somehow transform the original problem into a different problem that can be handled easily by a quantum computer, we can expect a performance improvement. This is shown in figure 1.4.

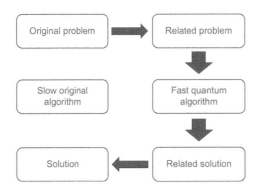

Figure 1.4   Transforming a problem to an area where quantum computers can make a significant difference

Note that we have to consider the cost of transforming the original problem into a different problem, and vice versa, for the final result. However, when talking about computation-intensive algorithms, this cost should be negligible.

> **NOTE**   When you see a quantum algorithm being explained, you may wonder why it seems to take a detour from the original problem. Quantum computers are capable of solving particular problems quickly, so moving an original problem to one of those particular problems allows for a much faster algorithm using QC.

Coming up with those algorithms often requires a deep mathematical background. Typically, developers do not create new quantum algorithms for applications that will benefit from quantum computers—they will use existing algorithms. However, developers who know the basics of quantum algorithms, why they are faster, and how to use them, will have an advantage.

1.1.4   Why start with QC today?

Programmers sometimes wonder why they should start learning QC when real, usable quantum computers are still years away. You have to realize, though, that writing software that involves QC is different from writing classical software. Although it is expected that there will be libraries that make it convenient for developers to use quantum computers, those libraries have to be written; and even then, it will require skills and knowledge to use the best tools for a particular project.

Any developer working on a project that requires encryption or secure communication can benefit from learning QC. Some existing classical encryption algorithms will become insecure when quantum computers are available. It would be a bad idea to wait until the first time a quantum computer breaks encryption before hardening the encryption software. On the contrary, you want to be prepared before the hardware is available. Because QC is really disruptive, it can be expected that most developers will need more time to learn QC than they typically need when using a new library.

Although we do not want to scare you with doom scenarios, it is important to understand that there is no need for a wide base of quantum computers to be installed before existing encryption techniques can be compromised. Cyberattacks do not require a large number of computers and can be carried out from anywhere.

> **TIP** There is a reasonable chance that some existing communication protocols and encryption techniques will be vulnerable once quantum computers become more powerful. It is essential for developers to understand what kind of software might be vulnerable and how to address this issue. This is not something that can be done overnight, so it is recommended that you start looking into this sooner rather than later.

The software examples we discuss in this book are basic applications. They illustrate the core principles of QC, and they make it clear what kind of problems can benefit from QC. But the gap between basic algorithms and fully functional software is significant. Hence, although it will be years before the hardware is ready, developers have to understand that it will probably also take a long time before they have optimized their software projects to use QC as much as possible, where applicable.

In the middle of the previous century, when the first digital computers were built, software languages needed to be created as well. The difference today is that we can use classical computers to simulate quantum computers. We can work on software for quantum computers without having access to a quantum computer.

This is an important benefit, and it highlights the importance of quantum simulators. Developers who start looking into QC today using simulators will have a huge advantage over other developers when quantum hardware becomes more widely available.

1.2 The disruptive parts of QC: Getting closer to nature

One of the main application areas of QC is anything related to physics. For a long time, scientists have been trying to understand the core concepts of modern physics by simulating the concepts on classical computers. However, because the most elementary particles of nature do not follow classic laws, it is complex to simulate them on classical computers. Using those quantum particles and their laws as the cornerstones of quantum computers makes it much easier to tackle those problems.

> **The nature of bits**
>
> The notion of a *bit* often seems to correspond with the smallest piece of information that can exist. Information such as music, books, videos, and functionality (applications) can be expressed in a sequence of bits. As we briefly explain later in this chapter, nature itself, including all matter that is contained in the universe, cannot be described purely as a sequence of 0s and 1s. At a small scale, particles behave differently, as rather successfully described by quantum mechanics. The fundamental building blocks of nature are not 0s and 1s but a set of elementary particles with different properties, and QC uses those particles and their properties.

1.2.1   *Evolutions in classical computers*

In recent decades, computers have become more powerful. Improvements in performance are often realized because of increases in

- Computer memory
- Processor performance
- Number of processors in a computer

These improvements typically lead to incremental, linear benefits. The potential performance gains that are expected to be realized using quantum computers have nothing to do with these improvements. A quantum computer is not a classical computer with smaller chips, more memory, or faster communication; instead, QC starts with a completely different fundamental concept: the *qubit*. We discuss the qubit in detail in chapter 3, but because it is a crucial concept, we introduce it here.

1.2.2   *Revolution in quantum computers*

In a classical computer, a bit is the smallest piece of information, and it can be either 0 or 1. Different operations are possible on those bits, and bits can be altered or combined. At any moment, though, all bits in a computer are in a clear state: 0 or 1. The physical analogy of a classical bit is related to current. A 0 state corresponds with no current, and a 1 state corresponds with current. All existing classical software development is based on the manipulation of those bits. Using combinations of bits and applying gate operations of bits is the essence of classical software development. We discuss this in more detail in chapter 3.

In QC, the fundamental concept is a qubit. Similar to a classical bit, a qubit can hold the values 0 and 1. But the disruptive difference is that the value of a qubit can be a combination of the values 0 and 1. When people first hear about this, they are often confused. It sounds artificial to have the qubit, the elementary component of quantum computing, be more complex than the elementary component of classical computing, the bit. It turns out, however, that a qubit is closer to the fundamental concepts of nature than the classical bit.

1.2.3   *Quantum physics*

As its name implies, the foundation of QC comes from quantum physics. In quantum physics, the smallest particles, their behavior, and their interactions are investigated. It turns out that some of those particles have properties with interesting characteristics. For example, an electron has a property called *spin*, which can take two values: up and down. The interesting thing is that the spin of an electron can, at a given moment, be in a so-called *superposition* of these two values. This is a hard-to-understand physical phenomenon, and it comes down to the easier-to-understand mathematical formula where the spin can be a linear combination of the up value and the down value—with some restrictions that we talk about in chapter 4.

The spin of an electron is one sample of a physical phenomenon that allows for a property to be in more than one state at the same moment. In QC, the qubit is realized by this physical phenomenon. As a consequence, the qubit is extremely close to the reality of quantum physics. The physical realization of a qubit is a real-world concept. Therefore, QC is often said to be close to how nature works.

One of the goals of QC is to take advantage of physical phenomena that happen at the scale of the smallest particles. Hence, QC is more "natural," and although it seems much more complex than classical computing at first sight, it can be argued that it is, on the contrary much simpler, as it requires fewer artificial constructs.

Understanding quantum phenomena is one thing; being able to manipulate them is another. It took lots of time and resources to be able to prove that quantum phenomena exist. To allow computational representations on qubits, we must be able to manipulate the elementary parts. Although this is done in large scientific research centers, it is still difficult to do in a typical computing environment.

1.3 *Hybrid computing*

We already mentioned that quantum computers are excellent for dealing with specific problems, but not for all kinds of problems. Therefore, the best results can probably be achieved using a new form of hybrid computing, where a quantum system solves part of a problem and a classical computer solves the rest.

Actually, this approach is not entirely new. A similar pattern is already being used in most modern computer systems, where the central processing unit (CPU) is accompanied by a graphics processing unit (GPU). GPUs are good for some tasks (such as doing vector operations that are needed in graphical or deep learning applications), but not all tasks. Many modern UI frameworks, including JavaFX, use the availability of both CPUs and GPUs and optimize the tasks they have to perform by delegating parts of the work to the CPU and other parts to the GPU, as shown in figure 1.5.

The idea of using different coprocessors for different tasks can be extended to QC. In the ideal scenario, a software application delegates some tasks to a CPU, other tasks to a GPU, and still other tasks to a quantum processing unit (QPU), as shown in figure 1.6.

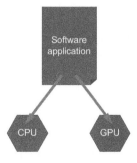

Figure 1.5   CPU and GPU sharing work

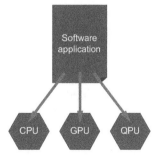

Figure 1.6   CPU, GPU, and QPU sharing work

The best results can be achieved when the best tools are used for a specific job. In this case, it means the software application should use the GPU for vector computations, the QPU for algorithms that are slow on classical systems but fast on quantum systems, and the CPU for everything that doesn't benefit from either the GPU or the QPU.

If every end application had to judge what parts should be delegated to which processor, the job of a software developer would be extremely difficult. We expect, though, that frameworks and libraries will provide help and abstract this problem away from the end developer.

If you are using the JavaFX APIs to create user interfaces in Java, you don't have to worry about what parts are executed on the GPU and what parts are executed on the CPU. The internal implementations of the JavaFX API do that for you. The JavaFX framework detects the information about the GPU and delegates work to it. Although it is still possible for developers to directly access either the CPU or the GPU, this is typically something that high-level languages like Java shield us from.

In figure 1.6, we oversimplified the QPU. Whereas a GPU easily fits in modern servers, desktop systems, and mobile and embedded devices, providing a quantum processor may be trickier due to the specific requirements for quantum effects to be manipulated in a controlled, noise-free environment (such as hardware that is maintained close to absolute zero in temperature). It is possible that, at least initially, most of the real QC resources will be available via specific cloud servers instead of via coprocessors on embedded chips. The principles stay the same, though, because the end software application can benefit from libraries splitting the complex tasks and delegating some tasks to a quantum system that is accessible via a cloud service, as shown in figure 1.7.

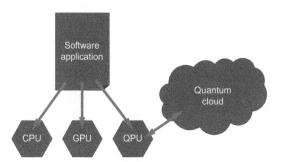

Figure 1.7   Quantum calculations relayed to cloud

1.4   *Abstracting software for quantum computers*

Although real quantum computers already exist, as we mentioned before, they are by no means ready for mass production. The steps in recent years toward creating hardware for QC are tremendous, but there is still a lot of uncertainty about implementing a real, useful quantum computer or quantum processor. However, this is not a reason to not start working on the software. We learned a lot from classical hardware and the software built on top of it. The high-level programming languages that have been created in the past decades allow software developers to create applications in a convenient way, such that they do not have to worry about or even understand the underlying hardware. Java, being a high-level programming language, is particularly good at making abstraction of the underlying low-level software and hardware. Ultimately, when a Java application is executed, low-level, hardware-specific instructions are executed. Depending on the hardware being used, specific machine instructions for different processors with different architectures are used.

Hardware for classical computers is still evolving. Software is evolving as well. Most of the changes in the Java language, however, are not related to hardware changes. The decoupling of hardware and software evolutions allows for much faster innovation. There are a number of areas where improvements in hardware ultimately lead to more specific evolutions in software, but for most developers, hardware and software can be decoupled. Figure 1.8 shows how a Java application ultimately results in operations on hardware, but different abstraction layers shield the real hardware (and the evolutions in the hardware) from the end application.

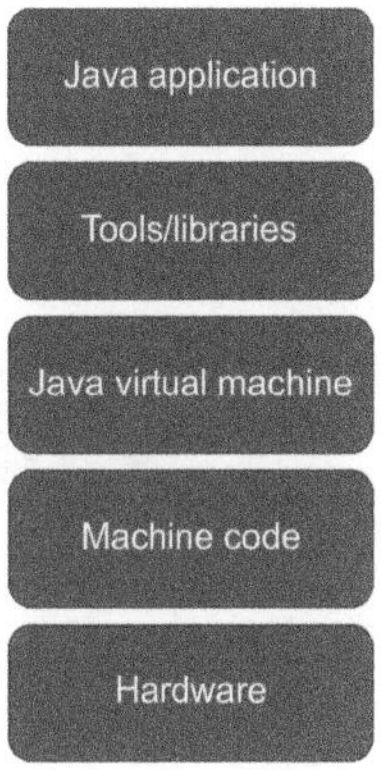

In large part, software for QC can be decoupled from hardware evolution. Although the hardware implementation details are far from certain, the general principles are becoming clear; we discuss them in chapters 2 through 5. Software development can be based on those general principles. Similar to how a classical software

| Java application |
| Tools/libraries |
| Java virtual machine |
| Machine code |
| Hardware |

Figure 1.8 Classic software stack

developer doesn't have to worry about how transistors (a low-level building block for classical computers) are combined on a single chip, a developer of quantum software does not have to think about the physical representation of a qubit. As long as the quantum software conforms with and exploits the general principles, it will be usable on real quantum computers or quantum processors when they become available.

A significant benefit while developing software for quantum computers is the availability of classical computers. The behavior of quantum hardware can be simulated via classical software: this is a huge advantage because it implies that quantum software can be tested today using a quantum simulator written in classical software on a classical computer. Obviously, there are major differences between a quantum computer simulator and a real hardware quantum computer—almost by definition, a typical quantum algorithm will execute much faster on a quantum computer than on a quantum simulator. But from a functional point, the results should be the same.

Apart from real quantum computers and quantum computer simulators, cloud services should be taken into account. By delegating work to a cloud service, an application doesn't even know whether it is running on a simulator or a real quantum computer. The cloud provider can update its service from a simulator to a real quantum computer. The results should be obtained much faster when a real quantum computer is used, but they should not be different from when a simulator is used.

These options are combined in figure 1.9: it shows that Java applications can use libraries that provide quantum APIs. The implementation of these libraries can do the work on a real quantum computer, use a quantum computer simulator, or delegate the work to the cloud. For the end application, the results should be similar. Also, when the hardware topology changes in the future (a quantum coprocessor is added, for example), the end application won't have to be modified. The library will be updated, but the top-level APIs should not be affected.

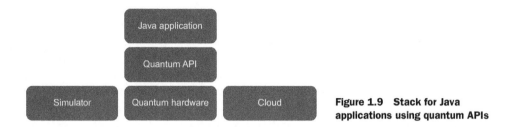

Figure 1.9   Stack for Java applications using quantum APIs

As we already discussed, quantum algorithms are particularly useful when dealing with problems that require nonpolynomial (exponential) scaling with classical computers. A typical example is integer factorization. A quantum computer will be capable of decomposing large integers into their prime factors (at least providing part of the algorithm), something that is not possible today even with all the computing power in the world combined. As a consequence, a quantum computer simulator written in classical software will not be able to factor those large numbers.

The same quantum algorithm can also, of course, factor small integers. Quantum simulators can thus be used to factor small integers. The quantum algorithm can be created, tested, and optimized using small numbers on a quantum simulator. Whenever the hardware becomes ready for it, that same algorithm can be used to factor numbers on real hardware. (A 5-qubit system has already factored 21.) As the quantum hardware improves (more qubits are added or fewer errors occur), the algorithm will allow larger numbers to be factorized.

In summary, the principles of quantum computers can be mimicked in software simulators running on classical computers. Developers can take advantage of this and run quantum experiments on those simulators. Throughout this book, we use an open source quantum simulator written in Java that works both locally on your laptop/desktop as well as in cloud environments. You don't have to worry about where the code is being executed.

We explain some of the QC principles by looking at the source code of the algorithms in the library. Although this is not strictly needed to write applications using QC, it will give you more insight into how and when quantum algorithms may lead to a real advantage.

1.5 From quantum to computing or from computing to quantum

There are several ways to use QC in IT projects, and different approaches are under investigation in parallel. Roughly speaking, there are two extreme points and lots of room for middle ground. Those options are shown in figure 1.10.

Figure 1.10 Finding the balance between a new, dedicated quantum language and existing languages

On one end of the spectrum is the idea of using a specific software language that directly corresponds to the physical characteristics of QC. An example is Q#, the quantum software language created by Microsoft. This approach has clear pros and cons:

- *Pro*—By building directly on top of quantum physical concepts, it is much easier to use these concepts in particular applications.
- *Con*—Many languages are already available to developers, and by not using an existing one, the hurdle to learn becomes bigger. Also, since most applications require a combination of quantum and classical computing, a dedicated quantum language alone is not sufficient for a project.

The other side of the spectrum sticks with existing languages and hides all quantum characteristics from the developer. This has pros and cons as well:

- *Pro*—Developers do not need to learn a new language, as their software will "magically" use the best implementation, be it classic, quantum, or hybrid.
- *Con*—The word "magically" in the previous sentence is hard to realize. It is already difficult to optimize a specific language to a specific use case (which just-in-time compilers typically do), but software that decides on the fly whether a quantum or classical routine should be used is even trickier.

In this book, we choose the middle ground. The Strange quantum simulator that we introduce in the next chapter allows Java developers to create applications that use QC. You do not need to learn a new language, but if you want to, you can create your own algorithms that directly benefit from quantum characteristics.

In the first part of this book, we mainly discuss the characteristics of quantum physics that make QC fundamentally different from classical computing. We use the low-level code in Strange to illustrate those concepts.

TY 411 6384

In the second part, we talk about how the fundamental concepts relate to (Java) code. This brings us a step closer to the "use an existing language" approach.

Finally, in the third part, the focus is on quantum algorithms that can be implemented in libraries and used by developers. This approach is shown in figure 1.11.

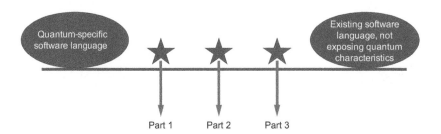

Figure 1.11   How the parts of this book correspond to the different approaches for developing quantum computing software

Ultimately, we expect that software platforms will become smarter and smarter and be able to find the optimal approach to implement a specific function using a combination of classical and QC. This will take a long time, though; in the meantime, knowledge of QC and its characteristics is definitely a competitive advantage for software developers.

Summary

- Quantum computing is not just an upgrade of classical computing.
- QC uses the fundamental core concepts of physics and is therefore more real than classical computing.
- It may be many years before hardware is powerful enough to gain the full benefits of QC.
- Quantum computers are expected to generate a massive speed-up in the execution of some algorithms that are practically impossible to solve in the classic way, but they won't replace classical computers because they are only good at particular (but important) tasks.
- Software development at a high level should not worry about the low-level quantum details.
- Software developers should be aware that moving some parts of an algorithm to a different area may lead to huge improvements.

"Hello World,"
quantum computing style
2

This chapter covers

- Introducing Strange, a quantum computing library in Java
- Trying the high-level and low-level APIs in Strange
- A basic visualization of a quantum circuit

This chapter introduces Strange, an open source quantum computing project including a quantum simulator and a library that exposes a Java API you can use in regular Java applications. Throughout the book, we discuss concepts of quantum computing (QC) and their relevance to Java developers, and we show how Java developers can benefit from these concepts.

Strange contains a pure Java implementation of the required quantum concepts. When discussing the concepts, we point you to the relevant code implementation of the concept in Strange. This is part of a low-level API.

Most Java developers will not have to deal with low-level quantum concepts. However, some may benefit from algorithms that take advantage of these concepts. For this group, Strange provide a set of high-level algorithms that can be used in regular Java applications. These algorithms are what we call the *high-level Java API*.

2.1   *Introducing Strange*

Figure 2.1 shows a high-level overview of the components of Strange. The Java Quantum API provides an implementation for a number of typical quantum algorithms. These are the high-level algorithms that you can use in regular Java applications. No knowledge of QC is required to use them.

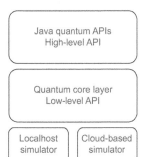

Figure 2.1   High-level overview of the Strange architecture

The quantum core layer contains the low-level API, which provides deeper access to the real quantum aspects. The high-level API does not contain a concept specific to QC, but its implementation uses the low-level quantum core layer. Whereas the high-level API shields you from the quantum concepts, the low-level API exposes those concepts to you.

The high-level API provides you with a ready-to-use interface to quantum algorithms. By using it, you can benefit from the gains realized by QC. However, if you want to be able to create your own algorithms or modify existing algorithms, the low-level API is the starting point.

2.2   *Running a first demo with Strange*

This book comes with a repository containing a number of examples that use Strange. You can find this repository on GitHub at https://github.com/johanvos/quantumjava. The requirements and instructions for running the examples are explained in appendix A. The first demo example is located in the hellostrange folder in the ch02 directory.

> **NOTE**   Keep in mind that all our examples require Java 11 or newer. In appendix A, you can find instructions for installing the required Java software.

Building and running the examples can be done using the Gradle build tool as well as the Maven build tool. The examples contain a build.gradle file that allows them to be handled by Gradle and a pom.xml file that allows them to be handled by Maven.

We recommend that you run the examples using your favorite IDE (IntelliJ, Eclipse, or NetBeans). The instructions for how to run Java applications are different for each IDE. In this book, we use the Gradle and Maven build systems from the command line; using the provided Gradle and Maven configuration files implicitly makes sure that all required code dependencies are downloaded. The code is compiled and executed as illustrated in figure 2.2.

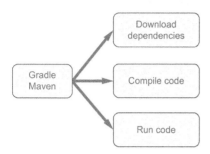

Figure 2.2   Using Gradle or Maven to run Java applications

NOTE   When running the examples using the command-line interface, we take a slightly different approach between Maven and Gradle. When using Maven, you need to cd into the example-specific directory (that contains a pom.xml file). When using Gradle, you stay at the root level (which contains a build .gradle file), and you run the examples by providing the chapter and project name. We will explain this with the HelloStrange example.

If you want to use the Maven build system to run the basic HelloStrange application, you need to move into the ch02/hellostrange directory. There, execute

```
mvn clean javafx:run
```

which will result in output similar to the following:

```
mvn clean javafx:run
[INFO] Scanning for projects...
[INFO]
[INFO] ------------------------------------------------------------------------
[INFO] Building hellostrange 1.0-SNAPSHOT
[INFO] ------------------------------------------------------------------------
[INFO]
[INFO] --- maven-clean-plugin:2.5:clean (default-clean) @ helloquantum ---
[INFO] Deleting /home/johan/quantumcomputing/manning/public/quantumjava/ch02
/hellostrange/target
[INFO]
[INFO] >>> javafx-maven-plugin:0.0.6:run (default-cli) > process-classes @ h
elloquantum >>>
[INFO]
[INFO] --- maven-resources-plugin:2.6:resources (default-resources) @ helloq
uantum ---
[INFO] Using 'UTF-8' encoding to copy filtered resources.
```

KE 237 1860

```
[INFO] skip non existing resourceDirectory /home/johan/quantumcomputing/mann
ing/public/quantumjava/ch02/hellostrange/src/main/resources
[INFO]
[INFO] --- maven-compiler-plugin:3.1:compile (default-compile) @ helloquantu
m ---
[INFO] Changes detected - recompiling the module!
[INFO] Compiling 1 source file to /home/johan/quantumcomputing/manning/publi
c/quantumjava/ch02/hellostrange/target/classes
[INFO]
[INFO] <<< javafx-maven-plugin:0.0.6:run (default-cli) < process-classes @ h
elloquantum <<<
[INFO]
[INFO] --- javafx-maven-plugin:0.0.6:run (default-cli) @ helloquantum ---
[INFO] Toolchain in javafx-maven-plugin null
Using high-level Strange API to generate random bits
\--------------------------------------------------
Generate one random bit, which can be 0 or 1. Result = 1
Generated 10000 random bits, 4967 of them were 0, and 5033 were 1.
[INFO] ------------------------------------------------------------------------
[INFO] BUILD SUCCESS
[INFO] ------------------------------------------------------------------------
[INFO] Total time: 1.790 s
[INFO] Finished at: 2021-08-18T14:52:58+02:00
[INFO] Final Memory: 13M/54M
[INFO] ------------------------------------------------------------------------
```

> **NOTE** Experienced Maven users might wonder why we don't simply use `mvn exec:java`, which would use Maven's Java plugin. We recommend using `mvn javafx:run` because that involves the Maven JavaFX plugin. This plugin allows us to run standard Java applications as well as JavaFX applications. We use the latter in a number of examples where a user interface is generated. Rather than switching between the Java and JavaFX plugins, it is more convenient to always invoke the JavaFX plugin, even if it is not strictly needed when we run Java applications without a user interface.

When using Gradle, you run Gradle from the root directory and need to pass the name of the project. You can inspect the contents of the settings.gradle file, which contains the name of all projects in the repository.

Running the example in Linux and macOS is done via

```
./gradlew ch02:hellostrange:run
```

If you are using Windows, you have to run it as follows:

```
gradlew.bat ch02:hellostrange:run
```

Both commands will result in the following output:

```
> Task :run
Using high-level Strange API to generate random bits
--------------------------------------------------
```

```
Generate one random bit, which can be 0 or 1. Result = 1
Generated 10000 random bits, 4961 of them were 0, and 5039 were 1.

BUILD SUCCESSFUL in 3s
```

> **NOTE** Gradle may add more output, especially if this is the first time you're using this Gradle version or when required dependencies are not yet installed on your system.

Congratulations! You just executed a program that involves quantum computing.

2.3 Inspecting the code for HelloStrange

To understand the output of the HelloStrange demo application, we recommend that you look at the source code for the application. Before we investigate the Java code, we have to look at the build.gradle and pom.xml files in the root directory of the example. The build.gradle file contains the instructions that allow Gradle to compile the Java classes, download and install dependencies, and run the application. The pom.xml file has the same goals, allowing us to deal with the application using Maven.

2.3.1 The build procedures

Typically, you shouldn't worry about the structure of the build.gradle file or the pom.xml file unless you plan to create applications or projects yourself. In that case, you can find great resources about using Gradle and Maven online.

BUILDING WITH MAVEN

The pom.xml file that contains the instructions for Maven to compile and run the application is shown in the following listing.

> **Listing 2.1 pom.xml file for the HelloStrange example**

```
<project xmlns="http://maven.apache.org/POM/4.0.0" xmlns:xsi="http://www.w3.
    org/2001/XMLSchema-instance"
  xsi:schemaLocation="http://maven.apache.org/POM/4.0.0 http://maven.apache.
    org/maven-v4_0_0.xsd">
  <modelVersion>4.0.0</modelVersion>          ◁───┐  The pom file requires some general
  <groupId>org.redfx.javaqc</groupId>                information about the project. The
  <artifactId>helloquantum</artifactId>              properties defined here are standard
  <packaging>jar</packaging>                         Maven properties and have nothing
  <version>1.0-SNAPSHOT</version>                    specific for our application, but they
  <name>grover</name>                                need to be defined.
  <url>http://maven.apache.org</url>

  <properties>
    <project.build.sourceEncoding>UTF-8</project.build.sourceEncoding>
    <maven.compiler.target>11</maven.compiler.target>
    <maven.compiler.source>11</maven.compiler.source>
  </properties>

  <dependencies>
    <dependency>
```

```
            <groupId>org.redfx</groupId>
            <artifactId>strange</artifactId>
            <version>0.1.1</version>
          </dependency>
        </dependencies>
        <build>
          <plugins>
            <plugin>
              <groupId>org.openjfx</groupId>
              <artifactId>javafx-maven-plugin</artifactId>
              <version>0.0.4</version>
              <configuration>
                <mainClass>
                    org.redfx.javaqc.ch02.hellostrange.Main
                </mainClass>
              </configuration>
            </plugin>
          </plugins>
        </build>
      </project>
```

The project depends on **org.redfx.strange.**

The life-cycle management of the project (compiling and running) is handled by the javafx-maven plugin, as described here.

The main class name needs to be specified so that the plugin can run it.

Users familiar with Maven can easily modify this .pom file, but in general, doing so is not necessary.

BUILDING WITH GRADLE

For clarity, the build.gradle file is shown next.

Listing 2.2   build.gradle file for the HelloStrange example

Declares what plugins Gradle should use. Gradle is a build system that allows third parties to provide plugins to make it easier to build and deploy applications. The demo application is an application and therefore uses the application plugin. Strange requires Java 11 and the modularity concepts introduced in Java 9. Our demo applications don't require knowledge of the modular system in Java. However, for the build tools to use the modularity, we also declare the use of the javamodularity Gradle plugin.

```
plugins {
    id 'application'
}

repositories {
    mavenCentral();
}

dependencies {
    compile 'org.redfx:strange:0.1.1'
}

mainClassName = 'org.redfx.javaqc.ch02.hellostrange.Main'
```

Declares where to download dependencies. Because our demo application is using a Java library, Gradle needs to know where to find this library to use it for compiling and running the demo application. The Strange library is uploaded to the mavenCentral repository, so we declare that in the repositories section.

Declares the dependencies. The HelloStrange demo application uses the Strange library. Here we declare that we need version 0.1.1 of the Strange library, which is defined by the combination of a package name (org.redfx) and an artifact name (strange). The compile keyword tells Gradle that this library is needed to compile the application, and by default, it will also use this library to run the application.

Declares the main class that should be executed when running the demo. We need to tell Gradle where it can find the main entry point to our application. In this case, the project has a single Java source file with a main method; hence, this is the entry point.

The build.gradle file is interesting to developers and code maintainers who are working on project development, deployment, testing, and distribution.

2.3.2 *The code*

The Java source files in a project are relevant to all developers. Maven and Gradle by default require that Java source files be placed in a folder whose name is src/main/java followed by the package name and the name of the Java source file. In the case of the HelloStrange application, the single source file is located at src/main/java/org/redfx/javaqc/ch02/hellostrange/Main.java. Note that every example has its own src directory so that it can easily be seen in isolation.

Before we show the code, we will briefly explain what we want to achieve. In this first example, we invoke a method on the high-level Strange API. This method is called `randomBit()` and generates a classic bit that is either `0` or `1`. We discuss the `randomBit()` method call shortly. Apart from this call, all Java code used in the example uses only the standard APIs that are part of the JDK.

The flow for the example is shown in figure 2.3. You can see that the Java class we create depends on the high-level Strange API. We don't have to worry about how it is implemented in the lower layers of Strange.

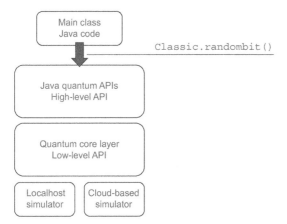

Figure 2.3 High-level overview of the first Java example

The complete source code for the application is shown in the following listing. We analyze this source code next.

Listing 2.3 Main.java file for the HelloStrange example

```
package org.redfx.javaqc.ch02.hellostrange;

import org.redfx.strange.algorithm.Classic;

public class Main {
```

```
          public static void main (String[] args) {
               System.out.println("Using high-level Strange API to generate random
          bits");
               System.out.println("-------------------------------------------");
               int randomBit = Classic.randomBit();
               System.out.println("Generate one random bit, which can be 0 or 1."+
                                   " Result = "+randomBit);
               int cntZero = 0;
               int cntOne = 0;
               for (int i = 0; i < 10000; i++) {
                    if (Classic.randomBit() > 0) {
                         cntOne ++;
                    } else {
                         cntZero ++;
                    }
               }
               System.out.println("Generated 10000 random bits, " + cntZero +
                                   " of them were 0, and "+cntOne+" were 1.");
          }
     }
```

Calls the Strange high-level API to generate one random bit — points to `int randomBit = Classic.randomBit();`

Generates 10,000 random bits — points to `for (int i = 0; i < 10000; i++) {`

This Java code follows the basic Java conventions, which we assume you are familiar with. For this example, we briefly mention the typical concepts in a Java application.

The Java code in this source file belongs to the package `org.redfx.javaqc.ch02 .hellostrange`, which is declared at the top of the file. We rely on functionality provided by the Strange library, and we import the Java class that provides the functionality we need:

```
import org.redfx.strange.algorithm.Classic
```

We take a deeper look at this `Classic` class later. For now, we simply assume that it provides the functionality we need.

The name of our example Java class is `Main`, as it has to match the name of the file. In Java, entry points in files need to be declared with a method `public static void main(String[] args)`. Build tools like Maven and Gradle invoke this method when asked to execute an application. When the `main` method is invoked, it first prints some information:

```
System.out.println("Using high-level Strange API to generate random bits");
System.out.println("-------------------------------------------------------");
```

In the next line of code in listing 2.3, we call a method on the `Classic` class that is part of the Strange library that we imported: `Classic.randomBit()`, which returns a Java integer that holds the value 0 or the value 1. After the statement

```
int randomBit = Classic.randomBit();
```

the value of `randomBit` is thus 0 or 1.

NOTE The classname `Classic` indicates that Strange offers this class for classic invocations. By this, we mean that code calling this class is not expected to contain any quantum-specific objects or functions. The calling code can be part of a project or a library that is entirely written using classic code. However, the implementation of the `Classic` class itself contains quantum implementations. Therefore, the implementation of `Classic.randomBit()` is not simply returning a default Java random bit but also using a quantum circuit to do so, as we show later in this chapter.

The next line prints this value. Note that when you execute the application, there is a 50% chance you will see a `0` printed and a 50% chance that you will see a `1` printed. As we said before, `Classic.randomBit()` is a Java method that under the hood uses quantum principles. We discuss the implementation later; for now, we assume that there is an equal chance for this method to return `0` and `1`.

To demonstrate this, the next part of listing 2.3 calls `Classic.randomBit()` 10,000 times and keeps track of how many times a `0` is returned and how many times a `1` is returned. Two variables are introduced to keep track of this occurrence:

```
int cntZero = 0;
int cntOne = 0;
```

Clearly, `cntZero` holds the number of times the returned value is `0` and `cntOne` holds the count for the calls that return `1`.

We create a loop in which the inner code calls the `randomBit()` method and increments the appropriate variable. This is done in the following code snippet:

```
for (int i = 0; i < 10000; i++) {
    if (Classic.randomBit() > 0) {
        cntOne ++;
    } else {
        cntZero ++;
    }
}
```

Finally, the results are printed. Because the random values are truly random, the final results will likely be different every time you run the application. The sum of the `cntOne` and `cntZero` values will always be 10,000, and it is expected that the `cntZero` and `cntOne` values will both be in the neighborhood of `5000`.

2.3.3 Java APIs vs. implementations

If you are familiar with Java development, the code we have shown and used so far should be familiar. No specific knowledge of quantum physics or QC has been required. We used `Classic.randomBit()`, which is a method similar to all the Java methods you see in Java applications. Under the hood, however, `Classic.random-Bit()` is using either a quantum simulator or a real quantum computer. The Java developer is not confronted with the implementation, though, one of the great things about Java is that the implementation is typically hidden for developers who program their applications using APIs. In this case, `Classic.randomBit()` is an API called by the developer.

Although you don't need to know the details of the underlying implementations, it often helps to have at least some insight into those details. This is not only the case for algorithms in QC but is applicable to many fields. Although documentation (such as Javadoc) is typically helpful for general cases, it may help to understand some of the details if you want to keep track of performance, for example. In the case of QC, it is recommended that Java developers have at least some basic knowledge of the underlying implementation of the quantum APIs, as this provides useful information that can be used to judge whether a quantum algorithm applies to a specific use case and what the performance impact will be.

Also, without this basic knowledge, you may worry about the initial performance of some of the algorithms. Indeed, if a quantum algorithm is executed on a quantum simulator, its performance will probably be worse than if a classic algorithm were used. However, if the quantum algorithm is well written and the problem applies to quantum speedup, its performance will dramatically improve when real quantum hardware is used.

2.4 Obtaining and installing the Strange code

As explained in the previous section, you typically don't need to understand the implementation details of an algorithm. However, in this book, we explain the basic concepts of QC by showing code snippets of quantum algorithms. By looking at the implementations of some algorithms, you'll learn more about the concepts of QC and become more knowledgeable about the areas where QC can make a big difference.

The Strange library we use throughout this book is written in Java. This allows you to use the quantum APIs in your own applications and enables you to have a deeper look at the implementations and modify or extend them when needed. If you are using a particular IDE (such as NetBeans, IntelliJ, or Eclipse), you should have no problem opening the library and reading the files.

2.4.1 Downloading the code

Similar to the examples and demos used in this book, the code for the Strange library can be downloaded from GitHub. The following command will provide you with a local copy of the Strange library:

```
git clone https://github.com/redfx-quantum/strange.git
```

Note that if you want to use the Strange library in your application, you don't need to download the source code. Binary releases of Strange are uploaded to Maven Central, and build tools like Gradle and Maven will retrieve them from this uploaded location.

If for some reason you want to make modifications to Strange and test them locally, you can easily compile the whole project. Similar to our demo application in the previous section, Strange uses the Gradle build system to create the library.

The following Maven command can be used to build the library:

```
mvn install
```

The result of this operation is a local copy of the Strange library, which you can use in local applications. Before you can use your own library, you need to take into account two things:

- The pom.xml file contains a `version` parameter. You can change that to whatever you want, but you have to be sure to use the same version in the `dependencies` section of your application.
- Your application needs to include `mavenLocal()` in the list of its repositories.

2.4.2 *A first look at the library*

You can open the code in your IDE, or you can browse through the files. For example, you can open the Classic.java file that we discussed in the previous section. The source code for the `Classic` class is in Classic.java, which is in the src/main/java/org/redfx/ strange/algorithm folder under the directory where you cloned the Git repository. We will discuss this file in detail in chapter 7, but the following snippet shows the link between the `Classic.randomBit()` call from the previous section to the implementation using a quantum computer or a quantum simulator:

```
public static int randomBit() {
    Program program = new Program(1);
    Step s0 = new Step();
    s0.addGate(new Hadamard(0));
    program.addStep(s0);
    QuantumExecutionEnvironment qee =
            new SimpleQuantumExecutionEnvironment();
    Result result = qee.runProgram(program);
    Qubit[] qubits = result.getQubits();
    int answer = qubits[0].measure();
    return answer;
}
```

This snippet shows that the random bit returned by the `randomBit()` method is not simply generated by a classic random function but involves steps specific to QC. Again, Java developers typically don't need to know much about the implementation, but by looking at it, you can learn a lot about QC.

2.5 *Next steps*

Now that you've downloaded the Strange library and run your first Java application using QC, it is time to learn more about the basic concepts of quantum computing. If you want to look into more code first, you're welcome to browse the files in the

Strange library. However, we recommended that you read about the basic concepts first. Whenever we introduce a concept, we will point to code in Strange where the concept is applied. By design, we avoid the high-level APIs in Strange, which contain quantum-specific concepts. In the following chapters, we explain the core concepts of QC by using the Strange low-level APIs.

Summary

- Strange is a quantum computing simulator with high-level and low-level APIs.
- You can easily create a HelloWorld application using the high-level API of Strange, and it will use quantum computing concepts under the hood.
- The implementation of high-level APIs requires low-level APIs. Typically, you do not have to be bothered about those low-level APIs, but if you want to get a deeper understanding about quantum computing concepts, they are very helpful.

Qubits and quantum gates: The basic units in quantum computing

This chapter covers

- Comparing qubits and (classical) bits
- Learning two notations for qubits
- Understanding how quantum gates allow us to perform operations on qubits
- Using StrangeFX to visualize the effect of a simple gate

When creating typical applications using classic computers, most developers don't think about the lowest-level transistors and operations that ultimately allow applications to execute on hardware. Classic hardware is a commodity in the sense that most developers take it for granted and don't think about it. The details about how it works are not relevant to most applications. High-level programming languages shield us from the low-level (assembly) code, and standards in chip design make it even less relevant for us to understand the physical working of the hardware in a computer.

This was not always the case. In the early days of classical computing, there were no high-level programming languages, and developers worked closer to the bare metal. When the hardware for classic computers became more mainstream and standardized, focus moved to higher-level programming languages.

It can be expected that quantum computing will follow a similar path. In the future, no knowledge of the basic concepts of quantum computing (QC) will be required for a developer who uses QC. Similar to the situation in classic computers, higher-level languages and intermediate layers will shield us from the implementation details in the hardware. Today, if we want to use QC, it definitely helps to have at least some basic understanding of the underlying principles.

In this chapter, we introduce those basic concepts. We discuss qubits and quantum gates, and we briefly touch the link to the physical world that allows their implementation. By no means is this chapter an introduction to quantum mechanics; the interested reader is referred to the specialized literature.

3.1   Classic bit vs. qubit

Suppose that you work for a bank, and you need to make sure the account number and balances for each customer are stored and can be retrieved. Developers need to be able to work with this information. How can you represent this information on a classic computer?

Previously, computers could work with information (numbers, text, images, videos, and so on) represented in a way that computers understood. The classic bit is one of the most common low-level structures that is understood and used by most developers. A bit contains the most granular information in classic computing; it has a value of either 0 or 1, as shown in figure 3.1. Usually, the bits are grouped in ordered sequences of 8 bits, called *bytes* (figure 3.2).

Figure 3.1   **A single bit can have a value of 0 or 1.**

Figure 3.2   **A single byte contains a sequence of 0s and 1s.**

At any moment in the execution of a classic algorithm, each bit is in a specific state: 0 or 1. As a consequence, a byte is, at any given moment, in a specific state as well. Each of the 8 bits in a byte is either 0 or 1.

The size of a computer's memory is expressed as the number of bits that can be accessed by the processor. The amount of memory is one of the main contributors to the quality and performance of computers. The more memory a computer has, the more data it can hold. The number of bits is an important characteristic for describing the length of CPU instructions and the precision of numbers. (A Java long has 64 bits, for example, whereas a Java int holds 32 bits.)

The core idea of a bit— the fact that its value at a given moment is either 0 or 1— is also one of its limitations. In QC, the equivalent of the bit is the qubit. Similar to a bit, a qubit can hold the values 0 and 1. But unlike a bit, a qubit can also hold values that are combinations of the 0 and 1 states. When this is the case, the qubit is in a so-called *superposition* state. Although this may sound counterintuitive at first, it is exactly what is happening in nature with a number of the most elementary particles, and it is directly linked to the core ideas of quantum mechanics. The fact that this superposition state occurs in nature with elementary particles is a good indication that building quantum computers is realistic. Classic computers ignore those quantum effects; therefore, classic hardware cannot be made smaller and smaller indefinitely without hitting the boundaries where quantum effects come into the picture.

When a qubit is measured, it returns 0 or 1, not something in between. The relationship between the superposition state of the qubit and the actual value when it is measured is explained in the next chapter. Roughly, the superposition relates to how likely it is that a given qubit, when measured, will hold the value 0 or the value 1, as shown in figure 3.3.

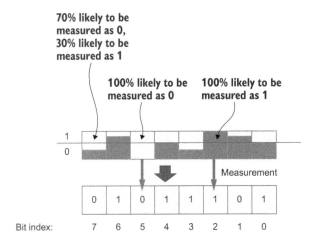

Figure 3.3 When measured, qubits fall back to 0 or 1. Note that even though the probability of measuring the qubit with index 1 as 1 is high, in this fictive example, we measure it as 0. We do this to illustrate that the link between probabilities and measurement is not just rounding.

We discuss the idea of superpositions of the 0 and 1 states in chapter 4. For now, the most important part is that as a consequence, a number of qubits can contain more information than the same number of classical bits because a single qubit contains information more complex than 0 or 1. This is important for problems or algorithms that theoretically require exponentially more bits for linearly increasing complexity.

3.2 Qubit notation

Although we haven't discussed superposition in detail yet, the previous paragraphs indicate that it is not (always) possible to identify the state of a qubit with a single 0 or a 1, which implies that we need a different notation to describe the state of a qubit. There are multiple notations for qubits, and depending on the use case (showing the state of a circuit, explaining how gates work, and so on), one notation may be preferred over another.

We will cover two notations: Dirac and vector. We look at only the simple cases in this chapter. When we discuss superposition in the next chapter, we will come back to these notations and extend them. For now, we consider only the basis states of a qubit, which represent the values 0 and 1.

> **Linear algebra**
> From this point on, we will sometimes use concepts and notations that are taken from linear algebra. If you want to get more background on these concepts, see appendix B for a short introduction to the linear algebra we use in this book.

3.2.1   *One qubit*

For the simple case in which a qubit is in one of its basic states, the vector representation of a single qubit is straightforward. We represent the qubit as a vector with two elements. If the qubit holds the value 0, the first element in the vector is 1, and the other is 0, as shown in equation 3.1.

$$\begin{bmatrix} 1 \\ 0 \end{bmatrix}$$

Equation 3.1

The Dirac notation of this qubit is as follows:

$$|0>$$

Equation 3.2

Because both notations are interchangeable, we can also write

$$|0> = \begin{bmatrix} 1 \\ 0 \end{bmatrix}$$

Equation 3.3

Similarly, if the qubit holds the value 1, we can represent it in a vector where the first element is 0 and the second element is 1. The Dirac representation of this single qubit is |1); hence, the representations can be written as

$$|1> = \begin{bmatrix} 0 \\ 1 \end{bmatrix}$$

Equation 3.4

3.2.2   *Multiple qubits*

In a system with more than one qubit, the state of the qubits in the Dirac notation is achieved by concatenating the individual qubits. Two qubits, each holding the value of 0, can be described by

$$|0> |0>$$

Equation 3.5

This is often abbreviated as follows:

$$|00>$$

Equation 3.6

The vector notation of a multiple-qubit system requires some vector operations. The resulting vector, representing the multiple-qubit system, is obtained by the tensor multiplication of the vectors of each qubit. Tensor multiplication is explained in appendix B. Although the appendix provides more insight, you do not need to know *how* those vectors are obtained:

$$|00>= \begin{bmatrix} 1 \\ 0 \end{bmatrix} \otimes \begin{bmatrix} 1 \\ 0 \end{bmatrix} = \begin{bmatrix} 1 \\ 0 \\ 0 \\ 0 \end{bmatrix}$$

Equation 3.7

In a system where the first qubit is 1 and the second qubit is 0, the notation of the qubits is as follows:

$$|10>= \begin{bmatrix} 0 \\ 1 \end{bmatrix} \otimes \begin{bmatrix} 1 \\ 0 \end{bmatrix} = \begin{bmatrix} 0 \\ 0 \\ 1 \\ 0 \end{bmatrix}$$

Equation 3.8

From binary to decimal

Classic computers work with bits, which are 0 or 1; but combined, they can represent more complex information. A decimal number (such as 5) can be described by a number of bits. When bits are put in sequential order, they can be considered indicators as follows:

$$0101 = 0*2^3 + 1*2^2 + 0*2^1 + 1*2^0 = 0*8 + 1*4 + 0*2 + 1*1 = 5$$

Hence, each bit in the sequence indicates whether a corresponding power of 2 should be added to the decimal number. When a bit is 1, the corresponding power of 2 is added; when the bit is 0, it is not added. The rightmost bit of a sequence is said to have an index of 0, the bit left of it has index 1, and so on. In general, a bit with index i corresponds with the value of 2^i.

There is another handy relationship between the Dirac notation and the vector notation. If we considered the qubits to be bits, the bits in the Dirac notation equal an integer value:

$$|00> = \quad 0$$
$$|01> = \quad 1$$
$$|10> = \quad 2$$
$$|11> = \quad 3$$

Equation 3.9

Let's compare this notation with the vector notation from equation 3.8. The only element in that vector that has the value of 1 occurs at position 2 (assuming that we start to count from position 0). As shown previously, $|10\rangle$ corresponds to the decimal value of 2, and this matches the second element in the corresponding vector (again assuming that we start to count from position 0). This is shown in figure 3.4. Hence, if we read the bits in the Dirac notation as a decimal number, such as n, the corresponding vector is all zeros except for the element at position n (starting from 0)—which is 1.

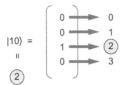

Figure 3.4   The correlation between the decimal value of a list of qubits and the position of 1 in the corresponding probability vector

If we add another qubit to the system, we need to add another tensor multiplication. A three-qubit system in which the first qubit is 1, the second qubit is 0, and the third qubit is 1 can be represented as follows:

$$|101\rangle = \begin{bmatrix} 0 \\ 1 \end{bmatrix} \otimes \begin{bmatrix} 1 \\ 0 \end{bmatrix} \otimes \begin{bmatrix} 0 \\ 1 \end{bmatrix} = \begin{bmatrix} 0 \\ 1 \end{bmatrix} \otimes \begin{bmatrix} 0 \\ 1 \\ 0 \\ 0 \end{bmatrix} = \begin{bmatrix} 0 \\ 0 \\ 0 \\ 0 \\ 0 \\ 1 \\ 0 \\ 0 \end{bmatrix}$$ Equation 3.10

Note that the previously mentioned relationship still holds: $|101\rangle$ is the digital representation of the integer 5, and if we start counting the first row in the vector as row 0, the element at row 5 equals 1.

The size of the resulting vector grows quickly when the number of bits increases. In general, for n bits, the resulting vector contains 2^n elements.

You may wonder why we make it so complex. Why do we need a vector with eight elements when we use only three qubits, and only one of those eight elements is 1? The answer will be given in chapter 4. So far, we've discussed qubits in a basic state; when we talk about qubits in a superposition state, it will become useful and even required to represent qubits in this way.

Physical representations of a qubit

Although it should not influence the behavior of an application, it is interesting to have a rough idea of how bits or qubits are created and maintained in the real physical world. It is essential to realize that there are different options for the physical realizations of bits and qubits and that developers are abstracted away from those physical realizations. A bit stored in the main memory of a computer can be realized by an electrical pulse that keeps the bit on. When a bit is stored on a hard disk, a different technique is used, such as using magnetic properties.

The general principle for storing qubits is similar to the principle for storing bits: we use phenomena that are encountered in nature and apply them to our goal. The electrical pulse that can be used to keep a bit on (giving it the value of 1) is a classic example. Quantum phenomena that describe a two-state system can be used to represent qubits. In such a system, the state is not simply 0 or 1; it can be in a more complex superposition of 0 and 1. (We discuss superposition in chapter 4.) The important thing to understand is that there are physical phenomena that exactly represent the behavior of a qubit. This is not a coincidence, of course, and the statement could well be reversed to read, "Qubits behave exactly like some phenomena encountered in quantum mechanics."

Different physical phenomena lead to a quantum two-state system. At this moment, most of the effort in creating and manipulating qubits is based on superconducting electronic circuits. The physical superconducting qubits that can be created in a superconducting environment can have diverse characteristics, so there are various possible implementations of qubits using superconducting circuits. Recently, more players have entered the market, and other technologies are being investigated, including trapped ions of photonic qubits. Since this is a fast-evolving topic, it is dangerous to give a static overview of the options. An interesting and entertaining overview of the state in the first half of 2021 is given in Sabine Hossenfelder's video "Quantum Computing: Top Players 2021" at https://www.youtube.com/watch?v= OGsu5Mlzruw. Most important to developers, though, is that this context allows us to create qubits that can be in a superposition until they are measured, as we describe in chapter 4.

3.3 *Gates: Manipulating and measuring qubits*

Being able to represent and store data is fine, but in computing, we need to be able to manipulate data: forms need to be processed, interest rates need to be applied, colors need to change, and so on. In a high-level software language like Java, a huge number of libraries are available to manipulate input data. At the lowest level, all of these operations come down to a sequence of simple manipulations of the bits in the computer systems. Those low-level operations are achieved with gates. It can be shown that with a limited number of gates, all possible scenarios can be achieved.

Gates are typically represented using simple pictures. A simple classical gate is the NOT gate, also known as the *inverter*. This gate is rendered in figure 3.5.

This gate has one input bit and one output bit. The output bit of the gate is the inverse of the input bit. If the input is 0, the output will be 1. If the input is 1, the output will be 0.

The behavior of gates is often explained via simple tables where the possible combinations of input bits are listed, and the resulting output is shown in the last column. Table 3.1 shows the behavior of the NOT gate.

Initial value is 1   NOT gate is applied   Resulting value is 0

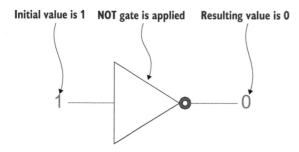

Figure 3.5 Representation of the NOT gate

Table 3.1 Behavior of the NOT gate

Input	Output
A	NOT A
0	1
1	0

When the input of the gate is 0, the output is 1. When the input of the gate is 1, the output is 0.

The NOT gate involves a single bit, but other gates involve more bits. The XOR gate, for example, takes the input of two bits and outputs a value that is 1 in case exactly one of the two input bits is 1, or 0 otherwise. This gate is shown in figure 3.6.

Figure 3.6 Representation of the XOR gate

Table 3.2 shows the behavior of the XOR gate.

Table 3.2 Behavior of the XOR gate

Input	Output	
A	B	A XOR B
0	0	0
0	1	1
1	0	1
1	1	0

Quantum gates have characteristics similar to classical gates, but there are also important differences. Like classical gates, quantum gates operate on the core concept (in this case, qubits): they can alter the value of qubits. One of the essential differences between classical gates and quantum gates is that quantum gates should be reversible. That is, it should always be possible to apply another gate and go back to the state of the system before the first gate was applied. The reason goes back to the laws of nature: quantum mechanics are reversible. If we want to use the hardware provided by quantum mechanics, our software rules should be consistent with the hardware restrictions. Hence, creating a nonreversible gate would make it impossible to implement the software stack on quantum hardware.

This restriction is not in place with classic gates. The XOR gate is not reversible, for example. If the result of an XOR gate is 1, it is impossible to know whether the first bit or the second bit was 0.

Because of the need for gate operations to be reversible, a quantum system needs different gates than a classical system. Therefore, low-level quantum applications require a different approach from low-level classical applications.

3.4 *A first [quantum] gate: Pauli-X*

Let's continue the example in which you work for a bank. You created a system that stores data (account numbers and balances). Now you are asked to modify balances, such as by applying interest. You need to manipulate data. How will you do this?

One of the core ideas of software development is writing functionality that manipulates data, such as adding 1 euro to all balances. This requires the ability to modify data, which happens at a huge scale in classic computers.

If you want quantum computers to execute your algorithm, those computers should be able to manipulate data. At a low level, this is what quantum gates do. A first example of a quantum gate is the Pauli-X gate, shown in figure 3.7.

Figure 3.7   Symbol of the Pauli-X gate

This gate inverts the value of a qubit. When we delve into superposition in the next chapter, we will come back to this example. For now, we take only the special cases into account, where a qubit is in the 0 or the 1 state. The Pauli-X gate flips the value of 0 to 1 and vice versa.

This process is reversible. If the value of a qubit is 1 after a Pauli-X gate has been applied, we know that it had the value of 0 before the gate was applied. If, on the other hand, the end value is 0, we know that the original value was 1. Hence, the principle of reversible gates holds so far. By applying a second Pauli-X gate after applying the first Pauli-X gate, we store the original state of the system, as illustrated in figure 3.8.

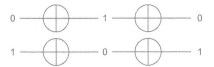

Figure 3.8   Two Pauli-X gates restore the system.

3.5   *Playing with qubits in Strange*

We haven't discussed superposition and entanglement yet, and our introduction to qubits was basic. The real power of QC will be demonstrated when we explain the concepts of superposition and entanglement. At this point, however, we can already create a simple application using Strange to see the Pauli-X gate in action.

In chapter 2, we used the high-level API of Strange to create an application that uses a quantum algorithm to return random values. In the following demo, we use the low-level API of Strange and work directly with qubits and gates. The code in listing 3.1 creates a single qubit (which has the initial value of 0), applies the Pauli-X gate, and measures the resulting value.

> **TIP**   The source code for this demo can be found in the ch03/paulix directory in the example repository. See appendix A for more information on how to obtain the example code.

Listing 3.1   Java application using a Pauli-X gate

```
public static void main(String[] args) {
    QuantumExecutionEnvironment simulator =          Creates an Environment
        new SimpleQuantumExecutionEnvironment();     for declaring and executing
                                                      a quantum application
    Program program = new Program(1);    Defines a
    Step step = new Step();              Program
    step.addGate(new X(0));
    program.addStep(step);                           After the Program is
    Result result = simulator.runProgram(program);   defined, it can be executed
    Qubit[] qubits = result.getQubits();             on the Environment and a
    Qubit zero = qubits[0];                          Result can be obtained.
    int value = zero.measure();
    System.out.println("Value = "+value);    The Result can be
}                                            processed and returned
                                             to the user.
```

Now let's run the code:

```
mvn javafx:run
```

As expected, the output of the program is as follows:

```
Value = 1
```

In this code, we introduce a number of concepts encountered in Strange. We talk about an execution environment, a program consisting of steps, and some results. Note that those concepts are typically used in all kinds of QC simulators and editors.

3.5.1 The QuantumExecutionEnvironment interface

The physical location and conditions of where and how a quantum application is executed are not relevant to the developer, and the options are still evolving. There are already cloud services offering real quantum infrastructure (such as IBM and Rigetti), but it is also possible to assume that a quantum co-processor will be able to execute quantum applications. Today, most quantum applications are executed on quantum simulators, which can run either locally or in a cloud environment. In summary, multiple different execution environments are capable of executing quantum applications.

Strange abstracts the differences in execution environments and provides an interface, QuantumExecutionEnvironment, in the org.redfx.strange package that provides the API for quantum applications to interact with the execution environment. Strange contains several implementations of QuantumExecutionEnvironment, but the most important thing is that quantum applications written with Strange can run on all current and future implementations without being modified.

The simplest execution environment uses a built-in simulator and is instantiated as follows:

```
QuantumExecutionEnvironment simulator = new
SimpleQuantumExecutionEnvironment();
```

SimpleQuantumExecutionEnvironment in the org.redfx.strange.local package provides a quantum simulator that executes quantum operations using classical software. Clearly, it is slower than real hardware, and because quantum simulators are memory-hungry when dealing with large numbers of qubits, it is not recommended for use with lots of qubits. For the demos in this book, SimpleQuantumExecution-Environment is more than good enough.

3.5.2 The Program class

If you want to create a quantum application in Strange, you have to create a new instance of Program. The Program class is in the org.redfx.strange package, and it provides an entry point to quantum applications you want to write.

The Program constructor requires a single integer parameter, defining the number of qubits you will use in the application. In the case of our simple application, we will use a single qubit, which explains this line:

```
Program program = new Program(1)
```

3.5.3 Steps and gates

A quantum Program is composed of one or more steps operating on the qubit. Each step is defined by an instance of Step. The Step class is in the org.redfx.strange package as well and has a zero-argument constructor. Inside a step, you define which gates are used.

In our example, we have a single step that is created like this:

```
Step step = new Step()
```

The step is further defined by adding a gate. Here we use the Pauli-X gate, which is defined by the X class in the `org.redfx.strange.gate` package. The constructor of the Pauli-X gate requires one integer to be passed, which is the index of the qubit the gate is acting on. In this case, because we have a single qubit, the index is 0. Creating this gate and adding it to the `Step` instance is done as follows:

```
step.addGate(new X(0));
```

In a single step, each qubit may be affected by no more than one gate. A gate may act on more than one qubit, but two gates in the same step cannot act on the same qubit. The following code snippet is wrong, as we add two gates to the same step, and both gates operate on the same qubit (with index 0):

```
step.addGate(new X(0));
step.addGate(new H(0));
```

If you try to use this snippet in an application, Strange will throw an `IllegalArgument-Exception` with the message "Adding gate that affects a qubit already involved in this step."

Note that we introduced another gate here: the Hadamard gate, represented by the H class. We cover this gate in the next chapter; we use it here only to show that it is not allowed to have two gates operating on the same qubit in a single step.

At this point, the single execution step in our program is ready. We have to instruct the `Program` instance that our `Step` instance should be added to the program:

```
program.addStep(step);
```

3.5.4   Results

When a quantum application or a `Program` has been executed, a result can be obtained. We briefly mentioned that a qubit can be in a so-called superposition, but that once it is measured, it will hold the value 0 or the value 1. Therefore, it is impossible to have intermediate results in quantum applications. Quantum simulators that are not using real physical qubits do not have this restriction, though; for debugging purposes, intermediate values can be used and can be useful, as we will demonstrate in chapter 7.

Strange defines the `Result` class in the `org.redfx.strange` package, and instances of it are created by the execution environment. The result is returned when the `run-Program()` method is called on the `QuantumExecutionEnvironment`:

```
Result result = simulator.runProgram(program);
```

The resulting instance of the `Result` class contains information about the final state of the quantum system. We talk about this in more detail in the following chapters. For now, we are interested only in the status of the single qubit that is in our system.

The `Result` class contains a method to retrieve the qubits:

```
Qubit[] qubits = result.getQubits();
```

Because we have only one qubit in the system, it can be obtained as follows:

```
Qubit zero = qubits[0];
```

We can ask for the value of this qubit after the program has been executed:

```
int value = zero.measure();
```

Finally, we print the value using simple Java commands:

```
System.out.println("Value = "+value);
```

Initially, qubits are in the 0 state. Our simple application sends the qubit through a Pauli-X gate and then measures the new value, which is always equal to 1. For some algorithms, you want a qubit to be in the 1 state initially: this is easily achieved by using a Pauli-X gate as the first step of the algorithm.

3.6 *Visualizing quantum circuits*

The code in the previous example is not hard to understand and follow, but it represents a simple quantum circuit involving only a single qubit and a single gate. When applications become more complex, it can be difficult to read the code and have a clear understanding of what is happening. Many quantum simulators or applications that allow us to generate quantum applications come with a visualization tool.

The Strange library has a companion library called StrangeFX that allows us to render programs intuitively. StrangeFX is written in Java as well, and it uses JavaFX, the standard Java UI Platform, for rendering. The `paulixui` example in this chapter's code shows this library in action.

When you have a `Program`, visualizing it is very easy. In case you are using the Maven build system, including the StrangeFX library is straightforward. We need to add two new dependencies in the pom.xml file:

```
<dependency>
  <groupId>org.openjfx</groupId>
  <artifactId>javafx-controls</artifactId>
  <version>15</version>
</dependency>
<dependency>
  <groupId>org.redfx</groupId>
  <artifactId>strangefx</artifactId>
  <version>0.0.10</version>
</dependency>
```

The javafx.controls module allows us to create graphical control components. This module depends on a few other javafx modules, which are loaded transitively.

Retrieves the org.redfx.strangefx artifact. It contains the code required to visualize quantum circuits.

The situation is similar when you are using the Gradle build system. You have to modify the build.gradle file and add a dependency to StrangeFX, like this:

```
plugins {
    id 'application'
    id 'org.openjfx.javafxplugin' version '0.0.10'
}
```
◁─┐ **Adds the**
   JavaFX plugin
   for Gradle

```
repositories {
    mavenCentral();
    jcenter();
}

dependencies {
    compile 'org.redfx:strange:0.0.17'
    compile 'org.redfx:strangefx:0.0.10'
}
```
┌ **Depends on**
│ **StrangeFX**
◁┘

```
javafx {
    modules = [ 'javafx.controls' ]
}
```
┌ **Uses the javafx.control**
│ **module in the**
◁┘ **application**

```
mainClassName = 'org.redfx.javaqc.ch03.paulixui.Main'
```

Note that we added this line to the `plugins` section:

```
id 'org.openjfx.javafxplugin' version '0.0.10'
```

This plugin makes sure that all the code required for running the JavaFX application can be used. Further, we have to add the dependency to StrangeFX to the list of dependencies:

```
compile 'org.redfx:strangefx:0.0.10'
```

Finally, because our application uses the JavaFX `controls` module, we have to tell the Java system to load it:

```
javafx {
    modules = [ 'javafx.controls' ]
}
```

The code required for rendering a program is simple. StrangeFX contains an `org.redfx.strangefx.render.Renderer` class that has the following static method:

```
Renderer.renderProgram(Program program);
```

This method analyzes the program and creates a visual representation of it in which each qubit is represented on a line. The initial state, with all qubits in the $|0\rangle$ state, is on the left. Going to the right, quantum gates are pictured when they are encountered. At the end of the line, the probability of this gate being measured with 1 is shown. Hence, if we want to render the circuit we composed before, we have to modify the end of our application as follows:

```
int value = zero.measure();
    System.out.println("Value = "+value);
    Renderer.renderProgram(program);
}
```

Running this program renders the user interface shown in figure 3.9. In this diagram, the visual components refer to the different components of the application, as we've marked.

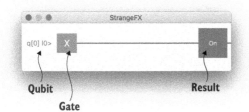

Qubit   **Result**
      Gate

Figure 3.9 **UI representation of a single qubit with a Pauli-X gate**

Summary

- The fundamental concepts of quantum computing are qubits (or quantum bits) and quantum gates.
- There are similarities and differences between those concepts and their counterparts in classical computing.
- The state of a qubit can be expressed in different notations: Dirac notation or a vector notation.
- Using the Java-based Strange quantum simulator, quantum gates can be composed into a quantum application.
- The Pauli-X gate is one of these quantum gates, and it can be used in a quantum application.

Part 2

Fundamental concepts
and how they relate to code

Now that we've narrowed down the term *quantum computing* to the parts that are relevant to developers, we can map the concepts of quantum computing to concepts that are familiar to developers.

In chapter 4, we introduce the concept of superposition, which is one of the things that makes quantum computing fundamentally different from classical computing. You will see how to deal with superposition by writing Java code. Chapter 5 discusses quantum entanglement, which—along with superposition—allows quantum computers to be so powerful. Similar to how superposition is explained, we show Java code that uses quantum entanglement. In chapter 6, we explain how classical networking can be affected by quantum computing and what a quantum network would look like.

Superposition 4

This chapter covers
- Understanding why superposition allows quantum systems to process exponentially more data
- Processing data via quantum gates
- Using the Hadamard gate

In the previous chapter, we briefly mentioned *superposition,* which is a fundamental concept of quantum computing. It is one of the reasons quantum computers are expected to be able to run some applications much faster than classical computers.

In this chapter, you learn what superposition is and how it is relevant in creating quantum algorithms. We talk about a specific gate that brings a qubit into a superposition state, and we show a simple but relevant example that demonstrates superposition. The flow of the chapter is explained in figure 4.1.

We try to keep the physical explanations to a minimum. The scientific work behind the physics is mind-boggling, but it requires different skills and is less relevant to software development. Keep in mind that even for the most knowledgeable people, quantum computing (QC) and its concepts are difficult to grasp, so do not worry if the physical concepts behind superposition are not clear. What matters to developers is how to use these concepts and write more suitable applications.

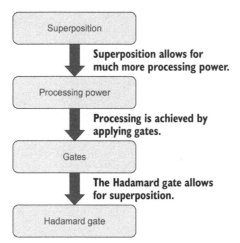

Figure 4.1   From superposition to the Hadamard gate

4.1   *What is superposition?*

A qubit can be in different states. We've mentioned before that a qubit can hold the value 0, the value 1, and also some sort of combination of the values 0 and 1. There are important restrictions on what combinations are allowed, though, and we discuss these now.

We said earlier that when a qubit is measured, it always returns the value 0 or the value 1. But that doesn't say everything about what is happening *before* we measure it.

To understand this, we'll make a short detour to the world of quantum physics. Remember that what software developers call a qubit is backed by real-world phenomena. The software behavior and properties of a qubit, therefore, have to correspond somehow with the behavior and properties of the real-world phenomena (figure 4.2).

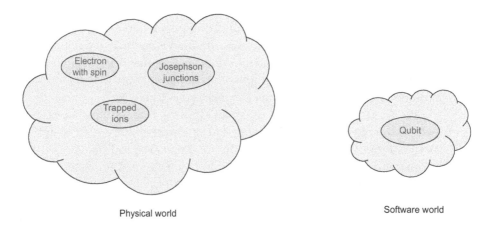

Figure 4.2   The characteristics of physical particles match the characteristics of software qubits.

In quantum physics, particles have interesting properties. An electron, for example, has a property called *spin*. When measured, this property can have two states: up and down, which we call the *basis states*. Note the similarity with bits, which can be 1 (corresponding to up) or 0 (corresponding to down). This is shown in figure 4.3.

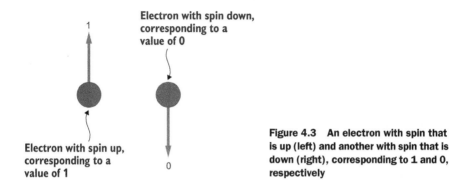

Electron with spin down, corresponding to a value of 0

Electron with spin up, corresponding to a value of 1

Figure 4.3 An electron with spin that is up (left) and another with spin that is down (right), corresponding to 1 and 0, respectively

The quantum theory, however, says that the spin of an electron can also be in a *superposition* of the up and down states. Symbolically, this can be represented by figure 4.4. Again, when it is measured, it always falls down to one of the two basis states.

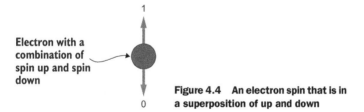

Electron with a combination of spin up and spin down

Figure 4.4 An electron spin that is in a superposition of up and down

There are some misconceptions about the superposition state:

- Being in a superposition does not mean the electron is in both the 0 (spin-down) state and the 1 (spin-up) state. Actually, the theory of superposition does not say what state the electron is in; rather, it describes the probability of states when the electron is measured at that particular point.
- Being in a superposition does not mean the spin of the electron is in either the up state or the down state and that we simply don't know yet. One of the fundamental (and weird) things about QC is that a system is influenced when it is measured. It is only when we measure the spin that it decides to be in the up state or the down state.

From the previous chapter, recall that a qubit that holds the value 0 is described in Dirac notation as |0>. In case the corresponding physical element is an electron, you can say that this is similar to the electrons having a spin-down property. Similarly, when the qubit holds the value 1, this is described in Dirac notation as |1>, which can correspond to the real-world situation in which an electron has a spin-up property.

> **NOTE** Most existing prototypes for quantum computers are not using electrons as qubit representations. However, the spin-up-/-down property of an electron is often easier to understand than the more complex phenomena used by most quantum computers (such as Josephson junctions). Because we try to make abstractions of the physical background as much as possible, we prefer to use an analogy with a simpler physical representation.

As we explained, an electron can be in a spin-up or spin-down state, but its spin can also be in a superposition of the up and down states. As a consequence, a qubit can be in a superposition as well.

We now give the qubit a name, similar to how we give variables or parameters in classical programs names. Greek symbols are often used, and to be consistent with most of the literature, we will use those symbols as well. Hence, a qubit named ψ (pronounced "psai") that holds the value 0 (corresponding to an electron with spin down) is described as follows:

$$|\psi> = |0>$$

Equation 4.1

Similarly, when the qubit named ψ holds the value 1 (corresponding to an electron with spin up), you can describe it as

$$|\psi> = |1>$$

Equation 4.2

The interesting thing is the description of a qubit in a superposition state, corresponding to an electron with a spin that is in a superposition of up and down. When a qubit is in a superposition state, this state can be described as a linear combination of the basis states:

$$|\psi> = \alpha|0> + \beta|1>$$

Equation 4.3

The equation tells you that the state of the qubit is a linear combination of the basis state |0> and the basis state |1>, where α and β are numbers related to probabilities, as we explain shortly.

This equation highlights one of the fundamental differences between classical computing and QC. Although the simple cases of a qubit holding the value 0 or the value 1 can also be reproduced with classical variables, the combination of both values is impossible for a classical computer, as explained in figure 4.5.

Quantum computer	Classical computer
|ψ>=|0>	boolean = false
|ψ>=|1>	boolean = true
|ψ>=α|0> + β|1>	boolean = ????

Figure 4.5 Variable assignments in quantum computers versus classical computers

You can also write equation 4.3 in vector notation. Using the definitions of Dirac notations for |0> and |1> you can rewrite equation 4.3 as follows:

$$|\psi> = \alpha \begin{bmatrix} 1 \\ 0 \end{bmatrix} + \beta \begin{bmatrix} 0 \\ 1 \end{bmatrix} = \begin{bmatrix} \alpha \\ \beta \end{bmatrix}$$

Equation 4.4

The Dirac notation and the vector notation refer to the same principle: the considered qubit is in a superposition of the |0> state and the |1> state.

There are a number of ways to try to explain what this equation means physically. At its core, the equation means the electron is in such a state that, if it were measured at that moment, there is a probability of α^2 that we would measure 0 and a probability of β^2 that we would measure 1.

Why is it α^2 and β^2 and not α and β? We discuss this in more detail in chapter 10 when we talk about the difference between the state vector and the probability vector. In short, probabilities need to be real, positive numbers, whereas the state variables can be complex numbers.

Because we will measure either 0 or 1, there is an additional restriction on the values of α and β: the sum of the probabilities should be 1 (because you measure something). So,

$$\alpha^2 + \beta^2 = 1$$

Equation 4.5

As we've said before, understanding quantum physics is hard. Fortunately, as a developer, you have to take into account only the equations—you can leave out the physical interpretation.

What we described for the spin of electrons also applies for other properties of other elementary particles. When we talk about a qubit, its underlying physical implementation uses the behavior of these properties. As a developer, you are shielded from the physical behavior. So, when we talk about a qubit in a superposition, you don't need to know anything about the physical representation of this qubit.

At this point, one of the most common questions asked by developers is the following: "Great, a qubit can be in a superposition of 0 and 1, but when we measure it, it is still either 0 or 1. What's the difference from a classical computer?" This is a reasonable question, and we give the answer in the following sections.

NOTE QC is sometimes linked to working with probabilities instead of certainties. A classical bit is either 0 or 1 and can always be measured. As you just learned, in QC, the state of a system is described by probabilities, which requires a different way of thinking.

4.2   *The state of a quantum system as a probability vector*

So far, we've talked mainly about qubits and the values that those qubits hold. Now that we've introduced superposition, you know that a single qubit can be in a combination of two basis states during processing, and it will fall back to one of the basis states (0 or 1) when measured. In classical computing, the value of parameters is the most important concept in processing. When we talk about quantum computers, however, those values are not uniquely defined during processing due to superposition. Therefore, it is often more convenient to talk about probabilities instead of values of qubits. This is what we explain in this section, and one of the consequences is the processing power of quantum computers.

In the previous chapter, you learned that the state of a quantum system can be represented by a vector. For a quantum system with one qubit, a vector with two elements describes the probabilities for the value of that single qubit when it is measured. A quantum system with two qubits can be represented by a vector with four elements, and in general, a quantum system with n qubits is represented by a vector with $2n$ elements. Figure 4.6 explains this principle.

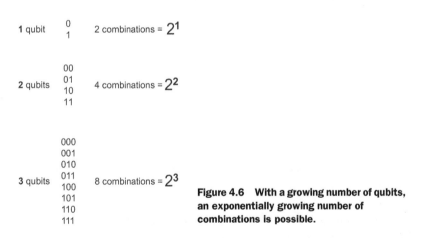

Figure 4.6   With a growing number of qubits, an exponentially growing number of combinations is possible.

The probability vectors we showed in chapter 3 representing the state of a quantum system with all qubits in a basis state were simple: all elements were 0 except for one element. That element defines the state of the system, and it corresponds to a clear value for each qubit: either 0 or 1.

You learned that a qubit can be in a superposition, in which its state is a linear combination of the 0 value and the 1 value. For a single-qubit system, the state can be described in Dirac notation and in vector notation as follows:

$$|\psi> = \alpha|0> + \beta|1> = \begin{bmatrix} \alpha \\ \beta \end{bmatrix}$$

Equation 4.6

A system with two qubits can be described as follows:

$$|\psi_0\psi_1> = \begin{bmatrix} \alpha_0 \\ \beta_0 \end{bmatrix} \otimes \begin{bmatrix} \alpha_1 \\ \beta_1 \end{bmatrix} = \begin{bmatrix} \alpha_0\alpha_1 \\ \alpha_0\beta_1 \\ \beta_0\alpha_1 \\ \beta_0\beta_1 \end{bmatrix}$$

Equation 4.7

This equation shows that a system with two qubits can be described by a (probability) vector with four values. Two qubits can hold four values simultaneously. When measured, only one value remains for each qubit. But all the computations in a quantum algorithm operate on the four values.

By extension, a system with n qubits corresponds to a vector with 2^n elements. This is an indication of why quantum computers are expected to help with *exponential* problems: with an increasing number of qubits, a quantum system can work with an exponentially increasing number of values.

Figure 4.7 shows a system with six qubits. In this picture, six qubits correspond to a vector with 64 (2^6) elements. Once measured, one of these elements holds the value 1, and all other elements have the value 0. From the index of the element that holds the value 1, the individual values for the six qubits can be calculated. So, you started with six values (each either 0 or 1) and ended with six values (each either 0 or 1).

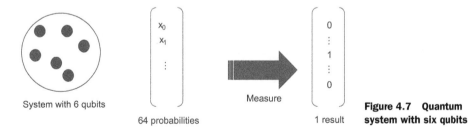

System with 6 qubits   64 probabilities   Measure   1 result

Figure 4.7 Quantum system with six qubits

At first sight, there might be no clear value due to superposition. You can hold an exponential number of elements in the system, but once you measure it, you seem to be back in the classical state where each bit has exactly one well-defined value.

The benefit of superposition for quantum computing

The real value of superposition for quantum computing lies in the fact that a quantum system can do processing while the qubits are in a superposition state. Hence, the operations defined by the quantum algorithms do not manipulate only six bits; they manipulate 64 probability values. One step in a quantum algorithm on a quantum computer with six qubits is modifying 64 values. Adding one qubit doubles the processing capabilities of the quantum computer. This explains the term *exponential*, which is often used in QC: adding n qubits adds processing power proportional to 2^n, where the n is in the exponent of this equation.

Let's compare a classical computer with six bits to a quantum computer with six qubits. Both computers have one value consisting of six bits as input to an algorithm, and after measuring the output of the algorithm, they both read a value of six bits again. Both computers can process 64 possible combinations as an input value. The key difference is that a quantum computer can process those 64 combinations at the same time. This is shown in figure 4.8.

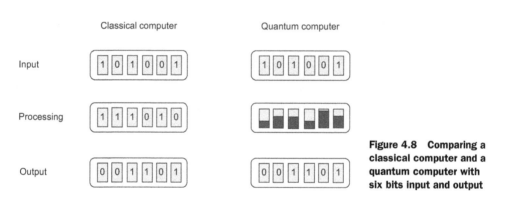

Figure 4.8   Comparing a classical computer and a quantum computer with six bits input and output

We can show this with some Java code. First, assume that you use a classical computer with a single bit, and you apply a function to that bit. You use the `boolean` type, as this Java primitive type can hold two values: false and true, corresponding to 0 and 1.

```
boolean input;
boolean output;

output = someFunction(input);
```

Here, `someFunction` is a Java function with the following signature:

```
public boolean someFunction(boolean v) {
    boolean answer;
    ... // do some processing          ◁——  The real
    return answer;                            processing is
}                                             done here.
```

To apply someFunction to all possible values of input, you have to invoke the function twice:

```
boolean[] input = new boolean[2];
boolean[] output = new boolean[2];
input[0] = false;
input[1] = true;

for (int i = 0; i < 2; i++) {
    output[i] = someFunction(input[i]);
}
```

You will now do the same for a quantum computer using pseudo Java code.

> **NOTE** This example doesn't use real Java code because we make some simplifications. There are more differences between classical algorithms and quantum algorithms than only the concept of superposition, as we see in the following chapters. One of the other essential differences that we explain in the next chapter is that qubits don't operate in an isolated way: an operation on one qubit may affect another seemingly unrelated qubit. As a consequence, when doing operations on qubits, the whole system (all qubits) needs to be taken into consideration.

You create an instance of a qubit and bring it into a superposition with a fictive super-position method. Later in this chapter, we explain how a qubit can be brought into a superposition:

```
Qubit qubit = new Qubit();
qubit.superposition();
```

someFunction now has to work with a qubit, so you define it as follows:

```
public Qubit someFunction(Qubit v) {
    Qubit answer;
    ... // do some processing
    return answer;
}
```

So far, this looks similar to the classical case. However, you can now evaluate the case where the qubit is 0 and the case where the qubit holds the value 1 with a single function evaluation by applying the function to the qubit in superposition:

```
Qubit qubit = new Qubit();
qubit.superposition();
qubit = someFunction(qubit);
```

The key element here is that the function someFunction takes a qubit as input and has a qubit as output. If the input qubit is in a superposition state, the function operates on both states. Similarly, if you have a function that has two qubits as input, it can operate on the four different combinations of the qubit states. In general, a function operating on n qubits can operate on 2^n possible states. This explains why the probability vectors are often used when talking about QC, as those vectors have 2^n elements describing the probability of finding the qubits in a specific state.

Now that you know why quantum computers allow for exponentially scaling, you need to find out how to benefit from this, as the exponential power applies only during processing—not during measurement. The trick when writing quantum algorithms is to come up with operations that, when applied, will lead to a measurement that tells more about the solution of a problem. This is shown in figure 4.9: before the quantum system is measured, processing is done by applying quantum gates. Those quantum gate operations modify the state of the probability vector.

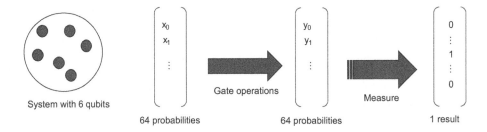

Figure 4.9   **Gates applied to a quantum system with six qubits**

NOTE   Suppose someone gives you 1,000 numbers and tells you that one of them is a prime number. You have to find the index of the prime number. Imagine that you can manipulate those numbers simultaneously and process them in such a way that all of them become 0 except the prime number, which becomes 1. A single measurement, then, reveals the position of the prime number. Although there is no easy quantum algorithm for this purpose, the analogy shows a benefit in being able to process a large number of values, even if the result is a single value.

We've talked several times about operations on quantum systems. This brings us closer to software, as we ultimately want to use software to manipulate the state of a quantum system. Before we turn our attention to software, we explain how quantum gates manipulate qubits and the probability vector.

4.3   *Introducing matrix gate operations*

We try to keep the mathematical parts in this book to a minimum. However, to understand the core concepts of quantum gates, it helps to have a basic understanding of linear algebra and matrix operations. In this section, we briefly describe the required background.

We explain this concept using the simplest (but still useful) quantum gate: the Pauli-X gate. After discussing how the Pauli-X gate corresponds to a matrix operation, we will generalize the concept to all gates.

At the beginning of this chapter, figure 4.1 showed the flow of the discussion. In this section, we add details to that illustration, as shown in figure 4.10.

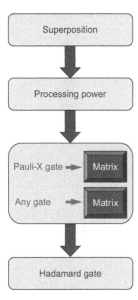

Figure 4.10   Detailing the gate concept: first we discuss the Pauli-X gate, and then we make the concept more general.

These steps are needed to get at the final part of this chapter: the discussion of the Hadamard gate. The Pauli-X gate is easy to comprehend, and you will get a clear understanding of how gates work after this section.

In the previous section, we explained that we can represent the state of a system with n qubits with a vector containing 2^n elements. We mentioned that a quantum computer can do processing on this vector, and in this section, we explain what we mean by this. The fact that a quantum computer can operate on a combination of states at the same moment is a great opportunity for performance, but it comes with some complexity: instead of thinking about individual qubits, you need to think about *probabilities* for the *combination* of qubits.

4.3.1   The Pauli-X gate as a matrix

In the previous chapter, we described the Pauli-X gate. We mentioned that the Pauli-X gate has similarities with the classical NOT gate, and we used the following simple table to explain the behavior of the NOT gate (repeated here for clarity):

input	output
A	NOT A
0	1
1	0

This table would also make sense when talking about the Pauli-X gate, but it takes into account only the basis states, where the input is either 0 or 1. As we mentioned earlier in this chapter, the general state of a qubit can be a linear combination of the basis states. The state is not simply 0 or 1 but a combination of probabilities: the probability that if you measure the qubit, you will measure 0 and the probability that you will measure 1. In this case, a simple table is no longer sufficient to describe the behavior of a gate. You need a table with an infinite number of rows, as shown in table 4.1, taking into account that there are already infinite values between 99% and 100%.

Table 4.1 Behavior of the NOT gate on a qubit

input	output
A	NOT A
100% chance of 0, 0% chance of 1	0% chance of 0, 100% chance of 1
99% chance of 0, 1% chance of 1	1% chance of 0, 99% chance of 1
98% chance of 0, 2% chance of 1	2% chance of 0, 98% chance of 1
...	...
0% chance of 0, 100% chance of 1	100% chance of 0, 0% chance of 1

In QC, a typical way to describe gates is using matrix operations.

4.3.2 *Applying the Pauli-X gate to a qubit in superposition*

The state of a quantum system with qubits can always be represented by a vector. When gates act on qubits, the values in the vector change. In linear algebra, this can be achieved by representing the gate with a matrix and multiplying the matrix with the qubit vector to obtain the new state of the qubit vector. In this section, we show that the Pauli-X gate can be represented by the following matrix:

$$\begin{pmatrix} 0 & 1 \\ 1 & 0 \end{pmatrix}$$

Equation 4.8

Let's start with something simple. First, suppose that the qubit originally held the value 0. You learned in the previous chapter that after applying a Pauli-X gate to this qubit, the qubit will hold the value 1. In Dirac notation, the qubit was originally written as |0>. In vector representation, this corresponds to

$$\begin{bmatrix} 1 \\ 0 \end{bmatrix}$$

Equation 4.9

Applying a gate to a qubit corresponds to multiplying the gate matrix and the qubit vector:

$$\begin{pmatrix} 0 & 1 \\ 1 & 0 \end{pmatrix} \begin{bmatrix} 1 \\ 0 \end{bmatrix} = \begin{bmatrix} 0 \\ 1 \end{bmatrix}$$

Equation 4.10

This equation introduces matrix-vector multiplication. Note that a vector is a special matrix, as it has exactly one column. The result of the matrix-vector multiplication is a new vector. When multiplying a matrix and a vector, there is a requirement that the number of columns in the matrix equal the number of rows in the vector. In this case, there are two columns in the matrix and two rows in the vector, so we have met that requirement. In addition, the resulting vector must have the same number of rows as the original matrix. The Pauli-X matrix has two rows, and the resulting vector has two rows as well.

The values in the resulting vector are calculated as follows: the element at position i in the resulting vector is the sum of the multiplications of all elements at row i of the matrix with the corresponding element in the original vector. The first element in the vector is obtained by $(0 * 1) + (1 * 0) = 0$ and the second element is obtained via $(1 * 1) + (0 * 0) = 1$.

So, the Pauli-X gate applied to a qubit in state |0> (the original vector in the equation) results in the qubit having state |1> (the result after applying the matrix multiplication). This is indeed what we learned in chapter 3.

Now, suppose that the qubit originally held the value 1 and thus is represented with Dirac notation |1> or by the vector

$$\begin{bmatrix} 0 \\ 1 \end{bmatrix}$$

Equation 4.11

In this case, multiplying the Pauli-X gate matrix with the qubit vector goes as follows:

$$\begin{pmatrix} 0 & 1 \\ 1 & 0 \end{pmatrix} \begin{bmatrix} 0 \\ 1 \end{bmatrix} = \begin{bmatrix} 1 \\ 0 \end{bmatrix}$$

Equation 4.12

The result is the vector representation for a qubit with a value of 0 or, in Dirac notation, |0>.

The two use cases we calculated here show that for the "simple" cases where the qubit holds the value 0 or 1, the matrix we created in equation 4.8 corresponds with what we expect from the Pauli-X gate.

But those are two edge cases, and we want to know what happens when a qubit is in a superposition state. In this case, the state of the qubit is written as follows:

$$\psi = \alpha |0> + \beta |1>$$

Equation 4.13

Or it is written like this in vector notation:

$$\psi = \begin{bmatrix} \alpha \\ \beta \end{bmatrix}$$

Equation 4.14

You will now apply a Pauli-X gate to this qubit by multiplying the matrix from equation 4.8 with this vector:

$$\begin{pmatrix} 0 & 1 \\ 1 & 0 \end{pmatrix} \begin{bmatrix} \alpha \\ \beta \end{bmatrix} = \begin{bmatrix} \beta \\ \alpha \end{bmatrix}$$

Equation 4.15

As you can see from this equation, the Pauli-X gate in general swaps the probabilities of finding 0 and finding 1 when the qubit is measured. In the extreme case that the qubit is either 0 or 1 before the Pauli-X gate is applied, the gate simply inverts the value.

4.3.3 *A matrix that works for all gates*

In the previous section, we showed how the Pauli-X gate operating on a single qubit can be described by a multiplication of the Pauli-X gate matrix with the probability vector of the qubit. In this section, you learn how this principle of matrix multiplications works for any gate. Throughout this book, we introduce new gates, and it helps to understand the general principle of how gates relate to matrices. The general action of applying a gate to a single qubit is shown in figure 4.11.

Figure 4.11 Applying a gate to a qubit

This is the equivalent of the following matrix multiplication:

$$\begin{bmatrix} \alpha \\ \beta \end{bmatrix} \rightarrow \begin{pmatrix} a_{00} a_{01} \\ a_{10} a_{11} \end{pmatrix} \begin{bmatrix} \alpha \\ \beta \end{bmatrix} = \begin{bmatrix} \alpha' \\ \beta' \end{bmatrix}$$

Equation 4.16

Originally, the qubit is in the state $|\psi>$, which can also be written as

$$|\psi> = \begin{bmatrix} \alpha \\ \beta \end{bmatrix}$$

Equation 4.17

The gate in figure 4.11 corresponds to this matrix:

$$\begin{pmatrix} a_{00} a_{01} \\ a_{10} a_{11} \end{pmatrix}$$

Equation 4.18

Applying the gate to the qubit corresponds to multiplying the matrix with the qubit probability vector:

$$\begin{pmatrix} a_{00} a_{01} \\ a_{10} a_{11} \end{pmatrix} \begin{bmatrix} \alpha \\ \beta \end{bmatrix}$$

Equation 4.19

The multiplication of the gate matrix with the qubit state results in a new vector describing the qubit state:

$$\begin{pmatrix} a_{00} a_{01} \\ a_{10} a_{11} \end{pmatrix} \begin{bmatrix} \alpha \\ \beta \end{bmatrix} = \begin{bmatrix} a_{00}\alpha + a_{01}\beta \\ a_{10}\alpha + a_{11}\beta \end{bmatrix}$$

Equation 4.20

After applying the gate to the qubit, the qubit is in the following state:

$$\begin{bmatrix} a_{00}\alpha + a_{01}\beta \\ a_{10}\alpha + a_{11}\beta \end{bmatrix} = \begin{bmatrix} \alpha' \\ \beta' \end{bmatrix}$$

Equation 4.21

Now that you've learned how gates correspond to a matrix operation, it is time to talk about a gate that is essential to the subject of this chapter: superposition.

4.4 *The Hadamard gate: The gate to superposition*

To bring a particle into a superposition state, some complex physics need to be applied. Fortunately, for a developer, bringing a qubit into a superposition state simply requires applying a specific gate to that qubit.

Figure 4.12 shows the gate that brings a qubit that is originally in the 0 state into a superposition state. This gate is called the *Hadamard gate*.

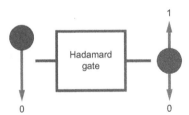

Figure 4.12 A Hadamard gate brings a qubit into a superposition.

The Hadamard gate is one of the most fundamental concepts in QC. After applying a Hadamard gate to a qubit that holds the value 0, there is a 50% chance that the qubit will be measured as 0 and a 50% chance that the qubit, when measured, will hold the value 1.

> **NOTE** We mentioned this before, but it can't be repeated enough: the wording *when measured* is extremely important in the previous explanation. As long as the qubit is not measured, it can stay in a superposition. Other gates can be applied, and the probabilities will change. Only when the qubit is measured will it have a value of either 0 or 1.

Similarly to the Pauli-X gate, the Hadamard gate acts on a single qubit and can be represented by a 2×2 matrix. The Hadamard gate is defined as follows:

$$\frac{1}{\sqrt{2}} \begin{pmatrix} 1 & 1 \\ 1 & -1 \end{pmatrix}$$

Equation 4.22

We want to find out what happens when we apply this gate to a qubit that is in the |0> state. This can be inspected by multiplying the gate matrix with the qubit vector:

$$\frac{1}{\sqrt{2}} \begin{pmatrix} 1 & 1 \\ 1 & -1 \end{pmatrix} \begin{bmatrix} 1 \\ 0 \end{bmatrix} = \frac{1}{\sqrt{2}} \begin{bmatrix} 1 \\ 1 \end{bmatrix} \qquad \text{Equation 4.23}$$

This equation shows that after applying the Hadamard gate to a qubit that is in the |0> state, the qubit enters a new state where the probability of measuring 0 is

$$\left(\frac{1}{\sqrt{2}} \right)^2 = \frac{1}{2} \qquad \text{Equation 4.24}$$

The probability of measuring 1 is also

$$\left(\frac{1}{\sqrt{2}} \right)^2 = \frac{1}{2} \qquad \text{Equation 4.25}$$

In conclusion, applying the Hadamard gate to a qubit that is in state |0> brings the qubit into a superposition state where the probability of measuring 0 is equal to the probability of measuring 1.

What will happen if you apply the Hadamard gate to a qubit that is in the |1> state? The vector representation of a qubit in that state is given by

$$\begin{bmatrix} 0 \\ 1 \end{bmatrix} \qquad \text{Equation 4.26}$$

Hence, applying a Hadamard gate to this qubit means multiplying the Hadamard matrix with the vector in equation 4.26:

$$\frac{1}{\sqrt{2}} \begin{pmatrix} 1 & 1 \\ 1 & -1 \end{pmatrix} \begin{bmatrix} 0 \\ 1 \end{bmatrix} = \frac{1}{\sqrt{2}} \begin{bmatrix} 1 \\ -1 \end{bmatrix} \qquad \text{Equation 4.27}$$

If you measured the qubit at this point, the chance of measuring 0 would be

$$\left(\frac{1}{\sqrt{2}} \right)^2 = \frac{1}{2} \qquad \text{Equation 4.28}$$

and the chance of measuring 1 would be

$$\left(\frac{-1}{\sqrt{2}} \right)^2 = \frac{1}{2} \qquad \text{Equation 4.29}$$

So, in both cases (qubit |0> or qubit |1>), applying a Hadamard gate gives an equal chance for the qubit to be 0 or 1 when measured.

4.5   *Java code using the Hadamard gate*

You learned the theory about the Hadamard gate; now it is time to use it in quantum applications. Let's use the Hadamard gate to create a random number generator; this is a useful application, as random numbers are helpful in cryptography. The code for this example can be found in ch04/hadamard. This example contains two parts. In the first part, you run the application only once. The relevant code for this part is shown next.

Listing 4.1   Running code with a Hadamard gate

```
public static void singleExecution(String[] args) {          At this point, the
    QuantumExecutionEnvironment simulator = new              environment is ready,
     SimpleQuantumExecutionEnvironment();                    and you can add gates.
    Program program = new Program(1);
    Step step = new Step();                      ←           Adds a Hadamard gate
    step.addGate(new Hadamard(0));               ←
    program.addStep(step);                                   Executes the
    Result result = simulator.runProgram(program);  ←┘      quantum program
    Qubit[] qubits = result.getQubits();
    Qubit zero = qubits[0];                                 Measures the qubit. It will
    int value = zero.measure();                  ←┘         have a value of 0 or 1.
    System.out.println("Value = "+value);
}
```

Note the similarity between this example and the Pauli-X example from chapter 3; we will skip detailed explanations about the steps that are similar to the Pauli-X example. You create the QuantumExecutionEnvironment, which runs your program. Next, you create a Program instance, which deals with a single qubit, and a Step instance.

Instead of adding the Pauli-X gate to that step, you add the Hadamard gate:

```
step.addGate(new Hadamard(0));
```

This applies a Hadamard gate to the qubit. By default, qubits are originally in the |0> state. You learned in this chapter that after applying a Hadamard gate to a qubit that is in that state, there is a 50% chance that the qubit when measured will be 0 and a 50% chance that it will be 1.

The remainder of the code is similar to the Pauli-X example. You add the step to the program and run the program on the simulator. Finally, you measure the qubit and print the value. If you run this program once, you will see either

```
Value = 0
```

or

```
Value = 1
```

After the example code prints out the measured value, it visualizes the quantum circuit with StrangeFX. This is done using the following line of code:

```
Renderer.renderProgram(program);
```

Figure 4.13 shows the window containing the quantum circuit. The resulting qubit has a 50% probability of being measured as 1.

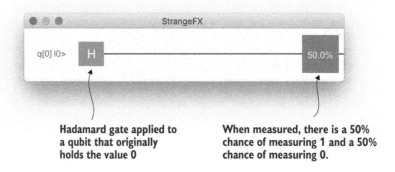

Hadamard gate applied to a qubit that originally holds the value 0

When measured, there is a 50% chance of measuring 1 and a 50% chance of measuring 0.

Figure 4.13   Rendering a quantum circuit with one qubit and one gate: the Hadamard gate

The second part of the example invokes the `manyExecution` function, which is similar to the `singleExecution` discussed earlier—but this time you run the program 1,000 times. The `QuantumExecutionEnvironment` and the `Program` have to be created only once. Add the following loop to the application.

Listing 4.2   Doing multiple runs of the Hadamard snippet

```
int cntZero = 0;
int cntOne = 0;
for (int i = 0; i < 1000; i++) {              ◁── Runs the following loop 1,000 times
    Result result = simulator.runProgram(program);   ◁── Runs the quantum program
    Qubit[] qubits = result.getQubits();
    Qubit zero = qubits[0];
    int value = zero.measure();               ◁── Measures the qubit
    if (value == 0) cntZero++;                ◁── Based on the measured value
    if (value == 1) cntOne++;                     (0 or 1), increments one
}                                                 counter or the other
```

The `runProgram` method is called 1,000 times on the simulator. Each time, you measure the resulting qubit. If the qubit holds the value 0, the `cntZero` counter is incremented. If the qubit holds the value 1, the `cntOne` counter is incremented. After applying this loop, print the results:

```
System.out.println("Applied Hadamard circuit 1000 times, got "
            + cntZero + " times 0 and " + cntOne + " times 1.");
```

The result of this application, therefore, is something similar to this:

```
==================================================
1000 runs of a Quantum Circuit with Hadamard Gate
Applied Hadamard circuit 1000 times, got 510 times 0 and 490 times 1.
==================================================
```

What you have created is a random number generator using the low-level quantum APIs. The single qubit in the program is brought into a superposition and then measured. When running this program on the quantum simulator—or, by extension, on any classical computer that simulates quantum behavior—the randomness is still somehow deterministic, as you use classic algorithms to generate a random number. Typically, simulators work with probability vectors; when a measurement is required, a random number is used to pick one of the probabilities, taking into account, of course, the value of the probabilities.

On real quantum hardware, nature itself will pick one value when we measure the qubit. This process is truly random (at least, that is what most quantum physicists currently assume). Although this simple application seems to be a complex way to generate a random number, it has real value: it shows how you can generate a truly random number using quantum hardware. Random numbers are extremely important in a number of areas, including encryption.

Summary

- The ability of qubits to enter a superposition state is a key concept in quantum computing.
- Quantum superposition is one of the reasons quantum computers can deal with algorithms that show exponential complexity.
- The state of the qubits in a quantum computer can be described by different notations.
- The mathematical equivalent of applying a gate to a qubit is to multiply the probability vector with a (gate) matrix.
- The Hadamard gate is a gate that brings a qubit from a basis state into a superposition state.
- Using Strange, you can deal with Hadamard gates and superposition in your Java quantum applications.

Entanglement 5

This chapter covers

- The analogy between flipping a coin and getting a random number
- Relating flipping coins and probability vectors
- The physical concept of quantum entanglement
- Using quantum entanglement to create connected random numbers
- Understanding how to use superposition and entanglement in Java applications

In the previous chapter, we introduced and explained the concept of superposition. This concept does not exist in classical computing, and it is one of the reasons quantum computing is fundamentally different from classical computing. Nevertheless, we managed to describe superposition in such a way that a Java programmer can use it in their code. In this chapter, we introduce quantum entanglement, a concept that is also not encountered in classical computing and that makes quantum computing powerful. Again, we show how you can simulate quantum entanglement and deal with it by using Java code.

5.1   *Predicting heads or tails*

Have you ever been at a magic show where the magician was able to predict a property that seemed to be random? Maybe a spectator chose a card from a deck, and the magician said which card it was without seeing it. Or perhaps the spectator tossed a coin and hid the result, and the magician could tell whether the coin landed heads or tails.

In this chapter, you learn to write code that does something similar. However, there is no magic involved here. You will use only the programmatic consequences of quantum physics.

Throughout this chapter, we use the analogy of a spinning coin that can land either heads or tails. First you will write classic code that simulates two spinning coins and measures the result. Next, you will write a quantum algorithm that achieves the same thing using the superposition principle explained in the previous chapter. Finally, you will use a new gate and entangle the two coins. Although the measured values are still random, measuring one coin will tell you the value of the other coin. This is shown in figure 5.1.

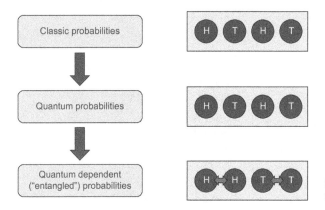

Figure 5.1   We use heads-tails coins throughout this chapter.

5.2   *Independent probabilities: The classic way*

Suppose you have two coins, coin A and coin B. Each coin can be heads or tails. You spin the coins, and while they're spinning, you move them into separate rooms. You wait for the coins to stop spinning, and you see whether they are heads or tails. What will be the result? We can't tell that with certainty, but we can say something about the probabilities. There is a 50% chance that coin A will be heads and a 50% chance that coin A will be tails. Similarly, there is a 50% chance that coin B will be heads and a 50% chance that coin B will be tails. If we link the outcome *heads* with the value 0 and the outcome *tails* with the value 1, there is a 50% chance that a coin will be measured as 0 and a 50% chance that a coin will be measured as 1, as shown in figure 5.2.

In total, there are four possible combinations we can measure:

- Coin A is heads (0), and coin B is heads (0). We denote this as 00 in binary representation, which is 0 in decimal representation.
- Coin A is heads (0), and coin B is tails (1). We denote this as 01 in binary representation, which is 1 in decimal representation.
- Coin A is tails (1), and coin B is heads (0). We denote this as 10 in binary representation, which is 2 in decimal representation.
- Coin A is tails (1), and coin B is tails (1). We denote this as 11 in binary representation, which is 3 in decimal representation.

A heads coin represents the value 0.

A tails coin represents the value 1.

Figure 5.2   Heads = 0, tails = 1

As we stated before, we often talk about probabilities when dealing with quantum computing. In this case, we have four possible outcomes, and each outcome has a specific probability. Hence, the probabilities can be stored in an array where the decimal representation is the index in that array. This array is also called the *probability vector*. The conversion between heads/tails, binary digits, and decimal numbers is shown in figure 5.3.

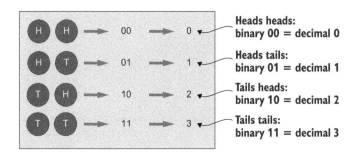

Heads heads:
binary 00 = decimal 0

Heads tails:
binary 01 = decimal 1

Tails heads:
binary 10 = decimal 2

Tails tails:
binary 11 = decimal 3

Figure 5.3   Different combinations of heads and tails

If the coins are totally fair, each of these combinations has an equal chance of occurring. Hence, because the total probability needs to be 100%, each combination has a 25% chance of being measured. In this case, the probability vector is written as follows:

$$p = \begin{bmatrix} 25\% \\ 25\% \\ 25\% \\ 25\% \end{bmatrix}$$

Equation 5.1

As a consequence, if we make 1,000 different independent measurements, we expect every combination to be measured more or less 250 times. We don't need a quantum computer to test this; we can use classical software. The classiccoin example contains a class TwoCoins, which does the bulk of the calculations.

Listing 5.1 Classic application for two coins

```
                              Performs the experiment
                                     1,000 times                        Generates
                                                                        random values
private static final int count = 1000;          ←┘                     using a Random
private static final Random random = new Random();      ←┘

private static boolean randomBit() {            ←        Creates and returns
    boolean answer = random.nextBoolean();              a random boolean
    return answer;
}
                                                         Calculates the probability
public static int[] calculate(int count) {      ←        vector for two coins that
    int results[] = new int[4];                          can be heads or tails
    for (int i = 0; i < count; i++) {
        boolean coinA = randomBit();            ←        Creates two random bits, which
        boolean coinB = randomBit();                     can be either true or false,
        if (!coinA && !coinB) results[0]++;     ←        independent of each other
        if (!coinA && coinB) results[1]++;
        if (coinA && !coinB) results[2]++;               Based on the values of the two
        if (coinA && coinB) results[3]++;                bits, increments one element
    }                                                    in the probability vector
    return results;        ←
}                                  Returns the probability vector
                                   to the caller of the function
```

The randomBit() function in this snippet returns a random boolean. The Math .random() Java function is used to generate a random number between 0 and 1. There is a 50% chance that this number will be smaller than 0.5, in which case the random boolean will be 0, and a 50% chance that the random number will be greater than 0.5, in which case the random boolean will return 1.

The calculate(int count) function takes an integer as input, which defines how many times the experiment needs to be done. It returns an array of four integers, each containing the number of cases in which the experiment led to a specific outcome. In each experiment, two random booleans (coinA and coinB) are obtained using the randomBit() function. Based on the conversion scheme shown in figure 5.3, one of the counters is incremented. If coinA is true and coinB is false, we have a tail-head outcome—equivalent to a 10 outcome—and the counter at index 2 will be incremented. The main method for this application is as follows:

```
                   Invokes the calculate function, returning the array
                   with occurrences of the different possible outcomes
                                                                         Prints the
public static void main(String[] args) {                                 different
    int results[] = TwoCoins.calculate(count);      ←                    outcomes
    System.out.println("We did "+count+" experiments.");   ←┘
```

```
System.out.println("0 0 occurred "+results[0]+" times.");
System.out.println("0 1 occurred "+results[1]+" times.");
System.out.println("1 0 occurred "+results[2]+" times.");
System.out.println("1 1 occurred "+results[3]+" times.");
Platform.startup(() -> showResults(results));
}
```

Shows the outcomes in a graph

NOTE   The code for showing the results in a graph uses JavaFX, but the details are outside the scope of this book.

If you run this application, you see a more or less evenly spread distribution:

```
We did 1000 experiments.
0 0 occurred 272 times.
0 1 occurred 239 times.
1 0 occurred 243 times.
1 1 occurred 246 times.
```

The application also shows a chart of this distribution; see figure 5.4. If you run this application multiple times, the individual probabilities will be different. But in general, all probabilities are equally possible; therefore, the numbers are in the same range.

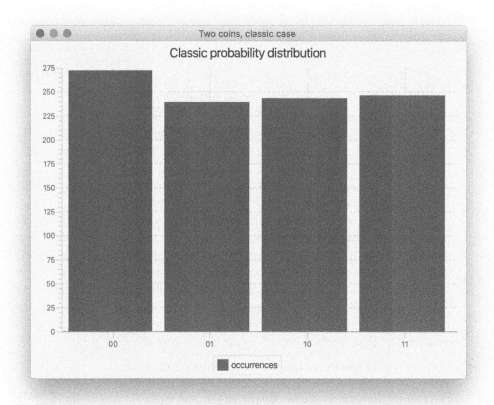

Figure 5.4   Distribution of probabilities

5.3 *Independent probabilities: The quantum way*

So far, there is nothing exciting about our experiment. We showed how we can simulate the random values of the coins by using a classic algorithm on a classic computer. Now we move to quantum computers and do something similar. In the previous chapter, we created a random number generator using quantum gates. More specifically, we learned that the Hadamard gate brings a qubit into a superposition state. When measured, the qubit falls down into one of its basis states, and we measure a value of 0 or 1.

If we extend our system from the previous chapter with another qubit and apply a Hadamard gate to that qubit as well, we can simulate the two coins from the previous (classic) example using qubits. The circuit is shown in figure 5.5.

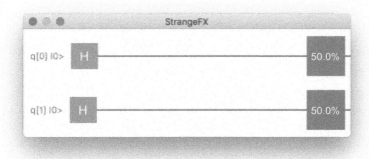

Figure 5.5 Quantum circuit with two qubits

Now let's write the code for generating this circuit and measuring the results. The code for this example is in the ch05/quantumcoin directory of the example repository and is shown next.

Listing 5.2 Quantum application for two coins

```
private static final int COUNT = 1000;

public static void main(String[] args) {
    int results[] = new int[4];
    QuantumExecutionEnvironment simulator = new
            SimpleQuantumExecutionEnvironment();
    Program program = new Program(2);
    Step step1 = new Step();
    step1.addGate(new Hadamard(0));
    step1.addGate(new Hadamard(1));
    program.addStep(step1);
    for (int i = 0; i < COUNT; i++) {
        Result result = simulator.runProgram(program);
        Qubit[] qubits = result.getQubits();
        Qubit zero = qubits[0];
```

Does 1,000 experiments

The results array contains the occurrences for the different possible outcomes.

Creates a quantumExecution-Environment, and constructs the program

Executes the program 1,000 times, and measures the results

```
        Qubit one = qubits[1];
        boolean coinA = zero.measure() == 1;
        boolean coinB = one.measure() == 1;
        if (!coinA && !coinB) results[0]++;          ◄────
        if (!coinA && coinB) results[1]++;
        if (coinA && !coinB) results[2]++;
        if (coinA && coinB) results[3]++;
    }
    System.out.println("We did "+COUNT+" experiments.");
    System.out.println("[AB]: 0 0 occurred "+results[0]+" times.");
    System.out.println("[AB]: 0 1 occurred "+results[1]+" times.");
    System.out.println("[AB]: 1 0 occurred "+results[2]+" times.");
    System.out.println("[AB]: 1 1 occurred "+results[3]+" times.");

    Renderer.renderProgram(program);
    Renderer.showProbabilities(program, 1000);          ◄────

}
```

Depending on the outcome, increments one of the counters

Shows the circuit for this program

Shows the probabilities for the different possible outcomes in a user interface

If you run this code, you see a distribution similar to the classical case. The program prints the following output:

```
We did 1000 experiments.
[AB]: 0 0 occurred 246 times.
[AB]: 0 1 occurred 248 times.
[AB]: 1 0 occurred 244 times.
[AB]: 1 1 occurred 262 times.
```

The program also visualizes this output. Figure 5.6 shows the circuit and the distribution.

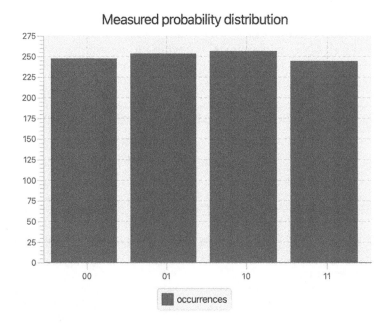

Measured probability distribution

Figure 5.6   Probability distribution for two quantum coins

All outcomes have a 25% probability. There is a 25% chance that an experiment will result in probability index 0, for example, corresponding to a measurement of 00. All other outcomes have a 25% chance as well.

This outcome can be expected if you analyze the code or look at the circuit in figure 5.5. In the code, you create a quantum program that involves two qubits by using the appropriate constructor:

```
Program program = new Program(2);
```

The program contains a single step. In this step, you assign a Hadamard gate to each individual qubit:

```
Step step1 = new Step();
step1.addGate(new Hadamard(0));
step1.addGate(new Hadamard(1));
```

The step is added to the program via

```
program.addStep(step1);
```

Hence, the program you created contains a single step, which contains a Hadamard gate on each individual qubit. Intuitively, it is clear that there is no connection between the qubits, and both qubits will be randomly 0 or 1 when measured, independent from each other. Again, this looks similar to what we showed in the previous section with classical bits.

5.4 The physical concept of entanglement

With the algorithm in the previous section, we showed that we can use a quantum algorithm to achieve the same result as a classic algorithm. But we promised we would go beyond the classic capabilities.

In this section, we make a detour to the physical world to explain the physical concept of quantum entanglement. After this, we go back to the software world and show how we represent this phenomenon.

With the physical representation of qubits, it is possible to achieve something that is impossible to achieve with the physical representation of classic bits, and we can use this in our software representation. In classic software, two different bits do not influence each other. Clearly, we can copy the value of one bit into another bit, but then we explicitly assign a value to the second bit.

The quantum phenomenon we use now is called *quantum entanglement*. This is one of the weirdest physical phenomena, and some of the brightest physicists in history had intense discussions about it. There is still ongoing debate about what quantum entanglement is and how it fits in with other physical concepts.

It's OK to find this weird

As physicist Richard Feynman said, "If you think you understand quantum mechanics, you don't understand quantum mechanics." Fortunately, you don't need to understand quantum mechanics if you want to use it. Although it is interesting to think about the quantum mechanical concepts behind quantum computing, you do not need to understand them before you can program quantum computers. Similarly, you can be a great developer in classical computing without understanding how a transistor works.

We said before that the physical representation of a qubit has a property (let's call it *spin*) that can be in either of two states but also in a superposition of those two states. We can create many qubits and bring them into a superposition state. This is the underlying physical approach in the previous section. If we send our application to a real quantum computer, the corresponding physical flow will be that two qubits are each brought into a superposition state and then measured. Figure 5.7 shows this distribution.

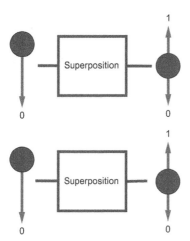

Figure 5.7   **Two particles, each brought into a superposition state**

If one of the particles is measured, there is a 50% chance that we measure spin up and a 50% chance that we measure spin down. If we measure the other particle, there is again a 50% chance that it is in spin up and a 50% chance that it is in spin down. The result of the second measurement is independent of the result of the first measurement. This is shown in figure 5.8.

As you can see, there are four possible outcomes from the measurement. This corresponds to what we showed in the previous section: when measuring the states of two qubits that are independent of each other in a superposition, there are four possible outcomes, each with a probability of 25%.

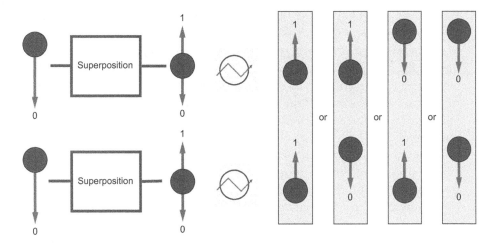

Figure 5.8 Measurement of two particles in superposition

It is already fantastic that this superposition state can be realized, but entanglement goes one step further. Entangled particles or entangled qubits share their state. They might appear to be independent particles in a superposition, but as soon as one of them is measured, the outcome of a measurement of the other is fixed as well. There are a number of ways to create two entangled particles, and we will stay away from discussing this creation process. Schematically, though, it can be represented as in figure 5.9.

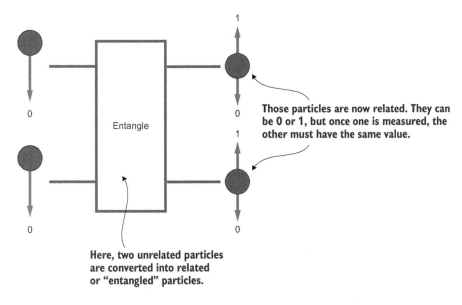

Figure 5.9 Two entangled particles being created

In this scheme, after the physical entanglement operation, both particles are in a superposition—and so far, it looks exactly the same as in the previous case. It turns out, however, that when one particle of an entangled pair is observed and its state is measured, the state of the other particle is determined as well. Depending on what entanglement technique is used, the state of the second particle will be the same as or the opposite of the state of the first particle. For simplicity, we assume that the entanglement technique that is used generates two particles that have the same state when measured.

When the first particle is measured, there is a 50% chance that we measure spin up and a 50% chance that we measure spin down. So far, this is exactly the same as in the previous case (with two particles in superposition). When the second particle is measured, there is also a 50% chance that we measure spin up and a 50% chance that we measure spin down. However—and this is the crucial difference from the previous case—the results are no longer independent. When the first particle results in a spin-up measurement, there is a 100% chance the second particle also results in a spin-up measurement. And when the first particle results in a spin-down measurement, there is a 100% chance that the second particle also results in a spin-down measurement. This is shown in figure 5.10.

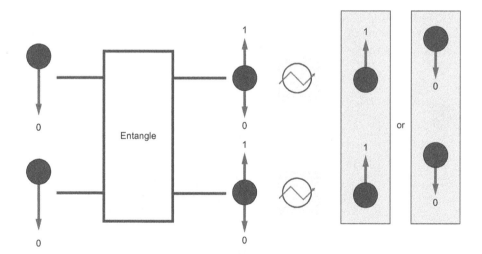

Figure 5.10   Measurement of two entangled particles

In this case, there are only two possible outcomes instead of the four in the previous case: {up, up} or {down, down}. Each of these outcomes has a probability of 50%. It is impossible to have an outcome of {up, down} or {down, up}. Hence, when we measure the individual particles, it seems that they produce a random value. Although that is true, the measurements are 100% dependent on each other.

The analogy of the entangled coins

This is something we can use to address the goal mentioned at the beginning of this chapter: we want to predict the outcome of a coin spin, which seems to be completely random. Indeed, the coin can land heads or tails, but the result will be the same as the result of our entangled coin. So while looking at our coin, we know the result of the other coin without looking at it. Again, note that this is an analogy; the quantum entanglement we are talking about here works with subatomic particles and cannot be extrapolated to large objects like coins.

NOTE   When two particles are entangled, that does not mean they are both in an up state or a down state and that we simply don't know which. They can be in a superposition until one of them is measured. This has significant consequences, as we see in the following chapters.

After this detour to the physical world, we now move back to software. We need to find a way to represent quantum entanglement by using gates so that we can create programs.

5.5   *A gate representation for quantum entanglement*

In the previous chapter, you learned that the physical concept of superposition can be used in quantum computing with the Hadamard gate. In this section, you see how the concept of quantum entanglement can be used in quantum computing as well by using a combination of two gates.

5.5.1   *Converting to probability vectors*

The result of the entanglement of two qubits is that when measured, the qubits are either both in spin up or both in spin down. We will write this information using a probability vector, as we did before. Remember that a qubit with spin up corresponds to a 1 and with spin down corresponds to a 0 value. Hence, the only possible combinations are 00 (both qubits in spin down) or 11 (both qubits in spin up). The probability vector we need to create contains the following:

- *00 (index 0)*— 50% chance that both qubits have spin down
- *01 (index 1)*— 0% chance that one qubit has spin down and the other spin up
- *10 (index 2)*— 0% chance that one qubit has spin up and the other spin down
- *11 (index 3)*— 50% chance that both qubits have spin up

This corresponds to the following matrix:

$$\frac{1}{\sqrt{2}} \begin{bmatrix} 1 \\ 0 \\ 0 \\ 1 \end{bmatrix} \qquad \text{Equation 5.2}$$

The square root of 2 is in this equation because a probability corresponds to the square of the value at a specific position. Indeed, the probability of measuring 00 (index 0) is the square of the value at index 0,

$$\left(\frac{1}{\sqrt{2}}1\right)^2 = 0.5 \qquad\qquad \text{Equation 5.3}$$

which corresponds to 50%. Similarly, the probability of measuring 11 (index 3) is the square of the value at index 0, which also leads to 50%.

The probability of measuring 01 (index 1) is the square of the value at index 1,

$$\left(\frac{1}{\sqrt{2}}0\right)^2 = 0 \qquad\qquad \text{Equation 5.4}$$

which corresponds to 0%.

5.5.2   *CNot gate*

We now need to find a combination of gates that leads to the probability vector we just created. It turns out that this can easily be achieved, but we need a new gate: the CNot gate. The CNot gate operates on two qubits and is symbolically depicted as shown in figure 5.11.

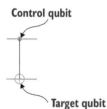

Figure 5.11   Schematic representation of a CNot gate

The two qubits involved in the CNot gate are often called the *control qubit* (top) and the *target qubit* (bottom). The behavior of the CNot gate is as follows:

- If the control qubit is $|0\rangle$, nothing happens. The state after the CNot gate is exactly the same as the state before the CNot gate.
- If the control qubit is $|1\rangle$, the target qubit is flipped: if the target qubit was $|0\rangle$, it is flipped to $|1\rangle$; and if the target qubit was $|1\rangle$, it is flipped to $|0\rangle$.

We can verify this with a simple application using Strange. The example called cnot shows a CNot gate in action in four different cases. The CNot gate acts on two qubits, and we check the outcome for the four different edge cases, where the qubits are in either the $|0\rangle$ or $|1\rangle$ state. The main method of the example invokes those four cases as follows:

```
public static void main(String[] args) {
    run00();
    run01();
    run10();
    run11();
}
```

The run00() method applies the CNot gate to two qubits in the |0⟩ state. The run01() method does the same for the case where the first qubit is in the |0⟩ state and the second is in the |1⟩ state. Similarly, the run10() method applies a CNot gate to a set of qubits where the first is in the |1⟩ state and the second in the |0⟩ state. Finally, the run11() method applies the CNot gate to two qubits that are both in the |1⟩ state.

In the first case, where we use the run00() method, we have both qubits in the |0⟩ state before we apply the CNot gate. Because the control qubit (the first qubit) is |0⟩, we don't expect anything to change in the outcome. Figure 5.12 shows the visual result. As expected, the outcome of this circuit always has the qubits in the Off value, which means when we measure, we always measure 0.

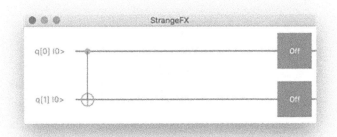

Figure 5.12 CNot gate applied to |00>

Let's have a look at the code that leads to this output. By now, most of the statements in the code should look familiar:

```
QuantumExecutionEnvironment simulator =
        new SimpleQuantumExecutionEnvironment();
Program program = new Program(2);
Step step1 = new Step();
step1.addGate(new Cnot(0,1));
program.addStep(step1);
Result result = simulator.runProgram(program);
Qubit[] qubits = result.getQubits();
Qubit q0 = qubits[0];
Qubit q1 = qubits[1];
int v0 = q0.measure();
int v1 = q1.measure();
System.out.println("v0 = "+v0+" and v1 = "+v1);
Renderer.renderProgram(program);
```

Creates a new environment to run our quantum program

Creates a quantum program working on two qubits

Adds a CNot gate to the first (and only) step in this program. Because the CNot gate operates on two qubits, we need to specify which ones. So, the CNot constructor takes two arguments: the control qubit (in this case, the first one, with index 0) and the target qubit (the second one, with index 1).

Executes the program, and measures the results

Renders the program and outcome

The other three cases require an additional step: before applying the CNot gate, at least one of the qubits needs to be brought into the |1⟩ state. As you learned in chapter 3, this can be done by applying the Pauli-X gate. The following snippet shows how to create the program for applying the case where the control qubit is |0⟩ and the target qubit initially is |1⟩:

Creates a first step

```
Program program = new Program(2);
Step step1 = new Step();
step1.addGate(new X(1));
program.addStep(step1);
Step step2 = new Step();
step2.addGate(new Cnot(0,1));
program.addStep(step2);
```

Applies a Pauli-X gate to the target qubit (with index 1) and adds it to this step

Creates a second step, this time with the CNot gate, and adds it to the program

Figure 5.13 shows the visual output for this circuit. The code for the cases where the input state is |01> and |11> is similar, and you can find it in the example.

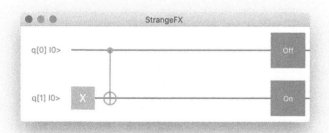

Figure 5.13   CNot gate applied to |10>

If you run the example, you will see four different visuals, with the outcome of the program applied to the four different input states. Figures 5.14 and 5.15 show the two visuals you have not yet seen. In summary, we can create table 5.1, showing how the CNot gate alters (or keeps) the value of the control qubit and the target qubit.

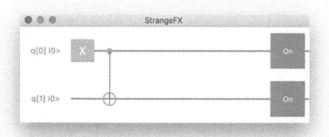

Figure 5.14   CNot gate applied to |01>

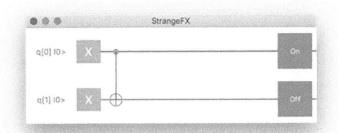

Figure 5.15 CNot gate applied to |11>

Table 5.1 Behavior of the CNOT gate

q0 (before)	q1 (before)	q0 (after)	q1 (after)
0	0	0	0
0	1	0	1
1	0	1	1
1	1	1	0

5.6   *Creating a Bell state: Dependent probabilities*

The four examples in the previous section were special cases where the input to the CNot gate was either |0⟩ or |1⟩. But what should we expect when the control qubit is in a superposition state, as shown in figure 5.16?

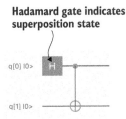

Hadamard gate indicates superposition state

Figure 5.16 CNot gate applied to a control qubit in a superposition

Remember from the previous chapter that you can use a Hadamard gate to bring a qubit into a superposition state. The code for creating this circuit can be found in the example named bellstate:

```
public static void main(String[] args) {
    QuantumExecutionEnvironment simulator = new
     SimpleQuantumExecutionEnvironment();
    Program program = new Program(2);
    Step step1 = new Step();
    step1.addGate(new Hadamard(0));
    program.addStep(step1);
```

```
        Step step2 = new Step();
        step2.addGate(new Cnot(0,1));
        program.addStep(step2);
        Result result = simulator.runProgram(program);
        Qubit[] qubits = result.getQubits();
        Qubit q0 = qubits[0];
        Qubit q1 = qubits[1];
        int v0 = q0.measure();
        int v1 = q1.measure();

        Renderer.renderProgram(program);
        Renderer.showProbabilities(program, 1000);
}
```

If you run this application, you will see one of the following lines as the output:

```
Result of H-CNot combination: q0 = 0, q1 = 0
```

or

```
Result of H-CNot combination: q0 = 1, q1 = 1
```

No matter how many times you run this application, you will see that the output is always one of those two outcomes. You will never see

```
Result of H-CNot combination: q0 = 0, q1 = 1
```

or

```
Result of H-CNot combination: q0 = 1, q1 = 0
```

When you run the application, in addition to the text output, you will also see the circuit output and the probability distribution. From the circuit output, shown in figure 5.17, you can tell that there is a 50% chance that qubit 0 will be measured as 0 and a 50% chance that it will be measured as 1. Similarly, the output shows that there is a 50% chance that qubit 1 will be measured as 0 and a 50% chance that it will be measured as 1.

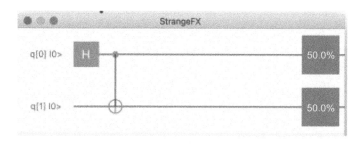

Figure 5.17   Result of a CNot gate applied to a control qubit in superposition

This result matches your observations when you run the example many times—both the first qubit and the second qubit can be measured as 0 and 1. However, this output does not show the additional restriction we observe: the *combinations* are limited. From our observations from the text output, if the first qubit is measured as 0, the second qubit is measured as 0 as well. And when the first qubit is measured as 1, the second qubit is measured as 1 as well. This is shown in the probability distribution, which is rendered in figure 5.18.

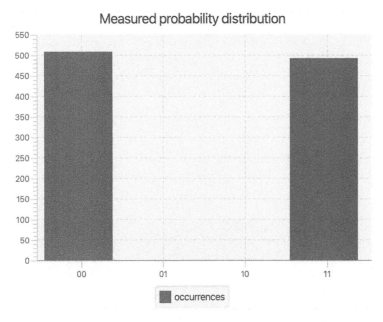

Figure 5.18 Probability distribution of a CNot gate applied to a control qubit in superposition

This is an interesting result. It seems that applying the CNot operator on a pair of qubits where the control qubit is in a superposition and the target qubit is in the $|0\rangle$ state always results in an entangled pair. The result we see here is exactly the state that we described earlier for an entangled pair. This result is also called a *Bell state.*

> **NOTE** When measuring individual elements of an entangled pair, the values you measure seem to be entirely random. Although that is true, there is a full match between the random values of bit elements of the entangled pair.

Hence, by using a combination of a Hadamard gate and a CNot gate, we can create quantum entanglement. The word *create* is not entirely correct, as we didn't physically create entanglement, but the circuit we created results in the same probabilities as the state of two entangled qubits. This means we found a programmatic way to represent the quantum entanglement behavior. In the following chapters, we use this behavior extensively.

5.7   *Mary had a little qubit*

Now that you've learned the basic concepts of quantum computing, you can begin using them in applications. To get you started, we created a simple game based on the Mary Had a Little Lambda application that Stephen Chin created to demonstrate the use of streams and lambdas in Java. (You can read more about this game at http://mng.bz/KoxP.)

We modified the game so that the lambs managed by Mary are actually qubits. The code is available in the ch05 directory in the repository, under the name maryqubit. You can start it by entering

```
mvn clean javafx:run
```

Doing so shows the start screen from figure 5.19.

Figure 5.19   Start screen for Mary Had a Little Qubit

You see Mary in a landscape with several elements. Some of them correspond to quantum gates: when a lamb visits the quantum gate while it is active, that gate is applied to the lamb qubit. At the top of the screen, the corresponding circuit is shown.

There are many things to be discovered in this game, and you are encouraged to browse through the source code. One particularly interesting exercise is the following:

walk with Mary through the gates, and create a three-qubit circuit that shows a Bell state and a third qubit with a Hadamard gate. The result is shown in figure 5.20.

Figure 5.20 Bell state with a Hadamard gate applied to a third qubit

If you look at the code for this game, you will see how you can combine the Strange simulator, the StrangeFX visualization, and your own application. The `StrangeBridge` class is where everything comes together.

Summary

- Quantum entanglement is a state shared between two qubits, where the properties of the qubits are not independent from each other.
- In quantum computing, we can use quantum entanglement and quantum gates that take entanglement into account.
- Using Strange, you can easily create two entangled qubits and measure their state.

Quantum networking: The basics

This chapter covers

- Understanding how quantum computers and quantum networks are related
- The challenges of creating a quantum network
- Writing a teleportation algorithm and a quantum repeater

So far, we've talked about quantum computing. Computing is indeed an important part of the software world, but most applications developed by today's software developers do not work in isolation. On the contrary, applications typically contain different modules that may not be located on the same server. They talk to external components, such as over REST interfaces. They read and write information from and to data storage systems. In general, software is distributed. One of the key elements to get a complete software application working is a reliable, predictable network of computers. Figure 6.1 shows a typical setup of a classical application that combines various modules over a network.

Classical computing relies heavily on a classical network. Similarly, quantum computing can benefit from quantum networks, as we learn in this chapter.

In the previous chapters, the focus was on a quantum computer. You learned how a quantum computer manages a set of qubits and applies gates to those qubits.

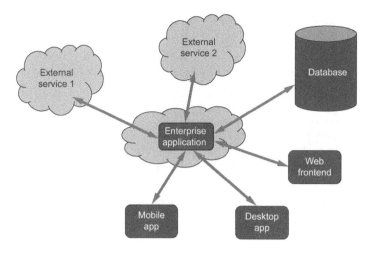

Figure 6.1   Classic application using modules in a network

You created small programs dealing with a number of qubits and gates. All qubits and all gates were local to the program. Although we did not make specific assumptions, it is reasonable to assume that the qubits are located in a single quantum computer and that the gates are in this quantum computer as well, as shown in figure 6.2.

Figure 6.2   A single quantum computer

Everything needed to execute the quantum programs we created in the previous chapters can be contained in a single quantum computer. A similar observation applies to our quantum simulator, Strange. So far, all applications we've created are executed in a `SimpleQuantumExecutionEnvironment`.

It is expected that most useful quantum applications running on a quantum computer require a large number of qubits. However, as you will experience in this chapter, there are also quantum applications that can work with a network of quantum computers that have a small number of qubits. Figure 6.3 shows an example of three small quantum computers connected by a quantum network. Actually, the small

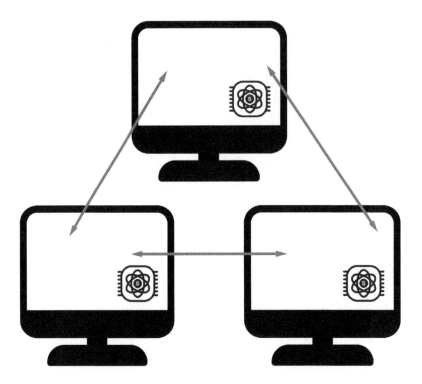

Figure 6.3   A quantum network combining three small quantum computers

quantum computers could be real classical computers with some quantum capabilities, such as the ability to measure or manipulate a single qubit or a few qubits.

The quantum network allows quantum computers to exchange qubits. As a consequence, a qubit from one computer may be transferred to another computer. This sounds similar to the classic case in which a computer sends a bit to another computer.

6.1   *Topology of a quantum network*

The simplest form of quantum networking is a direct connection between two quantum computers, as shown in figure 6.4. With some limitations that we discuss later in this chapter, existing fiber-optic connections can be used to transfer qubits from one quantum computer to another.

A more valuable quantum network contains more than two quantum computers. As in classical networks, opportunities often grow with the number of connected computers. Adding computers can spread the load of heavy computation between different computing instances or connect the system with different input. A possible setup is shown in figure 6.5.

Such a network topology would be harder to realize, as it would require direct connections between the computers. A typical networking approach is to use switches that

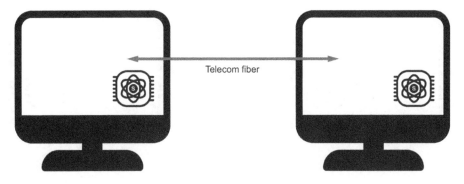

Figure 6.4   A quantum network combining two small quantum computers

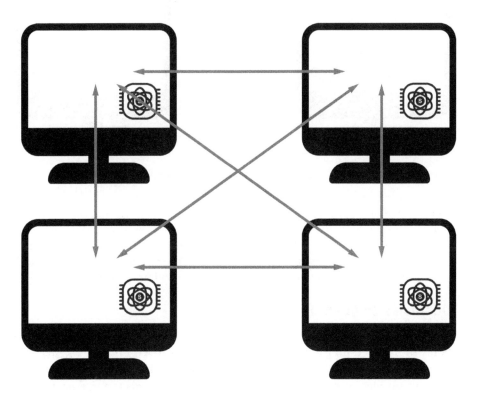

Figure 6.5   A quantum network combining a large number of small quantum computers

direct traffic to the right computer, as shown in figure 6.6. Although the network topology for a quantum network might look similar to the network topology for a classical network, there are important differences that on one hand, make it much harder to realize a quantum network, and on the other hand, open new opportunities.

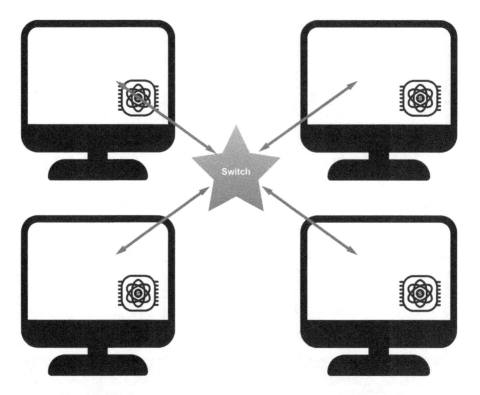

Figure 6.6   A quantum network using a switch to combine small quantum computers

TIP   One of the most intriguing aspects that you can think about for a moment is this: in the previous chapter, you wrote code showing that two qubits in a system can be entangled. The outcome of a quantum program depends on this entanglement. What happens when one of those two qubits is sent to another quantum computer, where it becomes part of another quantum program?

6.2   *Obstacles to quantum networking*

Before we talk about the benefits of quantum networking, we want to temper expectations. In this section, you learn that the typical approach for sending bits over a classical network does not apply easily to quantum networks. In the next section, you see that this problem can be solved. Moreover, doing so leads to huge new opportunities, including secure communication.

6.2.1   *Classical networking in Java*

In the typical case of classic networking, information is transferred from one computer to another computer. Let's look at how this would happen at the level of a Java application.

NOTE   In a typical Java application, developers use libraries on top of the low-level networking APIs that are part of the Java platform. These libraries typically provide convenience methods for easily transferring data from one computer to another, using languages or formats such as XML and JSON. The low-level networking APIs that we use in our examples help us understand how information is transferred from one computer to another.

Developers typically use high-level network libraries that shield them from low-level code. In most enterprise applications, Java developers hardly ever create an instance of the `java.net.Socket` class manually, but the libraries they use make use of this and related classes. Similarly, most developers writing applications using quantum computing do not deal directly with the low-level classes that enable quantum communication. High-level libraries hide the low-level complexity and allow us to take advantage of quantum communication without having to code for it manually.

The blueprint for such a quantum network stack is not yet finalized. A number of groups and standardization organizations are discussing a quantum version of the classical stack shown in figure 6.7. One of the interesting initiatives is the Quantum Internet Alliance (see http://quantum-internet.team). Figure 6.8 shows a proposal for a quantum network stack created by Axel Dahlberg from QuTech (https://qutech.nl), Delft University of Technology. More information about this stack can be found in the paper at https://arxiv.org/pdf/1903.09778.pdf.

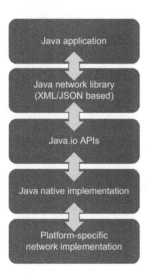

Figure 6.7   A typical approach in which a Java application uses libraries for networking

Application		
Transport	Qubit transmission	
Network	Long-distance entanglement	
Link	Robust entanglement generation	
Physical	Attempt entanglement generation	

Figure 6.8   A QuTech proposal for a quantum network stack

To understand the challenges and opportunities associated with quantum networks, it helps to see how they compare with classical networks. In the example in the ch06/classic directory, a main Java file demonstrates how networking at a low level is done in Java. The relevant code is shown next.

Listing 6.1   Classic network application for sending a byte

```
static final int PORT = 9753;                      ◄──┐  The PORT number defined here is
                                                        shared between the thread that
public static void main(String[] args)                  sends data and the thread that
                  throws InterruptedException {          reads data.
  startReceiver();
  startSender();                      ◄──┐  The code for sending
}                                          bytes is performed on
static void startSender() {                a second thread.
  Thread thread = new Thread(() -> {
    try {
      byte b = 0x8;
      System.err.println("[Sender] Create a connection
                          to port "+PORT);
      Socket socket = new Socket("localhost", PORT);   ◄──┐  The sender thread
      OutputStream outputStream =                            opens a low-level
                  socket.getOutputStream();                  Java network socket.
      System.err.println("[Sender] Write a byte: "+b);
      outputStream.write(b);              ◄──┐  The sender writes a
      outputStream.close();                    specific byte over that
      System.err.println("[Sender] Wrote a byte: "+b);  ◄──┐  socket to the receiver.
    } catch (IOException e) {                               │
      e.printStackTrace();                                     The value of the
    }                                                          transferred byte
  });                                                          can still be used
  t.start();                                                   (such as printed)
}                                                              by the sender

static void startReceiver()
        throws InterruptedException {

  final CountDownLatch latch = new CountDownLatch(1);
  Thread thread = new Thread(() -> {
    try {
      System.err.println("[Receiver] Starting to listen
                    for incoming data at port "+PORT);
      ServerSocket serverSocket =
                  new ServerSocket(PORT);        ◄──┐
      latch.countDown();
      Socket s = serverSocket.accept();          ◄──┐
      InputStream inputStream = s.getInputStream();
      int b = inputStream.read();
      System.err.println("[Receiver] Got a byte "+b);  ◄──┐
    } catch (IOException e) {
      e.printStackTrace();
    }
  }
```

The code for receiving bytes is performed on one thread.

The receiver opens a low-level Java network server socket, listening for incoming requests.

When a connection is discovered at the server socket, a direct socket connection is created between the sender and the receiver.

The receiver reads a byte from this connection.

The receiver prints the value of the byte they received.

```
    });
    thread.start();
    latch.await();
}
```

The output of this application is as follows:

```
[Receiver] Starting to listen for incoming data at port 9753
[Sender] Create a connection to port 9753
[Sender] Write a byte: 8
[Sender] Wrote a byte: 8
[Receiver] Got a byte 8
```

Note that after we send the byte to the other computer, we still have its value locally. Internally, the byte we declared in Java points to some memory in our computer. When the byte is transferred to the other computer, it is not removed from memory. Rather, the low-level network drivers of the operating system read the value of the byte at the specific memory location and send a copy of that value to the other computer.

To developers who are familiar with networking software, that sounds trivial—and indeed, in the case of classic computing it *is* trivial—but it is not trivial when we talk about quantum computers. To explain the challenges at a high level, take a look at the schematic representation of the Java program you just created, shown in figure 6.9.

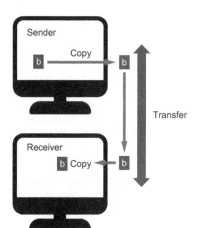

Figure 6.9 Transferring a byte from the sender to the receiver

NOTE The program creates two threads on the same computer, and the figure shows two different computers. The latter is of course more realistic, but in network demonstrations, it is common to use communication between two threads on the same computer that communicate over a socket. The endpoint of a socket is defined by a combination of hostname and portnumber. The hostname corresponds to the physical address of the computer, and the portnumber corresponds to an internal port of the computer. For our purposes,

MX 719 2352

it is enough to specify a port number only and keep the communication in one computer.

Figure 6.9 shows two major steps in classical networking:

1 The byte we want to transfer is copied.
2 The byte is transferred over a network to the other computer (where it is copied again).

The bad news is that there are issues with both of those steps in quantum computing:

- Qubits cannot be copied.
- Qubits cannot easily be transferred over long distances

In the following sections, we discuss these issues in more detail. After that, we explain how these issues can be solved and turned into opportunities.

6.2.2   No-cloning theorem

One of the core concepts of quantum computing is the *no-cloning theorem*, which states that it is impossible to make an exact copy of a qubit. In classical computing, you can inspect the value of a bit and create a new bit with the same value. By doing so, you don't alter the value of the original bit.

The following Java code demonstrates how we can copy the value of a `Boolean` object into another `Boolean` object in Java. Note that this can be done much more simply in Java, but we want to mimic the clone behavior so that we can try to apply that to a Qubit object as well:

```java
static Boolean makeCopy(Boolean source) {
  Boolean target;
  if (source == true) {
    target = new Boolean(true);
  } else {
    target = Boolean.valueOf(false);
  }
  return target;
}

public static void main(String[] args) {
  Boolean tr = Boolean.TRUE;
  Boolean trueCopy = makeCopy(tr);
  System.err.println("Source: "+tr+" and copy : "+trueCopy);


  Boolean fa = Boolean.FALSE;
  Boolean falseCopy = makeCopy(fa);
  System.err.println("Source: "+fa+" and copy : "+falseCopy);
}
```

The makeCopy method takes a Boolean object as a parameter and returns a new Boolean that holds the same value as the passed source parameter.

Makes a copy of a Boolean containing true and prints both the original and the copy

Makes a copy of a Boolean containing false and prints both the original and the copy

In this code snippet, which you can find in ch06/classiccopy in the example repository, we have a makeCopy method that takes a `Boolean` source as an argument and returns a new `Boolean` instance that has the same value as the `source` instance. When the `source` instance holds the value `true`, the returned instance will also hold the value `true`. If the `source` instance holds the value `false`, the returned instance will hold the value `false` as well.

The returned `Boolean` object is a new and independent object. After applying the `makeCopy` method, the values of the `source` and the returned instance are exactly the same. By repeating this procedure, we can make exact copies or a series of bits.

It is tempting to do this in quantum computing as well. Remember from equation 4.3 that we can write the state of a qubit as a linear combination of the $|0\rangle$ state and the $|1\rangle$ state:

$$| \psi > = \alpha\, |0\rangle + \beta\, |1>$$ **Equation 6.1**

If you look at the source code for the `Qubit` class in the Strange simulator in the package `org.redfx.strange`, notice that this class contains the following fields:

```
private Complex alpha;
private Complex beta;
```

These fields contain the information about the qubit needed for the simulator to perform operations. We could easily add a constructor to the `Qubit` class that does the following:

```
public Qubit(Qubit src) {
    this.alpha = src.alpha;
    this.beta = src.beta;
}
```

Doing so, we have a Java approach for copying the information from one qubit to another qubit. Our quantum applications could use it, and we can write code where we happily copy qubits all over the place. However, it would be impossible to implement this on a real quantum computer. Hence, your application could copy qubits in the Strange simulator, but it would not work on a real quantum computer. Therefore, there is no copy constructor for a Qubit in Strange.

It's all about probabilities
The real value of a qubit is not the value that you measure. What makes a qubit so powerful is that it holds a *probability* to measure 0 or 1. Simply measuring a qubit is not enough to reconstruct this probability.

In quantum computing, if you want to inspect the value of a qubit in a superposition, you have to measure it. And as you learned before, measuring a qubit destroys its superposition state, and it falls back into one of the basis states. Hence, by doing so, you destroy the original qubit and don't have enough information to create a new qubit with the same value. Let's show that with an example.

Suppose you have a qubit that has a 25% chance of being measured as 0 and a 75% chance of being measured as 1. The state of this qubit can be written as follows:

$$|\psi> = \frac{1}{2}|0> + \frac{\sqrt{3}}{2}|1>$$

Equation 6.2

Remember that if we want to obtain the possibility of measuring 0, we need to take the square of α. In this case, α equals 1/2; hence, the square of α is 1/4 or 25%. Similarly, the possibility of measuring 1 is obtained as the square of $\sqrt{3}/2$, which is 3/4 or 75%.

Next, suppose you measure the qubit and get the value 0. At that point, you still don't know whether that qubit was holding a value of 0 or was in a superposition with a 25% chance of a 0 measurement, a 95% chance of measuring 0, or any other state—apart from the state where α equals 0. To get an accurate idea of the original state of the qubit, you would need an infinite number of measurements on that qubit. However, the laws of quantum physics determine that you get only a single shot. After one measurement, the qubit is no longer in a superposition state, and the information is lost. In summary, you are not able to reconstruct the probability, and that is the number that matters when talking about qubits.

> **NOTE**   The no-cloning theorem is directly related to quantum physics. Using a software approach, we could easily circumvent this, but then your application would run only on the simulator, not on real hardware when that is available.

The no-cloning aspect of qubits makes a number of things challenging:

- Sending a qubit from one place to another cannot be done by taking a copy and transmitting that copy.
- The concepts of network switches and signal repeaters require that the bits be read, perhaps amplified, and put on a different wire again. If we can't copy a qubit, how can we deal with these networking requirements?

On the other hand, the cloning aspect leads to interesting opportunities. It is impossible to eavesdrop on a quantum communication channel without being notified, for example. When an attacker wants to intercept a qubit being sent from A to B, they have to measure the qubit. As a consequence, the information kept in the original qubit is gone, and the receiver knows that there was an issue. We discuss this opportunity in a later chapter, but we have a few issues to solve first.

In section 6.4, you will learn how to bypass the problem created by the no-cloning theorem. You will create a quantum circuit that allows you to send the information contained in one qubit to another qubit.

6.2.3 *Physical limitations on transferring qubits*

Let's start with some good news: qubits can be transferred via a number of existing physical communication channels. Qubits can be represented by photons that can be transferred via existing optical fiber or via satellite connections. This is interesting, as it means that the investment of telecom companies in classical physical communication infrastructure can largely be reused for quantum communication.

The bad news is that it is difficult to preserve the state of the qubits over a long distance. The longer a photon travels over a fiber-optic cable, the more likely it is that errors will occur. At present, the maximum distance that can be covered is in the range of 100 km. This is large enough to be practical but not large enough to allow for long-distance connections without additional solutions.

If we want to send qubits over long distances by using existing optical fiber, we somehow need to connect the different segments and have the qubits travel from the end of one segment to the beginning of the next segment, as shown in figure 6.10.

Figure 6.10 Sending a qubit over a long distance covering multiple segments

At first sight, this problem may look similar to an existing situation in classical communication: when using a signal to transmit data over a physical connection, the signal becomes weaker (the signal-to-noise ratio decreases) while traveling. At some point, the signal needs to be amplified to increase the signal-to-noise ratio again. This is done by *repeaters*.

The problem with quantum communication is that we cannot simply use a traditional repeater, as that will somehow measure the qubit and amplify it. But by measuring the qubit, the information it carries is gone. Hence, we need a different kind of repeater: a quantum repeater. The current technologies already allow us to create such quantum repeaters, and it can be expected that these components, which are crucial for a real long-distance quantum network, will become available in the upcoming years. In section 6.5, you will write a software solution that allows a quantum repeater to be created.

6.3 *Pauli-Z gate and measurement*

Before we can work on the quantum algorithm that allows us to overcome the obstacles described in the previous section, we have to introduce a new gate, and we need to spend a bit more time on what a measurement means in terms of a quantum program. We use the new gate and the measurement block in the upcoming algorithm.

6.3.1   *Pauli-Z gate*

In section 3.4, we introduced the Pauli-X gate, which is often called the quantum NOT gate. In section 4.3, we explained how this gate can be represented by this matrix:

$$\begin{pmatrix} 0 & 1 \\ 1 & 0 \end{pmatrix}$$

Equation 6.3

A variant to this gate is the Pauli-Z gate, which is represented by the following matrix:

$$\begin{pmatrix} 1 & 0 \\ 0 & -1 \end{pmatrix}$$

Equation 6.4

If you want to know what this gate does when applied to a qubit, you have to multiply this matrix with the probability vector of the qubit. The considered qubit is represented as follows:

$$\psi > = \alpha \left| 0 \right\rangle + \beta \left| 1 \right\rangle$$

Equation 6.5

This corresponds with the following probability vector:

$$\begin{bmatrix} \alpha \\ \beta \end{bmatrix}$$

Equation 6.6

After the Pauli-Z gate is applied to this qubit, the probability vector is calculated as follows:

$$\begin{pmatrix} 1 & 0 \\ 0 & -1 \end{pmatrix} \begin{bmatrix} \alpha \\ \beta \end{bmatrix} = \begin{bmatrix} \alpha \\ -\beta \end{bmatrix}$$

Equation 6.7

Hence, the qubit is now in this state:

$$\psi > = \alpha \left| 0 \right\rangle - \beta \left| 1 \right\rangle$$

Equation 6.8

When only this gate is applied to a qubit, the probability of measuring either 0 or 1 is not altered. Don't let the minus sign in front of β confuse you: the probability of measuring 1 is the square of $-\beta$, which is still β^2.

The physical relevance of this gate is beyond the scope of this book. It is important, though, to realize that there are physical ways to realize this gate, and it corresponds to real quantum physics behavior, so we can use it in software. The symbol for this Z gate is shown in figure 6.11.

Figure 6.11   Strange symbol for the Pauli-Z gate

Similar to how the CNot gate introduced in section 5.5.2 conditionally applies the Pauli-X gate when a control qubit would be measured as 1, the Controlled-Z gate (Cz) is a two-qubit gate that applies a Pauli-Z gate when the control qubit measures as 1. The symbol for this Controlled-Z gate is shown in figure 6.12.

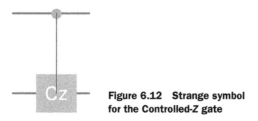

Figure 6.12 Strange symbol for the Controlled-Z gate

6.3.2 *Measurements*

We talked about measurements before. In section 3.1, we explained that when a qubit is measured, it will always have the value 0 or the value 1. If the qubit was in a superposition state before the measurement, that superposition state is gone after the measurement. In many quantum simulators, including Strange, it is possible to do a measurement on a qubit in a program. Once a measurement is applied, the qubit is destroyed, and the result is a classical bit. Hence, it is no longer possible to apply any gate that relates to superposition. In Strange, you can do a measurement on a qubit by applying a measurement operation to it. Although a measurement is not really a gate, Strange provides the `org.redfx.strange.gate.Measurement` class, which extends from the `Gate` interface. The reason is that by doing so, the `Measurement` class can benefit from functionality provided by the `Gate` interface and subclasses. We use the term *measurement operation* to make it clear that a measurement is not a gate.

When a measurement operation is applied to a qubit in Strange, the line representing the qubit flow becomes a double line. The measurement operation itself is marked with an *M*, as shown in figure 6.13.

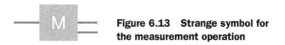

Figure 6.13 Strange symbol for the measurement operation

Exercise 6.1
You can create a simple quantum circuit with two qubits. First, apply a Hadamard gate to the first qubit. Next, apply a Controlled-Z gate to the two qubits, with the first qubit being the control qubit. Finally, measure the two qubits. The solution to this exercise can be found in the ch06/hczmeasure directory in the source code repository.

6.4   Quantum teleportation

Because of its name, quantum teleportation is a concept that easily attracts attention. Although we are not going to teleport a person from one physical location to another location, what we will discuss is an extremely important step toward a real quantum network.

6.4.1   The goal of quantum teleportation

In this section, you will send information from a qubit that is held by Alice to a qubit held by Bob. Alice's qubit stays with Alice, though, so you do not physically transfer the qubit. However, the result is that you transfer some quantum information from Alice to Bob. That sounds related to the core problem described in the previous sections: a qubit cannot be cloned, but if we have a way to transfer its quantum information over a distance, we get much closer to a quantum network.

The following sections will show the algorithm for teleportation. Step by step, you will create a program that achieves quantum teleportation using the techniques and gates discussed earlier. It can be mathematically proved that the algorithm you are about to program indeed teleports the information from Alice to Bob. However, this proof is not in the scope of this book. You will artificially give some initial values to the qubit you want to teleport so that you can check later whether the teleportation was successful.

6.4.2   Part 1: Entanglement between Alice and Bob

The qubit held by Alice is shown in figure 6.14 as qubit q. A prerequisite for quantum teleportation is that Alice and Bob share an entangled pair of qubits, as shown in figure 6.15.

Figure 6.14   Alice wants to send her qubit q to Bob.

Figure 6.15   Alice and Bob share an entangled pair of qubits.

From what you learned in the previous chapter, you can write the code to obtain this state. The following listing shows how to achieve the situation in figure 6.15.

Listing 6.2   Alice and Bob sharing an entangled pair

Adds a Hadamard gate to qubit a →

```
Program program = new Program(3);        ◁
Step step1 = new Step();
step1.addGate(new Hadamard(1));
Step step2 = new Step();
```

This program contains three qubits: q, the qubit to teleport to Bob; and a and b, the entangled qubits.

Adds a
CNot gate
to qubits a
and b

```
step2.addGate(new Cnot(1,2));
program.addStep(step1);
program.addStep(step2);
```

**Adds to the program the
steps (with the gates)
created so far**

Schematically, this code snippet is represented by the circuit in figure 6.16. Keep in mind that qubits q[0] (which is qubit q) and q[1] (which is qubit a) are located with Alice, whereas qubit q[2] (which is qubit b) is located with Bob.

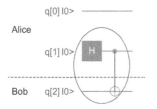

Figure 6.16 **Circuit showing Alice with
a qubit q and Alice and Bob sharing an
entangled pair (circled)**

6.4.3 Part 2: Alice's operations

In the second part of the teleportation algorithm, Alice will let qubit q interact with her component of the entangled qubit pair. Schematically, this is shown in figure 6.17.

Figure 6.17 **Alice lets her qubit interact
with her part of the entangled pair.**

It can be mathematically proved that the following steps will transfer the information from qubit q to qubit b, which is held by Bob. However, instead of the mathematical evidence, we build the required code here and then test it. First, Alice applies a CNot gate between her qubit q and her half of the entangled pair. Next, she applies a Hadamard gate to her qubit. The schematic representation of the quantum circuit created so far is shown in figure 6.18.

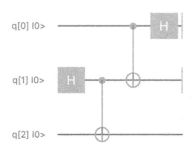

Figure 6.18 **Adding the interaction
between Alice's qubit and her half of the
entangled pair**

We added two steps to the quantum circuit, and in the code, this is achieved as follows:

```
Step step3 = new Step();
step3.addGate(new Cnot(0,1));
Step step4 = new Step();
step4.addGate(new Hadamard(0));
program.addStep(step3);
program.addStep(step4);
```

Adds a CNot gate to the qubits q and a

Adds a Hadamard gate to the qubit q

New steps (with the gates) we created

In the next step, Alice has to measure her two qubits. The schematic representation of the quantum circuit created so far is shown in figure 6.19.

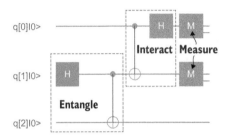

Figure 6.19   Alice measures her qubit and qubit a.

The code required to perform these measurements is

```
Step step5 = new Step();
step5.addGate(new Measurement(0));
step5.addGate(new Measurement(1));
program.addStep(step5);
```

6.4.4   *Part 3: Bob's operations*

Finally, based on the measurements done by Alice, Bob applies some operations on his qubit. If the measurement of the first qubit (the original qubit you want to teleport) is 1, Bob applies a Pauli-X gate to his qubit. If the measurement of the qubit a is 1, Bob applies a Pauli-*Z* gate to his qubit. The flow for these operations is shown in figure 6.20,

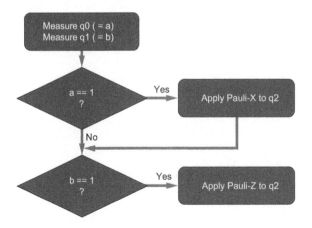

Figure 6.20   Flow for Bob's operations, depending on the values of Alice's qubits

and the schematic representation of the quantum circuit you created is shown in figure 6.21.

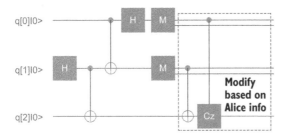

Figure 6.21 Depending on Alice's measurements, Bob applies a Pauli-X and/or a Cz gate.

The code for these conditional steps is

```
Step step6 = new Step();
step6.addGate(new Cnot(1,2));
Step step7 = new Step();
step7.addGate(new Cz(0,2));
program.addStep(step6);
program.addStep(step7);
```

If qubit q[1] (which is a) is measured as 1, apply a Pauli-X gate to q[2] (which is b).

If qubit q[0] (which is q) is measured as 1, apply a Pauli-Z gate to q[2].

That is all that is needed to teleport the information from qubit q to qubit b.

6.4.5 *Running the application*

Now you can run the entire program, which is in the ch06/teleport directory, by running

```
mvn javafx:run
```

You will see the output shown in figure 6.22.

The output contains two parts. In the top half of the screenshot, you see the circuit with three qubits, with the probability of measuring 1 on the right. This probability result shows several things:

- There is a 50% chance that qubit q (denoted by q[0]) will be measured as 1 and a 50% chance that it will be measured as 0.
- There is a 50% chance that qubit q_A (denoted by q[1]) will be measured as 1 and a 50% chance that it will be measured as 0.
- Qubit q_B (denoted by q[2]) is guaranteed to be measured as 0.

The last part is the most important. Initially, q was holding the value 0. At the end of the teleportation circuit, the value of q is not determined, but the value of q_B is now 0. Hence, the information from qubit q is teleported to qubit q_B.

The same information can be obtained by analyzing the bottom part of the figure, which shows the statistical results of 1,000 simulated executions of our quantum teleportation program. The x-axis shows the potential outcomes. The first value,

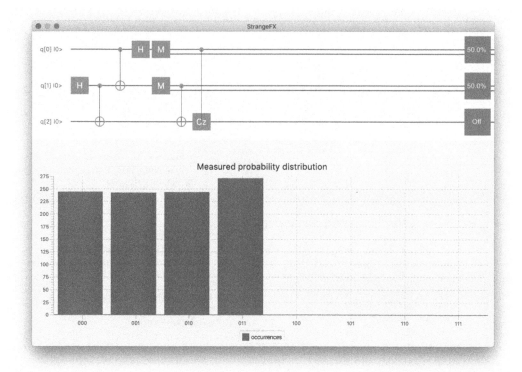

Figure 6.22   Output from the teleport program

000, corresponds to the case where the three qubits are all measured as 0. The second value, 001, refers to the case where the first qubit (q[0] or q) is measured as 1 and the other qubits are measured as 0.

> **TIP**   It is important to match the qubits in the top part with the outcomes in the bottom part of figure 6.23. In a quantum circuit, we show the qubit with index 0 (the least significant qubit) at the top. The qubit with the highest index (the most significant qubit) is at the bottom. When we write the qubits in a sequence, we start with the most significant qubit on the left and end with the least significant qubit on the right.

Of the 1,000 runs,

- About 250 had outcome 000 (hence, all qubits were measured 0).
- About 250 had outcome 001, which means q was measured as 1 and both q_A and q_B were measured as 0.
- About 250 runs had outcome 010, which means q was measured as 0, q_A was measured as 1, and q_B was measured as 0.
- About 250 runs had outcome 011, which means q was measured as 1, q_A was measured as 1, and q_B was measured as 0.

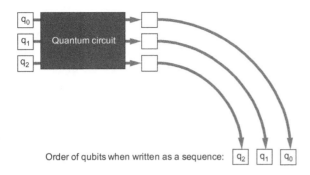

Figure 6.23 Link between qubit order and probability sequences

Note that in all those cases, q_B is measured as 0. The other qubits can hold either 0 or 1, but q_B is always 0.

These results seem to indicate that the algorithm you programmed is indeed teleporting a qubit from Alice to Bob. At least, when the value of Alice's qubit is 0, the resulting value of Bob's qubit is 0, too.

> **Exercise 6.2**
> You can check whether the algorithm also works when Alice's qubit has the value 1. In that case, we expect that the result of the algorithm always has the value of q_B be 1 as well.

If you did the exercise correctly, you added a Pauli-X gate to the first qubit so that Alice's qubit was holding a 1 before the whole teleportation algorithm started. This shows that the algorithm is also working when the qubit is in the 1 state. But what if it is in a superposition?

Fortunately, Strange can test this. Before a program is executed, you can initialize the value of a qubit using the `Program.initializeQubit (int index, double alpha)` method. In this method, `index` specifies the index number of the qubit we want to set, and `alpha` specifies the value we want to give to $alpha$. Add the following line to the program before the `runProgram` is invoked:

```
program.initializeQubit(0, .4);
```

Doing this sets the α value of the original qubit q[0] to 0.4. The probability of measuring 0 is the square of α, which means there will be a 16% chance of measuring 0 and an 84% chance of measuring 1.

If you run the modified program, you'll see something similar to the the output shown in figure 6.24. In the top half of the output, we see that there is now an 84% chance that Bob's qubit q[2] is measured as 1. The bottom part of the figure shows a similar result. This is exactly what we hoped for: it shows that the algorithm teleports the quantum information originally contained in the qubit held by Alice to a qubit held by Bob. Again, note that we didn't provide mathematical evidence, which is beyond the scope of this book. You can find evidence in a number of online resources, such as Ryan LaRose's seminar "The Quantum Teleportation Algorithm" (http://mng .bz/Rqav).

Congratulations; you just sent a qubit from one person to another!

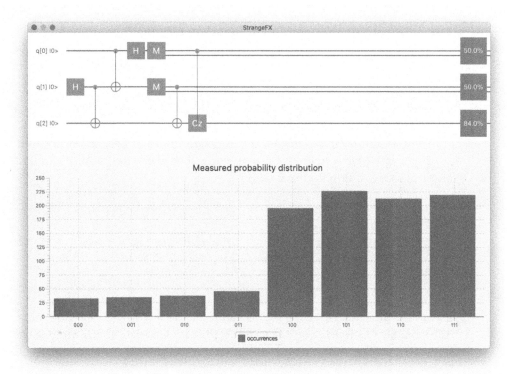

Figure 6.24   Output from the teleport program with an initialized qubit

6.4.6   *Quantum and classical communication*

An important thing to note is that there is only limited quantum interaction between Alice and Bob. In the first step of the algorithm, you created an entangled pair of qubits in which one part of the entangled pair is held by Alice and the other part is held by Bob. Apart from this step, no quantum communication is needed between Alice and Bob. Whether Bob needs to apply a Pauli-X gate, a Pauli-Z gate, or nothing at all depends on the outcome of two measurements done by Alice. The measurement result is always a classical bit, so the outcome can be transferred by using a classical network. Therefore, the communication aspects of the quantum teleportation algorithm can be split into two steps:

1 Make sure Alice and Bob each have a qubit that belongs to an entangled pair.
2 Perform classical communication to send the two measurement results (0 or 1) from Alice to Bob.

Schematically, this is shown in figure 6.25.

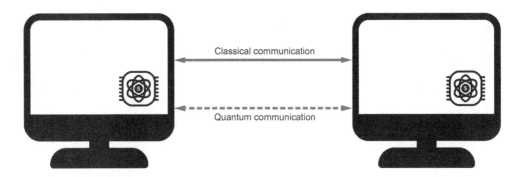

Figure 6.25   Communication between Alice and Bob is split between a classical channel and a quantum channel.

In this figure, the entangled qubit travels over a quantum channel, and the outcome of the measurements travels over a classical channel. As a result, if we have a device that can create an entangled pair of qubits, and if that device can send one of these qubits to Bob, we can transfer any qubit from Alice to Bob without requiring additional quantum interactions between Alice and Bob.

6.5   *A quantum repeater*

In the previous section, you managed to transfer information from one qubit to another qubit without violating the no-cloning theorem. If we can transfer entangled qubits, we can transfer the information contained in a qubit.

But what if Alice and Bob are located far away from each other (more than 1,000 km apart)? The classical data channel is not a problem. If the signal-to-noise ratio drops too much, classical repeaters can be used to amplify the signal. However, it becomes extremely difficult to send one of the entangled qubits from Alice to Bob. In this section, you create a software solution for this problem that uses the code you wrote earlier in this chapter.

We need to use quantum repeaters. A quantum repeater will not amplify the signal in a qubit (as that would require us to measure it and thus destroy the information), but it can use the same quantum teleportation to transfer the information from one segment to the next segment, as explained in figure 6.26.

Before we show the code for creating this quantum repeater, we'll take a high-level look at how to do this. Figure 6.15 shows the relatively simple case in which Alice and Bob are close to each other (that is, close enough to send half of an entangled pair from Alice to Bob). The case with a quantum repeater in between Alice and Bob is shown in figure 6.27.

Figure 6.26   A quantum repeater separating the distance between Alice and Bob into segments, transferring the qubit from one segment to the other

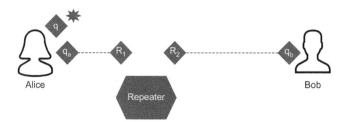

Figure 6.27   A quantum repeater between Alice and Bob

In this case, there are two entangled pairs:

- Alice and the repeater share an entangled pair with qubits q_A and R_1.
- The repeater and Bob share an entangled pair with qubits R_2 and q_B.

The code for the quantum repeater can be found in the directory ch06/repeater of the example repository. Because you are now dealing with five qubits (one qubit with information you want to teleport and two entangled pairs of qubits), the program is constructed as follows:

```
Program program = new Program(5);
```

Preparing the system requires the creation of two entangled pairs. In the quantum teleportation code, the entangled pair was created at the beginning of the code. We extend this code as follows (the lines we added are annotated):

```
Step step1 = new Step();
        step1.addGate(new Hadamard(1));
        step1.addGate(new Hadamard(3));            Adds a Hadamard
        Step step2 = new Step();                   gate to q[3]
        step2.addGate(new Cnot(1,2));              Adds a CNot gate
        step2.addGate(new Cnot(3,4));              between q[3] and q[4]
```

Note that you add a Hadamard gate to qubit 3 and a CNot gate between qubits 3 and 4, creating an entangled pair between qubits 3 and qubits 4. Apart from this preparation, the first part is to transfer the information from qubit q to qubit R1 using the teleportation algorithm created earlier. The flow of this first part is shown in figure 6.28. The code is identical to the code in the teleportation algorithm, and we won't duplicate it here.

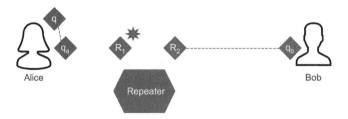

Figure 6.28 Alice interacts with the first entangled pair, teleporting her qubit to R1.

The information that was originally in Alice's qubit q is now in qubit R_1 at the repeater. Next, you repeat the teleportation algorithm, this time teleporting the information in R_1 to q_B. The flow of this second part is shown in figure 6.29.

Figure 6.29 The repeater let the R1 qubit interact with the second entangled part, thereby teleporting the information in the qubit to qB.

The code required is similar to the first part, but the gates operate on different qubits. In the first part, steps 3 to 7 were doing the teleportation. You add steps 8 to 12 to perform similar operations on the other qubits:

Measures q[2]

```
Step step8 = new Step();
step8.addGate(new Cnot(2,3));
Step step9 = new Step();
step9.addGate(new Hadamard(2));
Step step10 = new Step();
step10.addGate(new Measurement(2));
step10.addGate(new Measurement(3));
Step step11 = new Step();
step11.addGate(new Cnot(3,4));
Step step12 = new Step();
step12.addGate(new Cz(2,4));
```

Adds a CNot gate between q[2] and q[3]

Applies a Hadamard gate to q[2]

If q[3] is measured as 1, applies a Pauli-X gate to q[4]

If q[2] is measured as 2, applies a Pauli-Z gate to q[4]

Measures q[3]

Note that in the code in the example repository, we artificially initialized the original qubit (the one we want to transfer) similarly to how we did it before so that it has a 16% chance of being measured as 0 and an 84% chance of being measured as 1. This is achieved with the same code as in the quantum teleportation algorithm:

```
program.initializeQubit(0, .4);
```

Note that we do this only so that the results are easier to interpret.

When the program is executed, the result should be similar to the output in figure 6.30. From this output, it is indeed clear that the information originally contained in Alice's qubit q[0] is transferred to the qubit held by Bob, q[4].

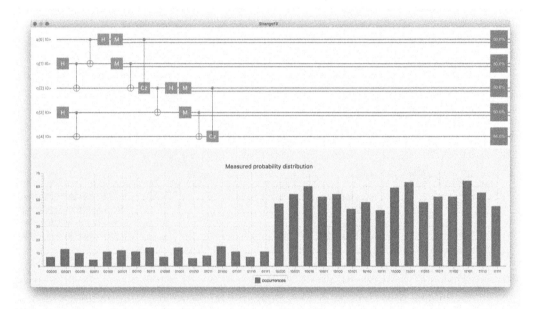

Figure 6.30 Result of the quantum repeater program

Summary

- Classical networks provide many benefits for classical computing; similarly, quantum networks can provide important benefits for quantum computing.
- To realize quantum networks, a number of low-level problems need to be fixed. This is currently being done, and standards are being discussed.
- You can create a Java application that simulates a quantum network and send a qubit from one part of the network to another part of the network.
- Using Strange, you can create a quantum repeater, allowing you to teleport qubits over longer distances.

Part 3

Quantum algorithms and code

Ultimately, developers write code that fixes problems. Now that we have explained the core ideas and fundamental concepts, it is time to see how traditional software problems can benefit from them.

Chapter 7 dives deeper into the HelloStrange example introduced in chapter 2. We study the example as part of a software application that uses quantum computing, bringing it closer to the daily work environment of a developer. In chapter 8, we implement an algorithm that allows for secure communication using quantum computing. The implementation is written in Java, and it can be used in many existing communication libraries. Next, in chapter 9, we create an implementation of the Deutsch-Jozsa algorithm, which is well known in the quantum computing field. Although the direct practical relevance of this algorithm is limited, the concept is important: it gives us an idea about what parts of typical applications may benefit from using quantum computing. Chapter 10 introduces Grover's search algorithm. In this chapter, we also look in detail at a quantum oracle and explain how it relates to classical black box functions. Finally, in chapter 11, we show a Java implementation of Shor's algorithm, which is one of the most famous quantum algorithms: it allows us to factor large integer numbers much faster than a classical algorithm can.

Our HelloWorld, explained

This chapter covers

- Introducing quantum computing simulators
- Using Strange for high- and low-level programming
- Debugging quantum applications using Strange and StrangeFX
- Understanding runtime targets: local, cloud, and real device

Tools in software development have specific goals. Some tools help with developer productivity; others help manage dependencies or give easy access to specific frameworks. Developers using those tools should be aware of what the tools they use can do and what their limitations are. In this chapter, we explain the benefits of quantum computer simulators, and we explore some of the specific features of Strange that make the use of quantum computing algorithms easy for existing (Java) developers. Strange, like any other quantum computer simulator, is not going to solve all our application issues by applying a quantum sauce to it. But it will help us benefit from quantum computing without being experts in quantum computing. To benefit maximally from the advantages Strange is offering, some understanding of quantum computing tools in general is helpful. That is the focus of this chapter.

The Java code for the HelloWorld example in chapter 2 is familiar to Java developers. The goal of Strange is to provide a library that is both familiar to Java developers and capable of using the quantum phenomena discussed in earlier chapters.

For some developers, quantum computing will be an implementation detail that they don't need to worry about. For others, using the right quantum computing concepts in the right place can be the main differentiator of their application.

With Strange, both options are possible. We discuss the typical stack for a high-level programming language on top of quantum hardware. Before we do that, we make the analogy with classical stacks. We do so for two reasons:

- The option to write low-level code that allows us to exploit specific hardware functionality or high-level code that is not dealing with any hardware specifics exists in the classical stack as well. We can learn from the classical approach to come up with options for a quantum stack.
- We explain why the quantum stack and the software stack are different and why we can't simply have a classical software stack on top of quantum hardware.

7.1   From hardware to high-level languages

There are typically many steps between the hardware operations of a computer and the high-level programming languages used by developers. Schematically, the flow in figure 7.1 shows a classical software stack running on top of hardware (a CPU).

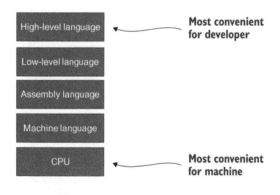

Figure 7.1   Typical software stack on top of a classical CPU. The hardware is at the bottom. The top of the stack is a high-level language used by software developers. The layers in between allow the next layer to be built on top of the previous layer.

> **NOTE**   The relevant hardware of a classical stack consists of more than the CPU. However, the goal of this chapter is not to explain the classical hardware-software stack; hence, we make this oversimplification.

The machine language is integrated with the CPU. Different types of CPUs have different kinds of machine language; assembly language is a more readable format, but it still depends on the CPU type. Low-level languages abstract most of the CPU-specific architecture but may still require differences for various types of CPUs (such as 32-bit or 64-bit). A high-level language like Java does not depend on hardware at all.

Figure 7.2 shows the relative amount of code reuse for code written in the different layers in the stack for two different CPUs: AMD64 and AARCH64. At the low level, the machine language for those CPUs is different, and there is no code reuse. The higher in the stack, the smaller the differences, and the more code can be reused. Finally, in the Java layer, there is 100% code reuse. A Java application that runs on an AMD64 CPU has the same source code as a Java application that runs on an AARCH64 CPU.

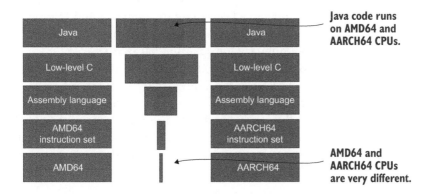

Figure 7.2 Comparison of code reuse when targeting two different CPUs. The wider the bar in the middle column, the more code reuse. Code for high-level languages typically runs on different kinds of hardware. Low-level code requires parts that are relevant only to a specific architecture (such as AMD64 or AARCH64).

Compilers and linkers make sure an application written in a high-level programming language can ultimately be executed using the specific hardware that belongs to a specific computer. One of the reasons for the success of the Java platform is that it allows us to write applications in a single language (such as Java) and then execute these applications on all kinds of hardware, ranging from cloud servers over desktops running Windows, macOS, or Linux to mobile and embedded devices. At the lower levels, there are many differences between the different target systems, but we are shielded from those differences. The Java platform achieves this thanks to the concept of Java bytecode. Java applications, created by developers, are translated into Java bytecode, which is a representation of the application in a platform-independent format. When the application is executed, this platform-independent bytecode is translated into machine-specific instructions, which are different on each platform.

> **TIP** Developer productivity increases if we can focus on issues specific to our application. Tools (such as quantum libraries) help shield us from implementation concepts that are important for the success of a project as a whole but not relevant to us.

7.2   *Abstractions at different levels*

Applications written in a high-level language like Java can use different types of hardware. Java applications can be executed on a Linux system with an AMD 64 CPU, but also on a Linux system with an AARCH64 CPU or a Windows system with an AMD64 CPU.

You may wonder whether a quantum chip can replace the existing classical chips and have existing applications running on top of those quantum chips. If that is the case, the schema in figure 7.2 also applies to the case where the CPU is a quantum computer. In that case, we can keep all our existing languages and libraries and add another low-level abstraction layer that translates the high-level language (such as Java) into sort of an assembly language for quantum hardware.

However, as you learned in the previous chapters, a number of things make quantum hardware different from classical hardware, such as superposition (chapter 3) and entanglement (chapter 4). If we want to use the quantum capabilities of quantum processors, the layers above the hardware should use these capabilities. That means we need to use superposition and entanglement in the higher layers of the stack and make it possible for high-level application languages to use them. Those concepts are not present in the classical assembly languages.

> **NOTE**   To use the real power of quantum computing, the core concepts (such as superposition and entanglement) need to be used inside the software stack. That does not mean they have to be exposed at the top level of any high-level language.

There are several approaches:

- Don't make abstractions, and propagate the quantum characteristics to the high-level application language. In this case, we need to understand and use quantum concepts such as superposition and entanglement.
- Make abstractions at the low level, and have high-level languages use these abstractions. In this case, high-level developers do not need to understand anything about quantum computing. This approach requires high-level languages to be aware of all aspects of quantum computing. It is up to the language (or its implementation) to decide what parts of an application need to be executed using a classical or quantum approach.
- Do something in between.

The first approach is followed by Microsoft, and the third approach is followed by most other initiatives. With Strange, we use the third approach as well. The second approach would allow most developers to use quantum computing without even understanding the basics of it. This is not unrealistic in the distant future, but it will take a long time before languages are capable enough to hide all quantum characteristics from high-level development. Even then, there will be use cases in which it is beneficial to use quantum characteristics directly.

7.3 Other languages for quantum computing simulators

Strange is not the only quantum computer simulator out there. A large and growing number of quantum simulators follow the same or a different approach. Several big IT companies (such as Microsoft, IBM, and Google) have also created quantum computer simulators.

7.3.1 Approaches

Microsoft created a domain-specific language (DSL) called Q# based on the analogy of C# and F#. The advantage of a DSL is that it allows us to add specific features in the language that we can use. By doing so, it is possible to optimize applications for quantum features such as superposition and entanglement. The drawback of this approach is that we need to learn yet another new language and also have a deep understanding of quantum computing.

IBM and Google took a different approach. They created simulators in Python, which is clearly an existing language. The advantage of this approach is that Python developers do not need to learn a new language to get started with quantum computing. This is the same advantage that Java developers have when using Strange.

7.3.2 Resources for other languages

As mentioned before, the research area related to quantum computer simulators is rapidly growing. It is impossible to write a list today that would still be complete by the time this book is published; however, some online resources are kept up to date as they evolve. Following are a few pointers to relevant resources, but keep in mind that these resources may become outdated or be moved to different locations:

- An exhaustive list of quantum simulators, sorted by programming language, can be found at https://www.quantiki.org/wiki/list-qc-simulators.
- The IBM Qiskit project is available at https://qiskit.org.
- Microsoft has information about its Q# programming language at https://docs .microsoft.com/en-us/quantum.
- Cirq, a quantum simulator in Python created by Google, can be found at https://quantumai.google.

7.4 Strange: High-level and low-level approaches

The HelloWorld example that you created in chapter 3 uses the top-level API of Strange. You also learned that the top-level API uses a low-level API. For convenience, we repeat the high-level architecture diagram in figure 7.3.

The high-level APIs focus on Java, and the low-level APIs deal with quantum gates. If you want to develop using the high-level APIs, you focus on Java code. If you want to develop using the low-level APIs, you focus on quantum circuits with quantum gates.

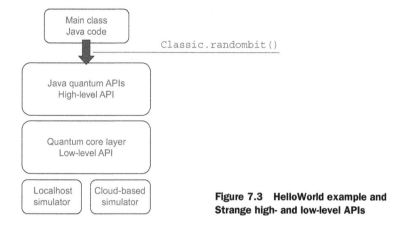

Figure 7.3   HelloWorld example and Strange high- and low-level APIs

Internally, the implementation of the high-level APIs depends on the low-level APIs, as explained in figure 7.4.

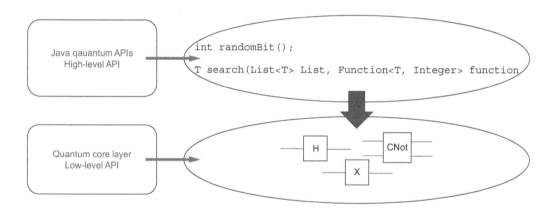

Figure 7.4   High-level and low-level APIs and their implementations

Hence, the high-level and the low-level APIs ultimately use the same low-level concepts. The difference is that the high-level API hides the complexity of these concepts from us.

7.4.1   *Top-level API*

The Strange top-level API is a typical Java API following the normal Java patterns. The API for this is in the class `org.redfx.strange.algorithm.Classic`.

> **NOTE**   At the time of writing, Strange is at version 0.1.0. Until the Strange 1.0 version is released, APIs may change location.

Some examples of methods in this class are as follows:

```
public static int randomBit();

public static int qsum(int a, int b);

public static<T> T search(List<T> list, Function<T, Integer> function);
```

The API deals with some of the restrictions of quantum computing. Once a qubit is measured, for example, it can no longer be used in a circuit. This restriction comes from the real quantum world, where measuring the physical representation of a qubit destroys the information in that qubit. However, we do not need to worry about this restriction. The Strange top-level APIs are created in such a way that they cannot enforce situations that are not compatible with real quantum systems.

Let's repeat the most important line of the HelloWorld example from chapter 2, where a random bit was generated:

```
int randomBit = Classic.randomBit();
```

`Classic.randomBit()` doesn't throw an exception. Hence, we can assume that the implementation does everything to ensure that there are no inconsistencies with the quantum world. Also, the concept of quantum gates is never exposed in the top-level API.

> **NOTE** The signature of the high-level APIs does not depend on quantum-specific objects. The return value of a high-level API call is never a qubit, for example.

7.4.2 Low-level APIs

The Strange low-level APIs are spread over different packages. Here is the typical approach followed when using those APIs:

1 Create a quantum program with a given number of qubits.
2 Add a number of quantum gates to this program.
3 Run the program.
4 Measure the qubits or process the probability vector.

In chapter 2, we showed how the high-level `Classic.randomBit()` method uses the low-level API, and we promised to go into more detail in this chapter. By now, you have seen more low-level code examples, so the implementation of the `Classic` `.randomBit()` method will probably look more familiar. Let's repeat the code here:

```
public static int randomBit() {

        Program program = new Program(1);     ◁──┐   Creates a new quantum
                                                    Program using 1 qubit
        Step s0 = new Step();              ◁────────  Creates a new step that will be
        s0.addGate(new Hadamard(0));       ◁──┐       added later to the Program
                                               Adds a Hadamard gate, working on the
                                               first qubit (with index 0), to the new step
```

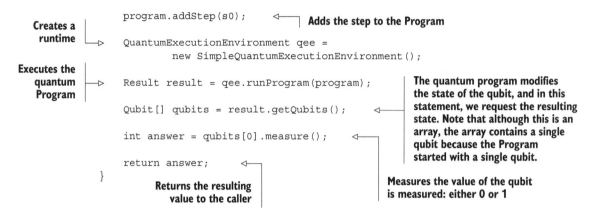

As you can see from this code, whenever the randomBit() function is invoked, a new quantum Program is created and executed. The return value, however, is a plain Java integer and has no quantum information associated with it. This marks the clear separation between the low-level APIs and the high-level APIs. This is another significant difference between the high-level and low-level APIs, and it is explained in figure 7.5.

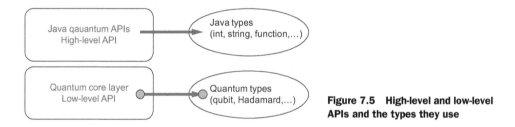

Figure 7.5   High-level and low-level APIs and the types they use

Java developers who wish to only use existing Java types can do this by using the high-level APIs. If you are more familiar with quantum concepts or want to experiment with those types, you can use the low-level APIs.

7.4.3   When to use what

We can choose to use the high-level APIs, or we can use the low-level APIs. In the previous sections, you learned about the differences between the high-level and low-level APIs. Here, we summarize the reasons for using either the high-level or low-level APIs. Keep in mind that it is okay to use both approaches. There are cases where the high-level APIs are more suitable and cases where the low-level APIs are more appropriate.

It is recommended to use the high-level APIs when

- You need to work on a project in which an existing, well-known, already-implemented quantum algorithm can provide an advantage—typically a performance advantage.
- You want to experiment with classical code that could benefit from quantum algorithms.

It is recommended to use the low-level APIs when

- You want to learn about quantum computing.
- You want to experiment with existing quantum algorithms.
- You want to develop new quantum algorithms.

7.5 StrangeFX: A development tool

The success of most popular classical programming languages is partly due to the availability of tools that allow us to be productive in that language. Almost all Java developers use an IDE when we create applications.

Similarly, to make programming quantum applications productive, there is a need for tools that make development easier. With StrangeFX, we can easily visualize and debug quantum applications.

7.5.1 Visualization of circuits

The quantum circuits discussed in the previous chapters were relatively simple. The programming approach is easy for us to follow. However, it often helps to get a visual overview of the created quantum circuit. Especially when programs become more complex, a visualization becomes important. As we explained in chapter 3, the StrangeFX library allows for a quick visualization of quantum circuits. A call to

```
Renderer.renderProgram(program);
```

generates a window with a graphical overview of the circuit.

The quantum program in the randombit directory in the example repository shows the visualization. It also contains the debug elements discussed in the next section; for now, we show the code without the debug elements:

```
Program program = new Program(dim);
Step step0 = new Step(new Hadamard(0), new X(3));
Step step1 = new Step(new Cnot(0,1));

program.addSteps(step0, step1);

QuantumExecutionEnvironment qee = new SimpleQuantumExecutionEnvironment();
Result result = qee.runProgram(program);
Qubit[] qubits = result.getQubits();
for (int i = 0; i < dim; i++) {
    System.err.println("Qubit["+i+"]: "+qubits[i].measure());
}
Renderer.renderProgram(program);
```

Running this program shows the measurements of the qubits and also the circuit, including the probabilities for the qubits. The output of the measurements can be either

```
Qubit[0]: 0
Qubit[1]: 0
Qubit[2]: 0
Qubit[3]: 1
```

or

```
Qubit[0]: 1
Qubit[1]: 1
Qubit[2]: 0
Qubit[3]: 1
```

The visualization of the circuit, which is shown in figure 7.6, helps us understand these two possible outcomes.

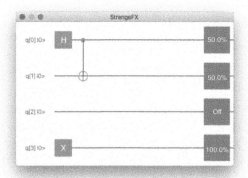

Figure 7.6   **Visualization of the circuit**

The visualization shows that the quantum program starts with four qubits. In a first step, a Hadamard and a NOT gate are added to the circuit. On the right side of the figure, the resulting qubits are shown, with the probability that they will be measured as 1.

7.5.2   *Debugging Strange code*

In the previous chapters, you learned how to create simple and more complex quantum circuits. One of the most important restrictions of quantum circuits is that measuring a qubit influences its state. If a qubit is in a superposition state and it is measured, it will fall back to either 0 or 1. It can't go back to the state it was in before it was measured.

Although this provides great opportunities for security (as we explain in the next chapter), it makes debugging quantum circuits difficult. In a typical classical application, you often want to follow the value of a specific variable during the program flow. Debuggers are popular with developers, and examining the change in a variable often provides valuable insight into why a specific application is not behaving the way we expect it to behave.

However, if measuring a variable changes the behavior of the application—as is the case in quantum computing—this technique cannot be used. To make it more complex, even if we were able to restore the original state of a qubit after measuring it, the measurement itself, being 0 or 1, doesn't give all the information. As we explained several times before, the real value in quantum programs is not the measured value of a qubit but mainly the probability distributions.

Fortunately, Strange and StrangeFX allow for a way to render the probability distributions. Strange allows us to use a fictive gate, `ProbabilitiesGate`, which can visualize the probability vector at a given moment in the program flow.

We'll reuse the program from the previous section, but this time we use `ProbabilitiesGate` to render the probabilities after a given step. The first part of the code is changed as follows:

```
Program program = new Program(dim);
Step p0 = new Step (new ProbabilitiesGate(0));
Step step0 = new Step(new Hadamard(0), new X(3));
Step p1 = new Step (new ProbabilitiesGate(0));
Step step1 = new Step(new Cnot(0,1));
Step p2 = new Step (new ProbabilitiesGate(0));

program.addSteps(p0, step0, p1, step1, p2);
```

Creates a new
step containing a
ProbabilitiesGate

The original
steps are still
created.

Running the example again shows the same circuit, but this time you see a probability vector displayed after each step (figure 7.7).

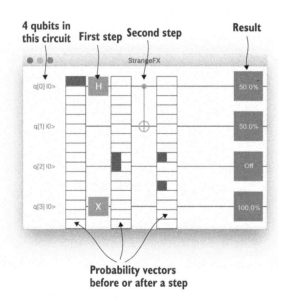

4 qubits in this circuit **First step** **Second step** **Result**

Probability vectors before or after a step

Figure 7.7 Visualization of the circuit with probabilities. Before and after each step, the probability vector is shown. This gives an indication of possible outcomes after each step without measuring the qubits.

Let's take a closer look at what is happening. The first step added to the program contains a `ProbabilitiesGate`. This does not change the probability vector at any point, but it triggers the renderer to display the vector. Zooming in on the left side of the visual output, we see in figure 7.8 a probability vector immediately after the qubit declaration and before the Hadamard and NOT gates are applied.

The probability vector is visualized as a rectangle divided into 16 parts. The first part represents the probability of measuring 0000 if a measurement was done at this point. The second part corresponds to the probability of measuring 0001, and so on.

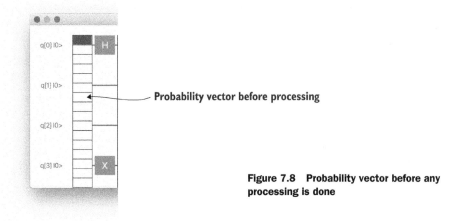

Figure 7.8   Probability vector before any processing is done

The more a part is colored, the higher the corresponding probability. In this case, the first part is entirely colored, which means the probability of measuring 0000 is 100%. This is indeed what you would expect from a quantum circuit with four qubits and no gates. All qubits initially are in the 0000 state, and that is what you would measure.

After applying the first real step, which contains a Hadamard gate and a CNOT gate, another probability vector is rendered. This vector is highlighted in figure 7.9 together with the corresponding qubit measurements.

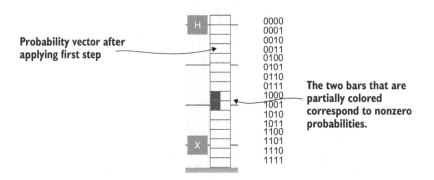

Figure 7.9   Probability vector after applying a Hadamard and a NOT gate. The 1000 and 1001 states are the only possible ones after this step, with an equal probability. Rendering this vector does not measure the qubits, so the processing can continue.

This figure shows the probabilities of measuring one of the 16 combinations if a measurement was made at this point. Again, keep in mind that we are talking about 16 probabilities, not the individual values of four qubits.

From the figure, it becomes clear that there are two possible outcomes for a measurement at this stage:

- A 50% chance that we would measure 1000
- A 50% chance that we would measure 1001

This corresponds to what we would expect when analyzing the single step that has been applied to this circuit so far. Applying the NOT gate to the most significant qubit (q_3) will cause that qubit to be measured as 1. Without applying the Hadamard gate to qubit q0, the status would thus be 1000. Applying the Hadamard gate to this qubit will result in a 50% chance of measuring this qubit as 0 and a 50% chance of measuring it as 1. In summary, there is a 50% chance that after this step, the system will be in the 1000 state and a 50% chance the system will be in the 1001 state, which is exactly what is shown by the probability vector.

The second step applies a CNOT gate on the qubits 0 and 1. The resulting probability vector is shown in figure 7.10.

This figure indicates two possible outcomes to measure at this point:

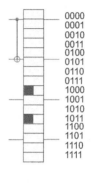

- A 50% chance to measure 1000
- A 50% chance to measure 1011

Figure 7.10 Probability vector after applying a CNOT gate

This corresponds with what you learned in chapter 5 when creating a Bell state. Applying a Hadamard gate followed by a CNOT gate brings the two involved qubits (q_0 and q_1) into an entangled state. Both qubits can be 0, and both qubits can be 1. If both qubits are 0, the total state of the quantum circuit is measured as 1000. If both qubits are 1, the total state is measured as 1011. This matches the final visualization of the circuit outcome, shown in figure 7.11.

From this figure, we know that q_2 will always be measured as 0, and q_3 will always be measured as 1. The other two qubits, q_0 and q_1, can be either 0 or 1. At first glance, this might correspond to what we learned by looking at the probability vector, but some important information is missing when we look at the possible measurements for the qubits only. Indeed, the probability vector states that the first two qubits can be either 00 or 11 but never 01 or 10 because they are entangled. There

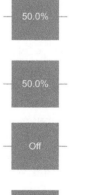

Figure 7.11 Possible measurements

are only two possible combinations, not four. This is something that cannot be seen simply by looking at the potential outcomes for qubit measurements.

NOTE The probability vector contains more information than the list of qubits with their individual probabilities. The latter misses the information about possible or impossible combinations, which is exactly what is available in the probability vector: there, each entry deals with all qubits.

7.6 Creating your own circuits with Strange

At this point, you have created several quantum circuits using Strange. There are still some steps between the simple circuits we've created so far and a real, useful quantum application, but it is essential to get a feeling for quantum computing. In this section, we write some basic code that introduces quantum arithmetic. You will notice that even simple operations, such as adding two numbers, are rather complex on a quantum computer, especially compared with how it is done on a classical computer. You may wonder why we don't use a classical computer for doing things such as addition and multiplication. Remember, though, that one of the key benefits of quantum computing is that we can have qubits in a superposition. Hence, we can add not only simple states where a qubit holds the value 0 or 1 but also any possible linear combination of these states. That makes a quantum computer powerful, and it can be compared with doing the same arithmetic operation on several possible values simultaneously.

7.6.1 Quantum arithmetic as an introduction to Shor's algorithm

One of the most popular potential applications that could benefit from quantum computing is integer factorization. Most of the widely used encryption techniques today rely on the fact that it is easy to calculate the product of two large prime numbers, but the reverse operation is hard and practically impossible for classical computers. We discuss integer factorization near the end of this book when we talk about Shor's algorithm. The mathematical background that leads toward the algorithm is beyond the scope of this book, but the programming challenges are difficult as well. Shor's algorithm relies on the efficient computation of modular exponentiation. In general, arithmetic on a quantum computer is more complex than arithmetic on a classical computer. In this section, we discuss the simple case of adding two qubits on a quantum computer. By doing so, you learn how to work with the low-level APIs of Strange, and you get a feeling for how quantum algorithms can be created. Although the example of adding two qubits is basic, the same techniques can be applied to create more complex arithmetic operations.

7.6.2 Adding two qubits

We start with a classical algorithm for a simple case: we have two bits, and we want to know the sum of those bits. Because each bit can be 0 or 1, there are four possible scenarios:

```
0 + 0 = 0
0 + 1 = 1
1 + 0 = 1
1 + 1 = 2
```

In a typical classical approach, the input of this circuit has two bits, and the output has two bits as well. One of the output bits contains the sum of the two bits, and the other contains the *carry* bit. If the resulting bit is supposed to be 2 (because it holds the result of $1 + 1$), that bit is set to 0, and the carry bit is set to 1. The classical circuit for this is shown in figure 7.12, and table 7.1 contains the possible values for the input and output bits.

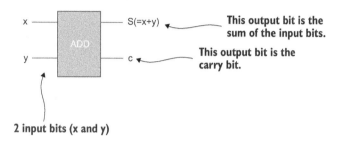

Figure 7.12 Classical addition

Table 7.1 Possible input/output values for classical addition

x	y	S =x+y	c
0	0	0	0
0	1	1	0
1	0	1	0
1	1	0	1

It would be a nice exercise to come up with a quantum circuit that does exactly the same thing, but that would be mean. There is no quantum circuit with two qubits that can achieve this result. Remember that one of the basic rules of quantum gates is that they are reversible. As a consequence, it should always be possible to go from the output back to the input. If you look closely at table 7.1, you see that two combinations lead to a sum of 1 and a carry bit of 0. Indeed, both the case where $x = 1$ and $y = 0$ and the case where $x = 0$ and $y = 1$ result in the same output. If we are given this result ($S = 1$ and $c = 0$), it is impossible to determine what the input was. Hence, this table cannot be implemented using quantum gates, as doing so would require a nonreversible gate.

To create a quantum adder, we will make this simple example even simpler. Let's forget about the carry bit for now. That alone doesn't solve our problem, as if we look only at the S output bit, it is impossible to uniquely identify what bits were used as input bits. However, if we create a circuit that keeps the first qubit intact and has the sum of the two input values in the second qubit, we can always go back from the result to the input. For every possible result, there is exactly one possible input. This quantum adder is schematically shown in figure 7.13, and table 7.2 shows the possible input values (x and y) and output values (the untouched x and the sum S).

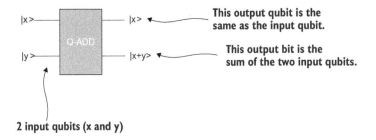

Figure 7.13   Quantum addition

Table 7.2   Possible input/output values for quantum addition

x	y	x	S = x + y
0	0	0	0
0	1	0	1
1	0	1	1
1	1	1	0

If you look at the output values (x and S), you see that it is now possible to reconstruct the input values (x and y) because every possible combination for x and S matches a single combination of x and y. This means the gate that transforms the input into the output is reversible. If you look closely at the table, the values will be familiar: this is the same table we used in chapter 5 to describe the CNOT gate! Hence, we can use a CNOT gate to do a simple addition of two qubits. Let's write the code to do that:

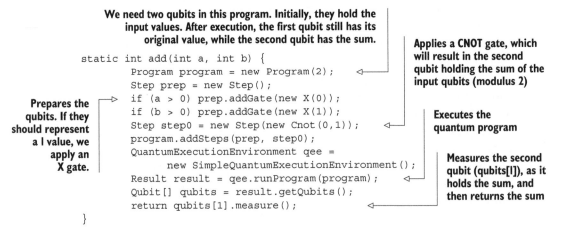

7.6.3 *Quantum arithmetic with a carry bit*

Remember that we gave up the carry bit used in classical addition because we needed to create a reversible quantum circuit. As a next step, we now reintroduce this carry bit in the result. We add a third qubit to the output; hence, we need to add a third qubit to the input. Moreover, we need to make sure it is always possible to transform every possible output back to the original input. We achieve this by adding an input qubit, also called an *ancilla qubit*. Ancilla qubits are regular qubits that do not directly help solve the functional goal but are often used to allow the quantum circuit to be reversible. Our new adder circuit will use this ancilla qubit to calculate the carry bit. Remember that the carry bit is set to 1 if and only if the input bits x and y are in the 1 state. This is a good moment to introduce the Toffoli gate, as this gate does exactly what we need here. The gates we discussed before operate on a single qubit (such as the X and H gates) or on two qubits (the CNOT gate). The Toffoli gate operates on three qubits and can be considered an extended version of the CNOT gate. Symbolically, the gate is depicted as shown in figure 7.14.

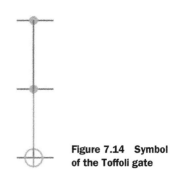

Figure 7.14 Symbol of the Toffoli gate

Comparing this image with the symbol for the CNOT gate already hints at what it is doing: the third qubit will be flipped if the first qubit and the second qubit are both in the 1 state. The first two qubits are untouched.

We describe what this gate is doing in three ways:

- We give some pseudocode.
- We show a table with the possible input/output combinations.
- We show the matrix that explains what is happening in a circuit.

Of these three approaches, only the last one is correct. In the first two cases, we take into account the values of 0 and 1, but as you know, qubits can be in a linear combination of these values. However, the pseudocode and combination table often help give us an intuitive idea of what is happening.

In pseudocode, the behavior of this gate can be described as follows:

```
out[0] = in[0];
out[1] = in[1];
if ((in[0] == 1) && (in[1] == 1)) {
    out[2] = !in[2];
} else {
    out[2] = in[2];
}
```

Table 7.3 describes the behavior.

From this table, it is clear that whenever either in[0] or out[0] is 0, nothing changes. Only when both inputs are 1 is the third input qubit flipped.

Table 7.3   Possible input/output values for a Toffoli gate

in[0]	in[1]	in[2]	out[0]	out[1]	out[2]
0	0	0	0	0	0
0	0	1	0	0	1
0	1	0	0	1	0
0	1	1	0	1	1
1	0	0	1	0	1
1	0	1	1	0	0
1	1	0	1	1	1
1	1	1	1	1	0

Finally, the matrix that describes the gate is given here:

$$\begin{pmatrix} 1 & 0 & 0 & 0 & 0 & 0 & 0 & 0 \\ 0 & 1 & 0 & 0 & 0 & 0 & 0 & 0 \\ 0 & 0 & 1 & 0 & 0 & 0 & 0 & 0 \\ 0 & 0 & 0 & 1 & 0 & 0 & 0 & 0 \\ 0 & 0 & 0 & 0 & 1 & 0 & 0 & 0 \\ 0 & 0 & 0 & 0 & 0 & 1 & 0 & 0 \\ 0 & 0 & 0 & 0 & 0 & 0 & 0 & 1 \\ 0 & 0 & 0 & 0 & 0 & 0 & 1 & 0 \end{pmatrix}$$

Equation 7.1

We will apply this Toffoli gate to enhance our simple quantum adder in such a way that it keeps track of the carry bit. Remember that the carry bit is expected to be true when the two input bits are true. This corresponds to applying a Toffoli gate to the two input qubits and to a third input qubit that is initially 0. Note that we have to apply this Toffoli gate *before* we apply the CNOT gate that does the addition, as that CNOT gate might change the value of the second qubit.

The resulting code for the addition algorithm now looks as follows:

Applies a Toffoli gate with the qubits at index 0 and index 1 as control qubits. The qubit at index 2 is the target qubit.

```
static int add(int a, int b) {
Program program = new Program(3);
Step prep = new Step();                      ◁──┐  We now need three qubits,
if (a > 0) {                                     │  as explained in the text.
    prep.addGate(new X(0));
}                                            ◁──┐  Prepares the two qubits that we
if (b > 0) {                                     │  want to add. The third qubit is
    prep.addGate(new X(1));                      │  initially in the 0 state.
}

Step step0 = new Step(new Toffoli(0,1,2));
```

```
Step step1 = new Step(new Cnot(0,1));

program.addSteps(prep, step0, step1);
QuantumExecutionEnvironment qee =
        new SimpleQuantumExecutionEnvironment();
Result result = qee.runProgram(program);
Qubit[] qubits = result.getQubits();
return qubits[1].measure()
        + (qubits[2].measure() <<1);
}
```

◄── **Similar to the code in the first step, applies a CNOT gate sum to the first two qubits and stores the value in the second qubit, leaving the first one unchanged.**

Executes the program and obtains the results

◄── **The value in the qubit with index 1 is the sum modulus 2, and the value in the qubit with index 2 has the carry bit, which is 1 if there was an overflow. In that case, the total sum is 2 + the sum in qubit with index 1.**

7.6.4 Next steps

You managed to calculate the sum of two bits on a quantum computer. In the process, you learned to take into account the opportunities of quantum computing but also its limitations. The fact that all quantum gates are reversible poses additional challenges and opportunities for many algorithms. It is recommended that you take some time now to play with Strange, create some quantum circuits, and find out whether they do what you would expect them to do.

7.7 Simulators, cloud services, and real hardware

Ultimately, the reason for creating quantum algorithms is to execute them on real quantum hardware. To take advantage of the special characteristics of quantum computing, we need to use real quantum devices. Understanding the real benefits of quantum computing and writing algorithms and code that use quantum computing takes time. Using a quantum simulator, you can learn the principles of quantum computing and create applications that can benefit from quantum hardware. If you master quantum algorithms by the time quantum hardware becomes available, you will have a competitive advantage.

It is desired and expected that applications written for a quantum simulator can also work on real quantum hardware without any change or with limited changes related to configuration. Therefore, as a developer, you focus on the application code, not on the execution environment. This is shown in figure 7.15.

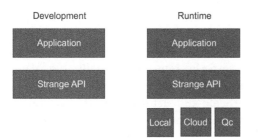

Figure 7.15 Development stack versus runtime stack

When developing applications that use quantum computing via Strange, you use the public APIs exposed by Strange. These can be the high-level APIs, the low-level APIs, or a combination. When running those applications, there are several options:

- Run your application on a local simulator.
- Run your application on a cloud simulator.
- Run your application on real hardware (or) in a cloud.

During the development phase, when you're writing the application, testing it, and integrating it with other components, running the application on a local simulator is the easiest approach. You don't need quantum hardware for this, and you don't need to set up a connection to a cloud service. The drawback is clear: a local simulator requires more resources and doesn't provide the performance that can be expected from a real quantum device.

The second option, running applications in a cloud simulator, is becoming available at the time of this writing. Several cloud companies are offering cloud APIs for doing quantum development. In the cloud, both simulators and real devices can be used. This adds another abstraction layer: applications can talk to cloud services, and their requests might be served by real quantum hardware or quantum simulators, as shown in figure 7.16.

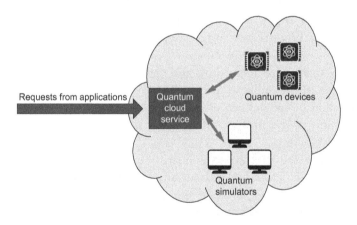

Figure 7.16   Cloud services with real quantum hardware or simulators

In this figure, the cloud service offers a single API. Based on a number of criteria, this cloud service can decide to forward the request internally to a real quantum device or to a quantum simulator in the cloud. Quantum simulators in cloud environments can benefit from the large scale and virtualization that typical cloud providers offer. They can thus use more memory and CPU power compared with local quantum simulators.

Many experts expect that the first batch of commercial quantum computers will be deployed mainly in cloud environments. This will address some of the challenges introduced by the current prototypes for quantum computers, such as cooling the environment to almost zero Kelvin. Dealing with infrastructure requirements is easier in a cloud facility than on a desktop or laptop in a private home environment. A quantum processor on a mobile phone is even harder to create. As long as cloud providers provide the same APIs for accessing real quantum devices in the cloud as well as classical quantum simulators, we don't have to worry about it.

The Strange APIs provide another level of abstraction. In chapter 3, we talked about the interface `QuantumExecutionEnvironment`. We explained that this interface defines the methods we can use to execute quantum applications without having to specify where the program is being executed.

At this moment, Strange contains a single implementation of `QuantumExecution-Environment`, and it is used throughout this book and the examples: `SimpleQuantum-ExecutionEnvironment`. However, work is underway to provide more implementations that communicate with external cloud services for accessing third-party quantum cloud environments. The major benefit of using Strange today is that our applications will work tomorrow on third-party cloud services with simulated or real hardware. The only change required is to change the `SimpleQuantumExecutionEnvironment` to `CloudQuantumExecutionEnvironment`. Based on the current draft work in Strange, this would require applications that are currently using the following snippet

```
Program program = new Program(...);
...

        QuantumExecutionEnvironment qee =
                new SimpleQuantumExecutionEnvironment();
        Result result = qee.runProgram(program);
```

to instead use this new snippet:

```
Program program = new Program(...);
        Map<String, String> params;
...

        QuantumExecutionEnvironment qee =
                new CloudQuantumExecutionEnvironment(params);
        Result result = qee.runProgram(program);
```

In this snippet, the `params` parameter provided to the `CloudQuantumExcecution-Environment` constructor contains information that allows Strange to select the most appropriate cloud service and provide relevant info (such as credentials) to this cloud service.

Summary

- Quantum APIs can be exposed at a low level or at a high level, and different language implementations take different approaches.
- Strange provides both a low-level API and a high-level API. The high-level API is very convenient to use and does not require specific knowledge about quantum computing. The low-level API does require this knowledge, but it is more flexible than the high-level API.
- Strange and StrangeFX contain features that allow you to debug quantum applications.
- Quantum applications can be executed on different execution environments: local simulators, cloud simulators, or real quantum devices. Thanks to the Java abstractions, code written for one execution environment can be executed on others as well.

Secure communication using quantum computing

This chapter covers

- Solving the bootstrap problem of secure communication
- Introducing quantum key distribution
- Understanding the BB84 algorithm
- Securely distributing shared keys between two parties

In this chapter, you create a useful quantum application. We show that quantum computing allows you to create a secret key that can be shared between two parties in a very secure way. This quantum key distribution (QKD) is the basis for a number of encryption techniques that are proven to be secure—even the best quantum computer can't break this security!

8.1 The bootstrap problem

We started chapter 6 by showing how classical networks are used to send classical information from one node (or computer) to another. We explained how different pieces of information travel from Java applications to a low-level implementation, where they are sent as bits to the other node and travel upward again. This is shown in figure 8.1.

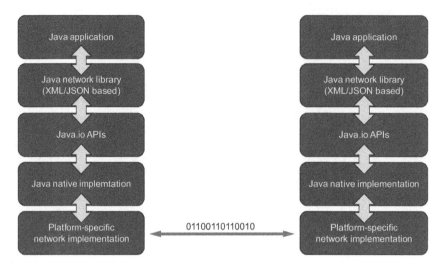

Figure 8.1   Java applications using classical communication

8.1.1   *Issues with sending bits over a network*

In this chapter, we focus on what happens at the communication level between the two nodes. Bits are transferred over a network connection: e.g., over optical fiber.

How secure is this? Security and privacy are gaining importance, and for many applications, it is crucial that the bits sent over physical networks between computers not be intercepted by third parties and also that they can't be altered by third parties.

The ideal situation is shown in figure 8.2: the bits are sent from Alice to Bob, and nobody is listening or altering the bits. Alice can send a message to Bob, and Bob will receive the message. No one else received or modified the message.

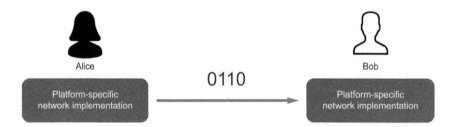

Figure 8.2   Ideal situation in network communication

READING MESSAGES

However, in practice, it is possible that an eavesdropper is on the line, as shown in figure 8.3. This can happen in various scenarios. The eavesdropper, who in examples is often depicted as "Eve," can physically cut the network cable, listen to the incoming bits, write them down, and then send the same bits to the other part of the cable.

Whatever technique Eve is using, the result is that she can read the bits sent over the communication channel between Alice and Bob.

Figure 8.3   Eve, the eavesdropper, reads the network communication.

Because the bits still arrive at Bob's end, neither Alice nor Bob know that Eve has been eavesdropping. Alice and Bob think they communicated in a secure way, but Eve listened to everything they exchanged.

MODIFYING MESSAGES

The other problem is that Eve might be altering the bits on the network line. For example, in figure 8.4, Eve switches the third bit from 1 to 0.

Figure 8.4   Eve, the eavesdropper, modified a bit.

This can lead to serious problems. For example, suppose Alice is sending the following message to Bob: "Can you pay me 500 EUR at account AL.1234?" Eve intercepts the message and alters it to say, "Can you pay me 500 EUR at account EV.1234?" Bob receives that message and isn't aware of any manipulation by Eve. He transfers money to Eve's account instead of Alice's.

   In many real-world situations, it is impossible to completely secure the physical channel that provides the low-level communication between two parties. Rather than assuming this communication is secure, we need techniques that allow us to create secure communication channels built on top of insecure networking channels.

   Fortunately, there are several classical techniques that improve the security and privacy of communication. We will not cover all of these techniques, but we'll pick one that is very popular: the *one-time pad*.

8.1.2   *One-time pad to the rescue*

The state of every message, every object, and every piece of data used in classical computing can be written down as a sequence of bits. A one-time pad is a series of bits at least as long as the original message that needs to be transferred. If the source (Alice) and the receiver (Bob) of the message have access to the same one-time pad, and if Eve has no access to it, it is possible to securely encrypt the message such that only Alice and Bob can decrypt it. The "one-time" part of one-time pad means the key should only be used once. If this is the case, it can be proven that the message encrypted with the one-time pad is transmitted in a secure way. Let's look at an example.

> **NOTE**   The following examples use very short sequences of bits to keep things simple. But the principles apply to very long sequences as well.

Suppose that Alice wants to send the following message (a bit sequence) to Bob:

```
0110
```

Before Alice and Bob started communicating, they agreed on a secret key (a one-time pad). We discuss later how they created this, but for now, let's assume this is their secret key:

```
1100
```

Only Alice and Bob know this key. Before Alice sends the message to Bob, she combines the message with the secret key—every bit in the original message is replaced by the XOR operation applied on the original bit and the corresponding bit in the key:

- If the original bit and the corresponding bit in the pad are equal (both 0 or 1), the resulting bit is 0.
- If the original bit and the corresponding bit in the pad are opposite (0 and 1 or 1 and 0), the resulting bit is 1.

The result of this combination is an encrypted bit sequence:

```
0110 (original message)
1100 (one time pad)
---- (XOR operation)
1010 (result)
```

Alice now sends the encrypted bit sequence 1010 to Bob, who needs to decode the sequence. To do this, Bob also applies an XOR operation on every bit he receives with the corresponding bit in the key:

```
1010 (encrypted message, received from Alice)
1100 (one time pad)
---- (XOR)
0110 (original message)
```

As you can see, the result of this operation is the original message sent by Alice. It can be proven that this is not a coincidence, and this technique always works regardless of

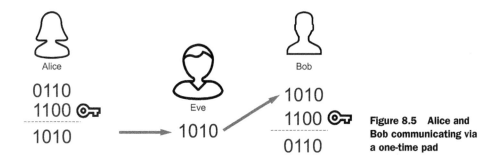

Figure 8.5 **Alice and Bob communicating** via a one-time pad

what message Alice sends. Schematically, the communication between Alice and Bob can now be represented by figure 8.5.

What happens if Eve still intercepts the message sent over the network? Instead of reading the original message (0110), she will read an encrypted message (1010); and since she doesn't have the key that Alice and Bob used, she can't decipher that message. Even if she knew that Alice and Bob used a secret key and encrypted their message by using a bitwise XOR operation, without the secret key itself, there would be no way Eve could decrypt the message.

You just learned that if Alice and Bob share a secret key, a sequence of bits that has the same length as the original message, their communication can't be intercepted—or rather, it *can* be intercepted, but the eavesdropper can't decrypt the intercepted message.

8.1.3 *Sharing a secret key*

The difficult question is how Alice and Bob can share a secret key. The naive approach would be to send a key over the network—but that brings us back to square one: we need a secret key to send our secret key in a secure way over the network. This recursive problem is visualized in figure 8.6.

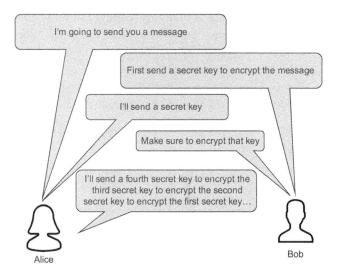

Figure 8.6 **Alice and Bob discover the bootstrap problem**

For real critical applications, secret keys are often shared not via the internet, but via traditional mail or other ways. In the remainder of this chapter, you learn how quantum computing can fix this bootstrap problem.

8.2   Quantum key distribution

In this section, you learn how quantum computing can be used to generate a secret key and share it *in a secure way* between two parties, Alice and Bob. Once Alice and Bob have such a key, they can use it to encrypt the messages they want to send to each other. If Alice and Bob can share a secret key in a secure way, the bootstrap problem explained in the previous section is fixed.

The generation and distribution of such a secret key using quantum techniques is called quantum key distribution (QKD), and it is often considered one of the hot topics and key advantages of quantum computing. Several algorithms can be used to generate QKD. Perhaps the best-known is the BB84 algorithm, named after its inventors, Charles Bennett and Gilles Brassard, who created it in 1984. We will eventually create this algorithm; but instead of starting from the physics behind it, we will use a software-oriented approach to arrive at it.

In the following section, we assume that we can *somehow* send qubits over a network. In chapter 6, we discussed quantum teleportation, which allows us to send the status of a qubit over a classical network connection, provided the two parties share an entangled qubit before the classical communication starts. Later in this chapter, we introduce a project that simulates (and eventually will provide) a real quantum network. Using this quantum network, we can send qubits from one node (or computer) to another node. Before we do that, though, the algorithms we develop will be executed on a single node. Keep in mind that the code you write and execute on a single node will also be capable of being executed on nodes that are connected to each other.

8.3   Naive approach

In a naive approach, Alice creates a sequence of qubits holding the value $|0\rangle$ or $|1\rangle$ and sends those to Bob. Bob then measures the qubits, thereby getting the original sequence of bits created by Alice. The sequence of qubits created by Alice (which can be done using random bits) is the secret key, and after Bob measures the qubits, he has the same secret key as Alice. Alice and Bob can then use this secret key as a one-time pad, as explained in the previous section. Schematically, this is explained in figure 8.7.

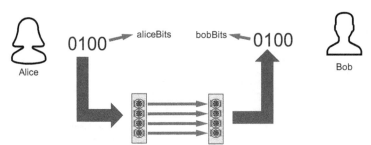

Figure 8.7   Alice generates random bits and uses qubits to send the values to Bob.

Using the techniques you learned in the previous chapters, you can create an application that does this. The following code is taken from the example ch08/naive.

Listing 8.1 Naive approach for generating and sending a quantum key

```
final int SIZE = 4;
Random random = new Random();

boolean[] aliceBits = new boolean[SIZE];
for (int i = 0 ; i < SIZE; i++) {
    aliceBits[i] = random.nextBoolean();
}


QuantumExecutionEnvironment simulator =
        new SimpleQuantumExecutionEnvironment();
Program program = new Program(SIZE);
Step step1 = new Step();
Step step2 = new Step();
for (int i = 0; i < SIZE; i++) {
    if (bits[i]) step1.addGate(new X(i));
    step2.addGate(new Measurement(i));
}

program.addStep(step1);
program.addStep(step2);

Result result = simulator.runProgram(program);
Qubit[] qubit = result.getQubits();

int[] measurement = new int[SIZE];
boolean[] bobBits = new boolean[SIZE];

for (int i = 0; i < SIZE; i++) {
    measurement[i] = qubit[i].measure();
    bobBits[i] = measurement[i] == 1;

    System.err.println("Alice sent "+(bits[i] ? "1" : "0") +
            " and Bob received "+ bobBits[i] ? "1" : "0");
}

Renderer.renderProgram(program);
```

- This example creates a key with a fixed size: 4 bits.
- Alice generates the key by assigning random values to each bit.
- Creates a program that involves 1 qubit for every bit in the key
- When a bit is TRUE, a Pauli-X gate is applied to the corresponding qubit.
- All qubits will be measured in step 2.
- Executes the program; the results are in an array of qubits.
- Measures the qubits and prints their value next to the original value of the corresponding bit used by Alice
- Renders the quantum circuit of this application

This program contains only simple quantum operations. Alice first generates the secret key, a series of random classical bits. She then creates qubits based on those bits. Initially, a qubit has the value $|0\rangle$. When a qubit needs to be created that corresponds to the bit 1, Alice applies a Pauli-X gate to the qubit. Next, qubits are sent to Bob one by one. Bob performs a measurement and reads the key bit by bit.

The quantum circuit representing the algorithm you created is shown in figure 8.8. When you execute this program—e.g., by running mvn javafx:run—you see the following output on the console:

```
Alice sent 0 and Bob received 0
Alice sent 1 and Bob received 1
```

```
Alice sent 0 and Bob received 0
Alice sent 0 and Bob received 0
```

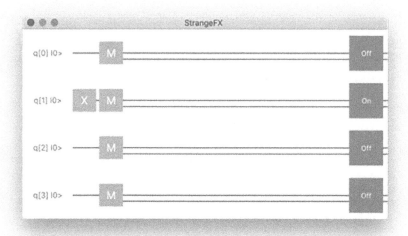

Figure 8.8   Quantum circuit showing the algorithm used by our application

NOTE   The exact output of this program is different each time you run it, since we used random values to initialize the bits used by Alice.

At the end of the previous section, we explained that for now, we are running the examples on a single node. That means both the part of the algorithm executed by Alice and the part executed by Bob are executed on the same node. Remember that there is an implicit point in the algorithm where we assume that the qubits are sent from Alice to Bob. This is shown in figure 8.9.

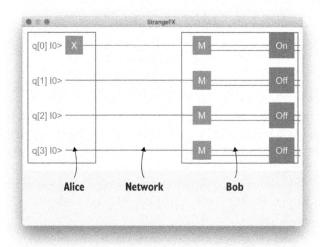

Figure 8.9   The first part of the algorithm is executed by Alice. Then the qubits are sent over a quantum network to Bob, where the second part of the algorithm is executed.

The output from the application shows that Alice can create a sequence of random bits and that Bob can receive the same sequence of random bits. You used qubits to transport the bits over a network cable.

If the quantum network is reliable and secure, this approach should work. You learned earlier that qubits can't be cloned and that once a qubit is measured, it falls back to one of its basic states. This behavior can be very helpful when dealing with quantum networks that should prevent eavesdropping.

However, the current application is far from secure. Suppose Eve is still in the middle, and she is measuring all qubit communication between Alice and Bob. We know that when Eve measures a qubit, the qubit will hold the value 0 or the value 1. If it was in a superposition state, the information about that superposition is lost. But in the current algorithm, there are no qubits in a superposition state. Hence, Eve knows that when she is measuring 0, the original qubit was in the state $|0\rangle$. She can then create a new qubit in the initial $|0\rangle$ state and put that back on the wire toward Bob. Similarly, when Eve measures a qubit and obtains the value 1, she knows that the qubit was in the $|1\rangle$ state. She can create a new qubit in the $|0\rangle$ state, apply a Pauli-X gate to bring it in the $|1\rangle$ state, and send it to Bob. This is shown in figure 8.10.

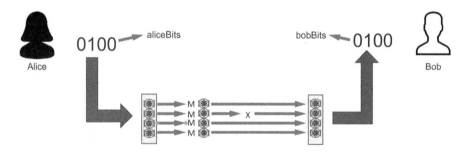

Figure 8.10 Eve reads the qubits and creates new qubits based on what she measures.

You can see that the eavesdropping part happens in the network layer. When Eve has access to the network, she can obtain the (not so) secret key that Alice and Bob share. She measures the same values that Alice used to generate the qubits, and those values *are* the secret key. What is especially dangerous is that Alice and Bob are not aware of what is happening. Bob receives qubits, measures them, and constructs the secret key. Bob and Alice successfully exchange a message encrypted with their secret key—but if Eve intercepts this message, she can decrypt it.

8.4   *Using superposition*

So far, our attempts to use quantum technologies to generate a real secure secret key shared only by Alice and Bob have not been successful. But we didn't really take advantage of the fact that qubits are very different from classical bits. If we are guaranteed that the qubits are in either the $|0\rangle$ state or the $|1\rangle$ state, many of the advantages that qubits offer are lost.

After measuring, Eve can easily reconstruct the original qubit (or at least create a new qubit in the same state as the original qubit) if she knows the original qubit is either $|0\rangle$ or $|1\rangle$. But if the qubit is in a superposition state, she will measure $|0\rangle$ or $|1\rangle$ without getting any information about the original state of the qubit. You will soon extend the initial naive algorithm by using superposition. The qubits sent by Alice will no longer be in the $|0\rangle$ or the $|1\rangle$ state, but in a superposition of these states. We will explain how Bob can retrieve the original state of the qubit after he receives it from Alice.

8.4.1   Applying two Hadamard gates

Before we modify the algorithm, we need to explain an interesting fact about the Hadamard gate. It can be proven that when a Hadamard gate operates on a specific qubit and another Hadamard gate operates on the result of this first operation, the resulting qubit will be in the same state it had originally.

Let's write some code to check if this is true. The code from ch08/haha does this, and the relevant snippet is shown here.

Listing 8.2   Applying two Hadamard gates in a row

```
QuantumExecutionEnvironment simulator =
            new SimpleQuantumExecutionEnvironment();

        Program program = new Program(2);          ⟵——  Creates a program
        Step step0 = new Step();                          with two qubits
        step0.addGate(new X(0));           ⟵——┐  Flips the first qubit to
                                                 │  be |1⟩ while we keep
        Step step1 = new Step();                 │  the second qubit at |0⟩
        step1.addGate(new Hadamard(0));
        step1.addGate(new Hadamard(1));

        Step step2 = new Step();           ⟵——┐  Applies another
        step2.addGate(new Hadamard(0));          │  Hadamard gate
        step2.addGate(new Hadamard(1));          │  to both qubits

        program.addStep(step0);
        program.addStep(step1);
        program.addStep(step2);
                                                        ⟵——┐  Executes the
        Result result = simulator.runProgram(program);      │  program
        Qubit[] qubit = result.getQubits();
                                                        ⟵——┐  Renders the results
        Renderer.renderProgram(program);                    │  graphically
```

- Applies a Hadamard gate to both qubits
- Adds all the steps to the program
- Measures the qubits

The result of this application is shown in figure 8.11.

The figure shows that if the original qubit was in the state $|0\rangle$, we are guaranteed that the qubit will be in the state $|0\rangle$ again after applying two Hadamard gates. Simi-

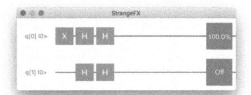

Figure 8.11   Result of applying two
Hadamard gates in a row

larly, if the original qubit was in the state $|1\rangle$, it will without doubt be in the state $|1\rangle$ again after the two Hadamard gates have been applied.

NOTE   While we only proved that this holds for qubits initially in state $|0\rangle$ or $|1\rangle$, it can be mathematically proven that the same applies to a qubit in any state.

We learn the following from this code: if Alice applies a Hadamard gate before she sends her qubit to Bob, and Bob applies another Hadamard gate before he measures the qubit, the qubit is back in the state that Alice prepared (either $|0\rangle$ or $|1\rangle$).

8.4.2   Sending qubits in superposition

We now modify our original algorithm to use this superposition benefit. Alice still creates a key with qubits that are based on random bits, but before she sends a qubit to Bob (in the $|0\rangle$ or $|1\rangle$ state), she applies a Hadamard gate. When Bob receives the qubit, he also first applies a Hadamard gate, which should bring the qubit back into the original state created by Alice.

A short notation for a qubit in a superposition state

Before we show this schematically, we'll introduce a short notation for a qubit that is transformed from a base state into a superposition. In chapter 4, you learned that applying a Hadamard gate to a qubit in the $|0\rangle$ state brings the qubit into a new state:

$$\frac{1}{\sqrt{2}}|0\rangle + |1\rangle$$

Since this state is often encountered in algorithms, it can also be denoted by the shortcut $|+\rangle$.

Similarly, applying a Hadamard gate to a qubit in the $|1\rangle$ state brings that qubit into the following state:

$$\frac{1}{\sqrt{2}}|0\rangle - |1\rangle$$

The short notation for this state is $|-\rangle$.

We use these notations throughout the text and figures in this book.

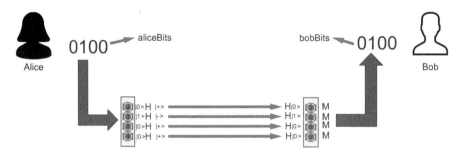

Figure 8.12 Alice applies a Hadamard gate before sending a qubit, and Bob applies a Hadamard gate before measuring the qubit.

Schematically, the situation where Alice and Bob both apply a Hadamard gate is shown in figure 8.12. The new code can be found in ch08/superposition, and the relevant part is shown in the following listing.

Listing 8.3   Using superposition to prevent easy reading of a secret key

```
final int SIZE = 4;
Random random = new Random();

boolean[] aliceBits = new boolean[SIZE];              Alice creates a
for (int i = 0 ; i < SIZE; i++) {                     key containing
    aliceBits[i] = random.nextBoolean();              random bits.
}
                                                     Alice performs a Hadamard
                                                     transformation to bring the
QuantumExecutionEnvironment simulator =              qubit into a superposition and
        new SimpleQuantumExecutionEnvironment();     sends it over the network.
Program program = new Program(SIZE);
Step prepareStep = new Step();                       She initializes her qubits
Step superPositionStep = new Step();                 according to these random bits.
Step superPositionStep2 = new Step();                A random bit of 0 will lead to a
Step measureStep = new Step();                       |0⟩ qubit; a random bit of 1 will
for (int i = 0; i < SIZE; i++) {                     lead to a |1⟩ qubit.
    if (aliceBits[i]) prepareStep.addGate(new X(i));
    superPositionStep.addGate(new Hadamard(i));
    superPositionStep2.addGate(new Hadamard(i));     Bob receives the
    measureStep.addGate(new Measurement(i));         qubit and performs a
}                                                    second Hadamard
                                                     transformation.
program.addStep(prepareStep);           Adds the
program.addStep(superPositionStep);     steps to the
program.addStep(superPositionStep2);    quantum
program.addStep(measureStep);           program

Result result = simulator.runProgram(program);      Executes
Qubit[] qubit = result.getQubits();                 the program


int[] measurement = new int[SIZE];
boolean[] bobBits = new boolean[SIZE];
```

Bob measures the qubit.

```
for (int i = 0; i < SIZE; i++) {
    measurement[i] = qubit[i].measure();
    bobBits[i] = measurement[i] == 1;
    System.err.println("Alice sent " +
        (aliceBits[i] ? "1" : "0") +
            " and Bob received " +
        (bobBits[i] ? "1" : "0"));
}
```

Bob's bit is measured, and both the bits from Alice and Bob are printed. They should be bitwise equal.

When you execute this application—e.g., using `mvn javafx:run`—you see the following output (again, the actual values are likely to be different since we generate the bits based on random values):

```
Alice sent 0 and Bob received 0
Alice sent 1 and Bob received 1
Alice sent 0 and Bob received 0
Alice sent 0 and Bob received 0
```

The application also shows the circuit that is created (figure 8.13).

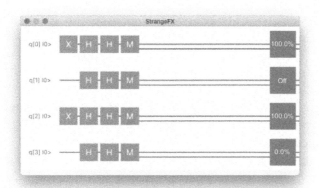

Figure 8.13 Using superposition to send qubits over a network

As expected, the qubits measured by Bob yield the same value that Alice used to prepare the qubits before the double Hadamard gate was applied. Hence, from a functional point, this algorithm still provides Alice and Bob with the same key. But is it secure?

If Eve can still listen on the network line, she can measure the qubits sent by Alice. However, regardless of whether the original bit Alice used to create the qubit was 0 or 1, Eve will always have a 50% chance of measuring 0 and 50% chance of measuring 1. Hence, she won't be able to reconstruct the incoming qubit and send it to Bob—at least, not the way she did before. This is shown in figure 8.14.

As you can see, things will go terribly wrong for Eve. When she measures the qubits from Alice, she randomly obtains a value of 0 or a value of 1. The qubits sent by Alice are all either in the $|+\rangle$ state or the $|-\rangle$ state. Both these states, when measured, will have a 50% chance of having the value 0 and a 50% chance of having the value 1. The real information is somehow *hidden* in the superposition composition. Eve is not

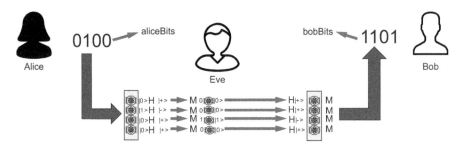

Figure 8.14 Eve measures the qubits sent by Alice and sends new qubits to Bob.

aware of this, and the values she reads may be correct or may be wrong. For example, the first qubit in figure 8.14, which originally was $|0\rangle$, is measured as $|0\rangle$ by Eve, so she is correct. However, the second value, which originally was $|1\rangle$, is measured as $|0\rangle$ by Eve. Hence, Eve will not obtain the correct shared key using this approach.

To make things worse, when Eve tries to hide her traces, she creates a new qubit based on her measurement and sends that to Bob. In the case of the first qubit, where she was lucky enough to measure 0, she constructs a new qubit $|0\rangle$ and sends that to Bob. Bob, not realizing what has happened, assumes Alice sent him a qubit in a superposition, and he applies a Hadamard gate. This brings the qubit sent by Eve into a superposition. When Bob measures this qubit, he can measure either $|0\rangle$ or $|1\rangle$. In the figure, Bob measures a 1, which is not what Alice sent.

In typical encryption algorithms, Alice and Bob use part of the transmitted bits to check if everything went correctly. They share the values of those bits (which makes those particular bits useless as they are no longer secure). If the values of the bits are different, Alice and Bob know something went wrong, and the whole key is not considered secure. Consequently, it is clear that using this approach, Eve can't obtain the secret without getting errors or being detected.

But Eve can learn. If Eve knows that Alice applied a Hadamard gate before sending the qubit over the wire, Eve might apply a Hadamard gate as well before measuring—doing exactly what Bob is doing. This will give her the information that would otherwise be obtained by Bob: the same bits that Alice used to prepare the qubits.

This won't help Eve, since Bob won't receive qubits. By measuring them, Eve destroys the superposition. However, now that Eve knows what Alice is doing, she can create new qubits by doing the same thing as Alice. Hence, Bob will receive a qubit in the same state as it would have come from Alice. He applies a Hadamard gate and then measures the qubit, and he gets the same bits used by Alice. This is schematically shown in figure 8.15.

As a consequence, using this approach, not only Alice and Bob share the bits of their secret key—Eve does, too. Hence, this approach is not secure either.

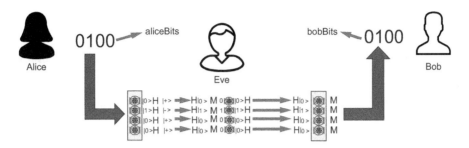

Figure 8.15 Eve applies a Hadamard gate before she measures the qubits sent by Alice and sends a new qubit to Bob after she applies another Hadamard gate.

8.5 *BB84*

The previous approach failed because Eve knew up front what Alice did and what Bob was going to do. In this section, we make it harder for Eve—or rather, impossible.

8.5.1 *Confusing Eve*

The reason Eve can go undetected is that she manages to send a qubit in the same state to Bob as the one she intercepted from Alice. If Alice only uses a Pauli-X gate or nothing at all before transferring her qubit to Bob, Eve can measure the qubit, and she will obtain the original information. If Alice also applies a Hadamard gate, Eve needs to apply a Hadamard gate as well before measuring the qubit.

But what if Eve doesn't know whether Alice used a Hadamard gate? Should she apply a Hadamard gate herself, or not? Let's analyze the situation. We have three variables that can each take two options, leading to eight scenarios:

- Alice sends a 0 or a 1.
- Alice applies a Hadamard gate or does not.
- Eve applies a Hadamard or does not.

The example in ch08/guess simulates the possible outcomes for the eight different scenarios. The relevant part of this algorithm is shown in the following listing.

Listing 8.4 Using superposition to prevent easy reading of a secret key

```
final int SIZE = 8;           ◁─┐ Considers the eight possible
                                 │ cases (numbered from 0 to 7)
...

for (int i = 0; i < SIZE; i++) {              │ In the first four
    if (i > (SIZE/2-1)) {                      │ cases, Alice applies
        prepareStep.addGate(new X(i));    ◁─┘ a Pauli-X gate.
    }
    if ((i/2) % 2 == 1) {                            │ In cases 2, 3, 6, and
        superPositionStep.addGate(new Hadamard(i));  ◁ 7, Alice applies a
    }                                                │ Hadamard gate.
```

```
if (i%2 ==1) {
    superPositionStep2.addGate(new Hadamard(i));
}
measureStep.addGate(new Measurement(i));
}
```

In cases 1, 3, 5, and 7, Eve applies a Hadamard gate.

Performs a measurement

The code in the for loop creates the eight scenarios. The visual output of the application, shown in figure 8.16, clarifies.

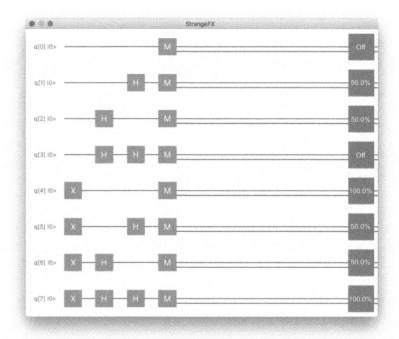

Figure 8.16   Different scenarios and their outcome

No Pauli-X gate was applied to the first four qubits, so they represent a bit value of 0. Let's look at those four scenarios in a bit more detail (see figure 8.17). The analysis we do here also applies to the last four qubits, with the difference that the initial value in that case is 1.

If both Alice and Eve apply a Hadamard operation or do not apply a Hadamard operation, Eve will measure a 0 value. But if either of them applies a Hadamard operation while the other doesn't, there is a 50% chance that Eve will measure a 0 and a 50% chance that Eve will measure a 1. These cases are circled in figure 8.17. The problem for Eve is that she can't tell whether her measurement is correct. She doesn't know if Alice applied a Hadamard gate, so she can't tell with certainty which scenario applies. To make things worse for Eve, she is also unable to create a qubit in the same state as the original one.

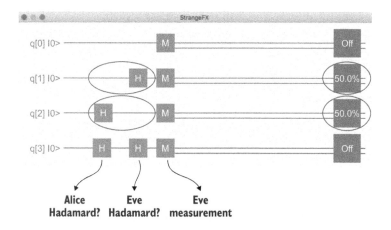

Figure 8.17 Alice is sending a 0, and the measurement depends on the presence of Hadamard gates.

For example, suppose Eve measures the qubit as a 0. From figure 8.16, it appears that there are six potential scenarios that would lead to a measurement of 0. The scenarios with q[0] and q[3] will absolutely lead to a measurement of 0, but each of the scenarios q[1], q[2], q[5], and q[6] also has a 50% chance of resulting in a measurement of 0. In the case of scenarios q[5] and q[6], the original bit was 1; and in the other scenarios, the original bit was 0. Since Eve knows whether she applied a Hadamard gate, she can exclude half of the scenarios, but there is always the possibility that the original bit was 0 and the possibility that the original bit was 1. Since Eve doesn't know the original scenario, she can guess and prepare a qubit that fits a valid scenario—but chances are, it is the wrong scenario, and Bob will receive a qubit in a different state than the one sent by Alice. We will shortly see how this can be detected.

8.5.2 Bob is confused, too

If Eve can't reconstruct the original scenario, the same must be true for Bob. We assume that Alice and Bob have no upfront knowledge—otherwise, we would have fixed the bootstrap problem already.

In our algorithm, we will instruct Bob to randomly either apply a Hadamard gate or not before measuring the incoming qubit. The situation for Bob is then very similar to the situation for Eve. If Alice and Bob both apply a Hadamard gate, or if neither of them apply a Hadamard gate, Bob's measurement is guaranteed to correspond to Alice's initial value. We can see this from figures 8.16 and 8.17 if we assume Bob is performing the second part instead of Eve. But if Alice applies a Hadamard transformation and Bob doesn't, or if Alice doesn't apply a Hadamard transformation but Bob does, the result can be wrong.

It seems that by making the situation complex for Eve, we made it equally complex for Bob. Both Alice and Bob randomly decide whether they apply a Hadamard gate.

But from the output of the previous application, it is clear that if Alice and Bob both decide to apply a Hadamard gate, or if they both decide not to use a Hadamard gate, they can share a key. In that case, the initial value used by Alice is guaranteed to be the same value measured by Bob.

8.5.3   *Alice and Bob are talking*

From the previous discussion, we can see that if Alice and Bob both use a Hadamard gate, or neither of them use a Hadamard gate, the original bit used by Alice and the measured bit used by Bob are guaranteed to be the same and can be used in a secret key. But how do they know that? The answer is simple: they tell each other whether they applied a Hadamard gate.

> **NOTE**   This might sound surprising. If Alice and Bob tell each other over a public channel whether they applied a Hadamard gate, Eve may be listening! The trick is this: Alice and Bob only share that information with each other *after* Bob has received and measured his qubit. At that moment, Eve can no longer do anything. If Eve knew the information up front, she could manipulate the system, since she could easily reproduce the qubit from Alice if she knew whether Alice applied a Hadamard gate. But she has to make a decision before sending a qubit to Bob—and that decision is made based on a measurement of the qubit she intercepted from Alice. Hence, all information in that qubit is destroyed. It's a pity for Eve, but the public information is useless.

When Alice and Bob have each other's information about the Hadamard gates, they simply remove the values measured on qubits that had non-matching Hadamard gates. The remaining values are guaranteed to be correct.

> **NOTE**   Alice and Bob only share the information about the Hadamard gates. They do not share the initial value (in Alice's case) or the measured value (in Bob's case). They know, though, that those values are equal, and they can use them as part of a shared secret key.

Typically, Alice and Bob use part of their secret key to check whether the connection was eavesdropped on, for example by reserving some space to add a checksum. If Eve isn't discouraged by the fact that she can't get the original key without getting noticed, she might still try to get the key—but she will have to make wild guesses about whether to apply a Hadamard gate. If she makes the wrong guess, she will send a qubit to Bob that is in a different state from the one Alice sent to Bob. So, there is a chance that Bob will measure a different value than Alice used. If both or neither Alice and Bob apply a Hadamard gate and the initial value from Alice is different from the value measured by Bob, Alice and Bob know that the connection was tampered with.

8.6   QKD in Java

The combined knowledge obtained in the previous sections allows you to create a QKD application in Java. The example in ch08/bb84 does exactly this.

8.6.1   The code

We won't include all of the example code here, but we'll highlight a few important snippets.

INITIALIZING VARIABLES

First we initialize some arrays:

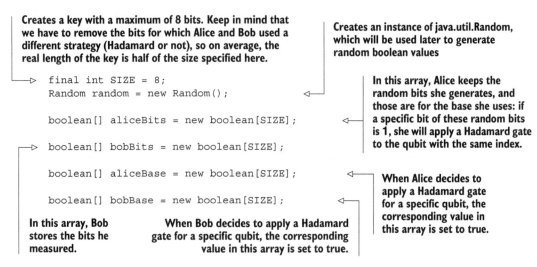

Creates a key with a maximum of 8 bits. Keep in mind that we have to remove the bits for which Alice and Bob used a different strategy (Hadamard or not), so on average, the real length of the key is half of the size specified here.

Creates an instance of java.util.Random, which will be used later to generate random boolean values

```
final int SIZE = 8;
Random random = new Random();

boolean[] aliceBits = new boolean[SIZE];

boolean[] bobBits = new boolean[SIZE];

boolean[] aliceBase = new boolean[SIZE];

boolean[] bobBase = new boolean[SIZE];
```

In this array, Alice keeps the random bits she generates, and those are for the base she uses: if a specific bit of these random bits is 1, she will apply a Hadamard gate to the qubit with the same index.

When Alice decides to apply a Hadamard gate for a specific qubit, the corresponding value in this array is set to true.

In this array, Bob stores the bits he measured.

When Bob decides to apply a Hadamard gate for a specific qubit, the corresponding value in this array is set to true.

PREPARING THE STEPS

The quantum application we create contains different steps. The first two steps are performed by Alice, and third and fourth steps are performed by Bob:

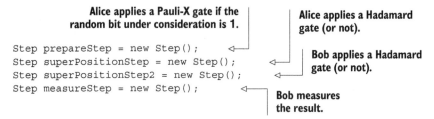

Alice applies a Pauli-X gate if the random bit under consideration is 1.

Alice applies a Hadamard gate (or not).

Bob applies a Hadamard gate (or not).

```
Step prepareStep = new Step();
Step superPositionStep = new Step();
Step superPositionStep2 = new Step();
Step measureStep = new Step();
```

Bob measures the result.

FILLING THE STEPS

All the steps are created for each bit that can be part of the key. Three of those steps depend on random values.

Based on a first random value, a Pauli-X gate is applied to prepareStep. There is a 50% chance that the Pauli-X gate is applied, causing the qubit to be in the $|1\rangle$ state, and a 50% chance that no gate is applied and the qubit stays in the $|0\rangle$ state.

The second random value defines whether a Hadamard gate is applied to `super-PositionStep`, which is executed by Alice. The next step, `superPositionStep2`, uses a random value to decide whether Bob applies a Hadamard gate:

```
                     The following steps are applied for each
                     bit that is a candidate for the secret key.        A random value determines
                                                                        whether Alice's bit is 0 or 1.
for (int i = 0; i < SIZE; i++) {          ◄─┘
                                                                        If Alice's bit is 1, applies an X
    aliceBits[i] = random.nextBoolean();      ◄─┘                       gate to the |0⟩ state
    if (aliceBits[i]) {
        prepareStep.addGate(new X(i));        ◄─┘                       A random value (stored in
    }                                                                   the aliceBase array) decides
                                                                        whether Alice applies a
    aliceBase[i] = random.nextBoolean();          ◄─┘                   Hadamard gate.
    if (aliceBase[i]) {
        superPositionStep.addGate(new Hadamard(i));                     A random value (stored
    }                                                                   in the bobBase array)
                                                                        decides whether Bob
    bobBase[i] = random.nextBoolean();            ◄─┘                   applies a Hadamard gate.
    if (bobBase[i]) {
        superPositionStep2.addGate(new Hadamard(i));
    }

    // Finally, Bob measures the result                                 Bob measures
    measureStep.addGate(new Measurement(i));      ◄─┘                   the qubit.
}
```

EXECUTING THE APPLICATION

We now have to execute the application in our quantum simulator. This is done using the techniques you learned in previous chapters:

```
QuantumExecutionEnvironment simulator =                                 Creates a
        new SimpleQuantumExecutionEnvironment();      ◄─┘               QuantumExecutionEnvironment
    program.addStep(prepareStep);             ◄─┐
    program.addStep(superPositionStep);         │  Adds the steps created
    program.addStep(superPositionStep2);        │  in the previous phases
    program.addStep(measureStep);

    Result result = simulator.runProgram(program);    ◄─┘               Runs the quantum
    Qubit[] qubit = result.getQubits();       ◄─┐                       program on the simulator
                                                │  Assigns the results to
                                                │  an array of qubits
```

PROCESSING THE RESULTS

Now that the program has been executed and the results are in, we can process those results. In this phase, we decide whether a specific bit should be part of the key, both for Alice and for Bob:

```
                                              For each candidate bit, we run the
                                              following steps that evaluate whether
int[] measurement = new int[SIZE];            the bit should be part of the key.
    for (int i = 0; i < SIZE; i++) {      ◄─┘
        measurement[i] = qubit[i].measure();
        bobBits[i] = measurement[i] == 1;     ◄─┐   Sets the bit in the bobBits array to
                                                │   the measurement value of the qubit
```

If the random bases chosen by Alice and Bob for this bit are different, ignores values and prints a message

```
if (aliceBase[i] != bobBase[i]) {
    System.err.println("Different bases used,
        ignore values "+aliceBits[i]+
        " and "+ bobBits[i]);
    } else {
        System.err.println("Same bases used.
            Alice sent " + (aliceBits[i] ? "1" : "0")
            + " and Bob received "
            + (bobBits[i] ? "1" : "0"));
        key.append(aliceBits[i] ? "1" : "0");
    }
}
```

Otherwise, Alice and Bob used the same Hadamard strategy. The initial value from Alice matches the measurement from Bob.

This bit now becomes part of the secret key.

8.6.2 Running the application

You can run the application from the ch08/bb84 directory with the command `mvn clean javafx:run`. The results when running this application vary each time; the following output is just one example of the many possibilities (see figure 8.18):

```
Same bases used. Alice sent 1 and Bob received 1
Same bases used. Alice sent 0 and Bob received 0
Same bases used. Alice sent 1 and Bob received 1
Different bases used, ignore values false and true
Same bases used. Alice sent 1 and Bob received 1
Different bases used, ignore values false and true
Same bases used. Alice sent 1 and Bob received 1
Different bases used, ignore values true and true
Secret key = 10111
```

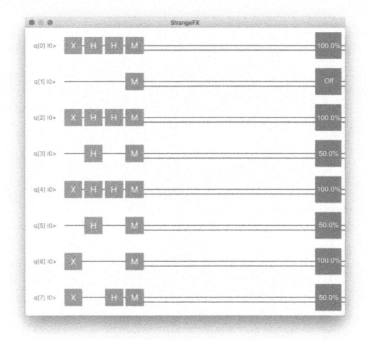

Figure 8.18 Output obtained by running the BB84 application

From both the text output and the graphical output, it is clear that Alice and Bob used the same Hadamard strategy for bits 0, 1, 2, 4, and 6. Those five bits are thus part of the secret key. The other bits are useless since Alice and Bob used a different Hadamard strategy (either Alice applied one and Bob didn't, or the other way round).

Introducing SimulaQron

So far, all of our code runs in a single quantum execution environment. This way, we could explain the concepts that led to the BB84 algorithm. In practice, though, secure communication requires two different nodes. We need to be able to send a qubit from one node to another if we want to generate a shared secret key between those two nodes. This requires a distributed version of a quantum execution environment.

An interesting project that provides a way to transfer qubits from one node to another is the SimulaQron project from QuTech (http://qutech.nl). One of the goals of QuTech is to build a network of quantum computers using fiber optic cables. From the code we have shown so far, it should be clear that even with a very limited number of qubits available, quantum networking has huge benefits. A single qubit can be used to generate a shared secret bit between two parties. By repeating this process as often as necessary, a shared secret with as many bits as required can be obtained.

While work on the physical quantum network is being carried out, QuTech is also building a protocol stack similar to a protocol stack for classical networking. Such a stack makes abstraction of the hardware implementation and shields developers from the low-level implementations. Developers using the top layer of such a protocol stack can create applications that can then run on a different implementation of the protocols. This is useful because the same code can work with different kinds of hardware; plus it allows code to use simulators while the hardware is not yet available.

SimulaQron provides a protocol called CQC that allows high-level programming languages (Java, Python, C, and so on) to interact with the implementation and use quantum networking functionality. Support for the CQC protocol is being added to the Strange simulator. As a consequence, applications you write using Strange will work on a distributed system. In the first phase, this will be a network containing quantum simulators, but in a later phase—once there are real quantum nodes in a network—this should also work on real hardware.

Summary

- Secure communication is an important aspect in today's IT landscape, and hackers are eager to intercept messages and security keys.
- Using a one-time pad, a message can be encrypted with a key that is not reused later. Every message uses a new key, making it harder for hackers to intercept.
- The BB84 algorithm is a famous quantum algorithm that generates a one-time pad.
- Using Strange, you can implement the BB84 algorithm in Java.

Deutsch-Jozsa algorithm

This chapter covers

- Obtaining information from classical functions
- Function evaluations vs. function properties
- Quantum gates that correspond to classical black box functions
- Understanding the Deutsch algorithm and the Deutsch-Jozsa algorithm

The Deutsch-Jozsa algorithm that we discuss in this chapter demonstrates some of the characteristics of typical quantum algorithms. The direct practical use cases may be limited, but the algorithm is a great tool for explaining the logic that quantum algorithms often follow.

9.1 When the solution is not the problem

Do you know if the number 168,153 can be divided by 3? There are a number of ways to find out. For example, you can simply take a calculator and obtain the result:

```
168153 / 3 = 56051
```

YJ 896 0498

The result of the division is 56,051. But that was not the question. Actually, we don't care about this result. But thanks to this evaluation, we know the real answer: there are no digits after the decimal point, so we can conclude the number can indeed be divided by 3.

There is another simple approach to find the answer to this question, and you might know this simple trick: take the sum of the individual digits that compose the number, and see if that sum can be divided by 3. If so, the original number can be divided by 3 as well. Let's do that:

```
1 + 6 + 8 + 1 + 5 + 3 = 24
```

Since 24 can be divided by 3, we can conclude that 168,153 can also be divided by 3.

The first approach (using the calculator) gave us a result of a division, and it provided us with the real answer. The second approach (sum of the individual digits) only provided the real answer, not the outcome of the division.

The relevance of this is that in many cases, we are interested in a specific property of something (e.g., a number or a function). We are not interested in a function evaluation, but we somehow want to obtain information about the function. Evaluating the function is often the easiest way to do so, but it can be more efficient to indirectly look at the properties of the function and draw conclusions from there.

This is of particular interest in quantum computing. A quantum computer with n qubits that needs to examine a specific function can only do one function evaluation at a time. Applying the quantum circuit to a given specific set of input qubits will result in a modified state of these qubits. Measuring them gives a particular result, and if you want a new result, you need to run the circuit again. Even though we can apply Hadamard gates to the input qubits to bring them into superposition—which allows us to evaluate the qubits in the 0 and 1 states simultaneously—we can't magically create new qubits that will hold the information of the different cases. This is shown in figure 9.1 for a system with two qubits.

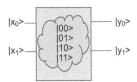

Figure 9.1   A quantum system with two qubits can do many evaluations, but only two qubits can be measured.

The internal computations can contain the equivalent of many evaluations, but we can't obtain those simultaneously. We are limited to a result of n qubits. But that is often enough to solve problems. In the case of our number being a multiplicator of 3 or not, a single qubit is enough to store the answer. We don't need to evaluate the division function.

In this chapter, we demonstrate this approach using quantum computing. We investigate a property of a function f acting on n bits, without being interested in the individual function evaluations. We show that retrieving the property in the classical way requires $2^{n-1} + 1$ function evaluations. With the quantum algorithm, the property can be obtained with a single evaluation.

The functions we use are very simple, and there is no direct use case for this problem. But it demonstrates an essential aspect of quantum computing, and it explains why quantum computing is often associated with "exponential" complexity. You can easily see that the more input bits the function has, the harder it becomes to solve the problem in a classical way. The number n is indeed in the exponent, and as we showed in chapter 1, exponential functions quickly result in huge values. If a quantum algorithm can fix the same problem in just a single evaluation (or, in general, in less than an exponential number of equations), this is a huge advantage for a quantum computer.

We will gradually come to the algorithm that achieves this. We will follow the approach shown in figure 9.2.

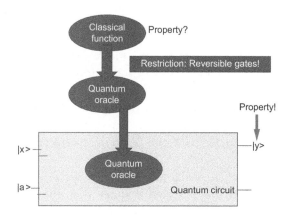

Figure 9.2 Approach for finding the property of a function

First we talk about properties of functions and how to obtain them in a classical way. Next, we convert the functions into quantum blocks called *oracles*. We show that there are some requirements for doing this. Once we can create a quantum oracle that represents a classical function, this oracle can be used in a quantum circuit. Evaluating this quantum circuit once results in the property of the function we are looking for.

9.2 *Properties of functions*

In most typical cases where functions are involved, you are interested in finding the result of a function. For example, consider the function $y(x) = x^2$.

If we want to know the value of this function for, for example $x = 4$ and $x = 7$, we need to evaluate this function:

$$y(4) = 4^2 = 16$$
$$y(7) = 7^2 = 49$$

In some cases, though, the function evaluations are not important, but the characteristics of the functions are. In this area, quantum algorithms can be helpful. An example that we will discuss in chapter 11 is the periodicity of a function. We are not interested in the individual evaluations of a function, but we are interested in the periodicity. A *periodic function* is a function where the same pattern of values comes back with a fixed periodicity. Here's an example:

x	0	1	2	3	4	5	6
y	7	9	5	7	9	5	7

From this table, you can tell that the function has a periodicity of 3: for every value of x, the result of the function is the same as the function applied to $x + 3$. This is an example where the property of a function can be more interesting than the function evaluations themselves.

9.2.1   *Constant and balanced functions*

In general, the functions we consider are noted as $f(x)$, where f is the function that operates on an input variable called x. The evaluation of a function for a specific input is also called the *result* and sometimes noted as y, where $y = f(x)$.

   In this chapter, we start with a very simple family of functions that have simple properties. We start with a function with only a single input bit, and we extend it later to a function with n input bits. In all cases, the result of the function is either 0 or 1.

   The functions we discuss here have a special property: they are either balanced functions or constant functions. A function is called *constant* when the result is not dependent on the input. In our case, that means the result is either 0 for all input cases or 1 for all input cases. A function is called *balanced* when the result is 0 in 50% of the cases and 1 in the other cases.

   The Deutsch algorithm, which we discuss shortly, deals with a function called f that takes a single bit (a Boolean value) as its input and produces a single bit as well. The function only operates on 0 and 1, and its result is either 0 or 1. The combination of two input options and two output options leads to four possible cases for this function, which we name *f1*, *f2*, *f3*, and *f4*:

   f1: f(0) = 0 and f(1) = 0
   f2: f(0) = 0 and f(1) = 1
   f3: f(0) = 1 and f(1) = 0
   f4: f(1) = 1 and f(1) = 1

From those definitions, it appears that *f1* and *f4* are constant functions, and *f2* and *f3* are balanced functions.

In many classical algorithms, it is important to know the output of a function for specific values. In many quantum algorithms, on the other hand, it is useful to know the properties of the function under consideration.

This is part of the "different thinking" that is required when considering quantum algorithms. Thanks to superposition, a quantum computer can evaluate many possibilities simultaneously; but since obtaining a result requires a measurement, the superposition is gone, and we are back to a single value. Hence, the added value is in the function evaluation and not in the result of the function evaluation.

In the Deutsch algorithm, a function is provided, but we don't know what function it is. We know it is *f1*, *f2*, *f3*, or *f4*, but that's all we know. We are now asked to find out if this function is constant or balanced. Our task is not to determine whether the provided function is *f1*, *f2*, *f3*, or *f4*. We are asked about a property of the function, not the function itself. Schematically, the problem is explained in figure 9.3.

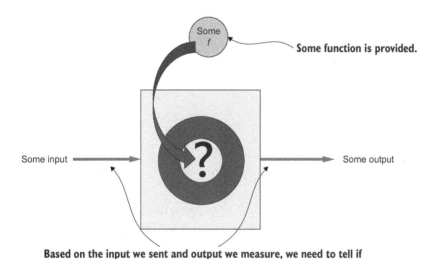

Figure 9.3 Finding the properties of an unknown function by doing evaluations

How many function evaluations do we need before we can answer this question with 100% certainty? If we do only a single evaluation (we only calculate either *f(0)* or *f(1)*), we don't have enough information.

Suppose we measure *f(0)* and the result is 1. From the earlier table, it seems that, in this case, our function is either *f3* (which is balanced) or *f4* (which is constant). So, we don't have enough information. If the result of measuring *f(0)* is 0, the table shows that the function is either *f1* (which is constant) or *f4* (which is balanced). Again, this proves that measuring *f(0)* is not enough to conclude whether the function is constant or balanced. It can be either.

Exercise

Prove that measuring *f(1)* is not sufficient, either.

It turns out we need two classical function evaluations before we can determine whether the provided function is constant or balanced. Let's write a Java application that demonstrates this. You can find this application in the ch09/function directory of the examples.

Listing 9.1 Two evaluations to declare a function constant or balanced

```
static final List<Function<Integer, Integer>> functions = new ArrayList<>();

static {
    Function<Integer, Integer> f1 = (Integer t) -> 0;
    Function<Integer, Integer> f2 = (Integer t) -> (t == 0) ? 0 : 1;
    Function<Integer, Integer> f3 = (Integer t) -> (t == 0) ? 1 : 0;
    Function<Integer, Integer> f4 = (Integer t) -> 1;
    functions.addAll(Arrays.asList(f1, f2, f3, f4));
}

public static void main(String[] args) {
    Random random = new Random();
    for (int i = 0; i < 10; i++) {
        int rnd = random.nextInt(4);
        Function<Integer, Integer> f = functions.get(rnd);
        int y0 = f.apply(0);
        int y1 = f.apply(1);
        System.err.println("f" + (rnd + 1 + " is a "
                + ((y0 == y1) ? "constant" : "balanced")
                + " function"));
    }
}
```

Prepares the four possible functions. This step needs to be done only once.

We will do 10 experiments.

Performs two function evaluations: one for input 0 and one for input 1

Picks a random function, not knowing anything about its implementation

If the results of those two evaluations are similar, the function is constant; otherwise, the function is balanced.

In this code, we create the four possible functions in a static block. We do this is because we want to stress that the creation of the function and the determination of whether they are constant or balanced should be considered two independent processes.

After the functions are created, the application really starts. Inside the for loop, a random function is picked. Based on the two function evaluations, we can determine whether the function is constant or balanced.

A possible output of this application is the following:

```
f4 is a constant function
f4 is a constant function
f3 is a balanced function
f1 is a constant function
f2 is a balanced function
f2 is a balanced function
f1 is a constant function
f4 is a constant function
```

```
f3 is a balanced function
f2 is a balanced function
```

As expected, the application has the correct answers for every loop. But in every loop, we performed two evaluations of the function. As we showed earlier, a single evaluation would not be sufficient to conclude whether the function is balanced.

9.3 Reversible quantum gates

So far, we have talked about classical functions and their properties. Before we can discuss the quantum equivalent of those functions, we need to look into the requirement of quantum gates in more detail.

In the previous chapters, you learned about and used several quantum gates. These gates have many similarities with gates you encounter in classical computing. However, there are some fundamental differences.

Quantum gates are physically achieved using properties of quantum mechanics, and therefore they must obey the requirements and restrictions that are related to quantum mechanics. One of the key requirements for a quantum gate is that it should be *reversible*. This means when a quantum gate is applied to a given *begin* status, there should exist another quantum gate that brings the result back to the *begin* status. In a quantum system, information can't simply disappear. The information that was in a system before a specific quantum gate is applied should be recoverable. We briefly touched on the concept of reversible gates in chapter 7. Since this is such an important concept, we'll go a bit deeper into the topic now.

All the gates we have discussed so far are reversible. Let's show that with a simple example: the Pauli-X gate. The gate that brings a system back to its original state after a Pauli-X gate is applied is another Pauli-X gate. We can explain this in two ways:

- Experimental evidence
- Mathematical proof

9.3.1 Experimental evidence

Let's create a simple quantum application that applies a Pauli-X gate on a single qubit, followed by another Pauli-X gate. Instead of only taking the special cases into account where the qubit is either |0> or |1>, we will artificially initialize the qubit so that it has a 75% chance of being measured as 1. The circuit is shown in figure 9.4.

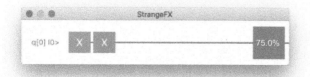

Figure 9.4   Quantum program containing two Pauli-X gates

The code for this example can be found in the example repository under ch09/ reversibleX. The relevant code is shown next.

Listing 9.2   Two Pauli-X gates applied to a single qubit

```
QuantumExecutionEnvironment simulator =
            new SimpleQuantumExecutionEnvironment();
Program program = new Program(1);
Step step0 = new Step();
step0.addGate(new X(0));

Step step1 = new Step();
step1.addGate(new X(0));
program.addStep(step0);
program.addStep(step1);
program.initializeQubit(0,.5);

Result result = simulator.runProgram(program);
Renderer.showProbabilities(program,1000);
Renderer.renderProgram(program);
```

Creates a quantum application with a single qubit

Adds the steps to the quantum program

The first step (step0) applies a Pauli-X gate to the qubit.

The second step (step1) applies another Pauli-X gate to the qubit.

Initializes the single qubit with an alpha value of 0.5, which leads to a probability of 25% of measuring 0

Executes the quantum program

Renders the statistical results of running this program 1,000 times

The result of running this circuit 1,000 times is shown in figure 9.5. As expected, after applying two Pauli-X gates, the probability of measuring 0 is about 25%, and there is about a 75% chance of measuring 1. This matches the artificial initial value that we applied to the qubit.

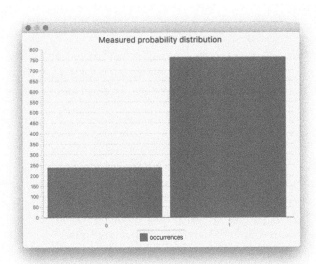

Figure 9.5   Statistical results of a quantum program containing two Pauli-X gates

9.3.2   *Mathematical proof*

In chapter 4, we explained the mathematical equivalent of applying a gate to a qubit: we multiply the gate matrix and the probability vector of the qubit. Let's assume the initial qubit is described as follows:

$$\psi = \alpha|0> + \beta|1>$$

Or in vector notation:

$$\psi' = \begin{bmatrix} \alpha \\ \beta \end{bmatrix}$$

Equation 9.1

Applying two Pauli-X gates to this qubit brings it into the following state

$$\psi' = XX \begin{bmatrix} \alpha \\ \beta \end{bmatrix}$$

where X is the matrix defining the Pauli-X gate. From chapter 4, we know the structure of the matrix, so we can write

$$\psi' = \begin{pmatrix} 0 & 1 \\ 1 & 0 \end{pmatrix} \begin{pmatrix} 0 & 1 \\ 1 & 0 \end{pmatrix} \begin{bmatrix} \alpha \\ \beta \end{bmatrix}$$

Using matrix multiplication (explained in appendix B), we can write this as follows:

$$\psi' = \begin{pmatrix} 1 & 0 \\ 0 & 1 \end{pmatrix} \begin{bmatrix} \alpha \\ \beta \end{bmatrix} = \begin{bmatrix} \alpha \\ \beta \end{bmatrix}$$

Equation 9.2

From equation 9.2, it can be seen that the end state of the qubit, denoted by ψ, is written as

$$\psi' = \begin{bmatrix} \alpha \\ \beta \end{bmatrix}$$

This is exactly the same as the *begin* state of the qubit, which was shown in equation 9.1.

This shows that after applying two Pauli X-gates, the quantum system is in the exact same state as in the beginning—before the two Pauli-X gates were applied. Hence, we have proven that the Pauli-X gate is indeed a reversible gate, and that the changes to a quantum system caused by applying a Pauli-X gate can be undone by applying another Pauli-X gate. Now that you have learned that the Pauli-X gate is a reversible quantum gate, you can use the same technique to prove that the other gates you have learned about are reversible as well.

> **NOTE** The gates we've introduced so far have the special property that they are their own inverse. This is not always true, and there is no restriction that a quantum gate should be its own inverse.

9.4 Defining an oracle

In many quantum algorithms, the term *oracle* is used. We will use an oracle when we create the Deutsch algorithm, so some explanation is needed now.

An oracle is used to describe a *quantum black box*—similar to how each of the earlier functions (*f1, f2, f3,* and *f4*) can be described as a *classical black box*. Internally, the functions had some computational flow; but in the main loop of the program, we pretended we didn't know about the internals—we simply evaluated the functions for different input values.

The same concepts can be applied to an oracle. Internally, an oracle is composed of one or more quantum gates, but we typically don't know which gates. By querying the oracle (e.g., by sending input and measuring the output), we can learn more about the properties of the oracle. Because an oracle is composed of quantum gates, the oracle itself also needs to be reversible.

An oracle can thus be considered the quantum equivalent of the black-box functions we discussed earlier in this chapter. Both an oracle and a function perform some calculations, but we don't know the internal details about these calculations. This is shown in figure 9.6.

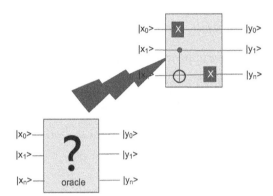

Figure 9.6 A quantum oracle, acting as a black box in a quantum circuit, is internally composed of a number of gates.

Let's look at an example of an oracle used in a simple quantum application. Using the Strange simulator, you define an oracle by providing the matrix that is the mathematical representation of the oracle. That sounds like we are cheating: are we really defining something that we later claim we don't know anything about? The answer is yes. We indeed create this oracle, since *someone* has to do it. In real quantum applications, the oracle is an external component given to us.

> **NOTE** The creation of the function and the creation of the oracle should be considered totally separated processes. In the upcoming algorithms, we assume that someone created an oracle for us. The algorithm itself has no clue how the oracle was created, how complex or simple it is, etc. This is often confusing, since to demonstrate the algorithm, we obviously need an oracle. However, the complexity of creating the oracle should not be considered part of the complexity of the algorithm. Just assume that someone (yourself, another developer, a real piece of hardware, or nature itself) created the oracle and provided it to you.

We learned before that all gates can be represented by a matrix. An oracle contains zero or more gates, and therefore the oracle itself can also be represented by a matrix. An oracle can be considered part of the quantum circuit that is given to you. You can't see the gates that together constitute the oracle, but you can use them in your quantum programs.

In Strange, an oracle is defined by providing the matrix that represents it. In a real hardware situation, the oracle is available as is. In a software simulation, we somehow need to define the oracle's behavior, so a matrix needs to be provided. Figure 9.7 shows how an oracle can be part of a quantum program.

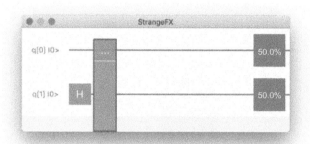

Figure 9.7   An oracle, pictured as a vertical box, is used in this quantum circuit. First a Hadamard gate is applied, followed by the oracle.

We will create some code in which we apply an oracle in a quantum program. We create the oracle by providing a matrix that may look familiar to you. It is recommended that you not look at the contents of the matrix, though, as doing so takes away the mystery of the oracle. Instead, you can look at the result of the entire program and try to find out what the oracle is doing.

Let's consider the following snippet, which is taken from the example in ch09/oracle.

Listing 9.3   Introducing an oracle in quantum applications

```
QuantumExecutionEnvironment simulator =
        new SimpleQuantumExecutionEnvironment();
    Program program = new Program(2);
    Step step1 = new Step();
    step1.addGate(new Hadamard(1));


    Complex[][] matrix =  new Complex[][]{
        {Complex.ONE, Complex.ZERO,
            Complex.ZERO, Complex.ZERO},
        {Complex.ZERO, Complex.ONE,
            Complex.ZERO, Complex.ZERO},
        {Complex.ZERO, Complex.ZERO,
            Complex.ZERO, Complex.ONE},
        {Complex.ZERO, Complex.ZERO,
            Complex.ONE, Complex.ZERO}
    };

    Oracle oracle = new Oracle(matrix);

    Step step2 = new Step();
    step2.addGate(oracle);
```

Creates a quantum program that requires two qubits

The first step applies a Hadamard gate to the second qubit.

Creates a matrix containing complex numbers. For now, we don't interpret these numbers.

Creates an oracle based on this matrix

Creates a second step in which the oracle is applied

```
program.addStep(step1);
program.addStep(step2);
```
◁──┐ **Adds both steps to the quantum program**

```
Result result = simulator.runProgram(program);
Renderer.showProbabilities(program,1000);
Renderer.renderProgram(program);
```
◁──┐ **Executes the program and displays its circuit and the results of 1,000 runs**

The circuit created here is the one shown in figure 9.7. The result of running this circuit 1,000 times is shown in figure 9.8.

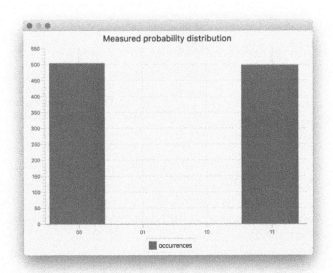

Figure 9.8   Statistical results of a quantum program containing an oracle

If you look at those statistical results, it seems that there are only two possible outcomes: |00> or |11>. Remember from chapter 5 that a circuit with two entangled qubits has the same probabilities: there is a 50% of measuring |00> and a 50% chance of measuring |11>. This is an indication that the oracle we created, combined with the initial Hadamard gate, results in two entangled qubits. In chapter 5, you created two entangled qubits by applying a CNot gate after a Hadamard gate. So, we learn that the oracle we created behaves like a CNot gate. If we cheat and look at the contents of the oracle, we see that the matrix that represents the oracle matches the matrix of the CNot gate. This exercise shows that we can apply oracles to a quantum circuit. We can apply an oracle without knowing its internal details.

9.5   *From functions to oracles*

In the Deutsch algorithm, we show that a single evaluation is enough to find out if a provided function is constant or balanced. Before we can do that, we need to convert the classical function into a quantum operation.

We can't simply apply a function to a qubit. Remember, we explained that all quantum gates need to be reversible. A function that, after being applied, makes it impossible to retrieve the original input can't be used in a quantum circuit. Therefore, the function first needs to be transformed into a reversible oracle.

In this section, we demonstrate how oracles can be created that can then be used in the Deutsch algorithm we explain in the next section. Similar to how a classical function is handed to the classical algorithm, an oracle is handed to the quantum algorithm.

Every classical function that we described earlier in this chapter can be represented by a specific oracle. Since we had four possible functions, we also have four possible oracles.

The general way to construct an oracle based on a function is shown in figure 9.9. In this approach, we have an input qubit called |x> and an additional qubit named |a>.

Figure 9.9 Oracle used in the Deutsch algorithm

The oracle leaves the |x> qubit in its original state, and the |a> qubit is replaced by the XOR operation between a and f(x). Let's examine this oracle in a bit more detail: we will investigate what it looks like for the four functions we defined earlier.

9.5.1 Constant functions

The first function, *f1*, is a constant function that returns 0 regardless of the input. Hence, since $f(x) = 0$ for any value of x, the output status of the second qubit can be simplified as follows:

$$a \oplus f(x) = a \oplus 0 = a$$

The resulting oracle can be pictured as in figure 9.10. In this case, the oracle is simply the Identity matrix. Both |x> and |a> are unaltered between the input and the output. The hidden logic inside the oracle can thus be represented by the scheme in figure 9.11.

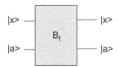

Figure 9.10 Oracle used in the Deutsch algorithm for *f1*

Figure 9.11 Oracle circuit for *f1*

As a result, the matrix representing the oracle is written as follows:

$$\begin{pmatrix} 1 & 0 & 0 & 0 \\ 0 & 1 & 0 & 0 \\ 0 & 0 & 1 & 0 \\ 0 & 0 & 0 & 1 \end{pmatrix}$$

This matrix is an Identiy matrix: it does not alter the probabilities when measuring the qubits. Multiplying this matrix with any probability vector yields the original probability vector.

> **NOTE** The circuit shown in figure 9.11 isn't the only possible circuit that results in the Identity matrix. Many other circuits operate on two qubits and return the two qubits in the same state. For example, applying two Pauli-X gates on each qubit results in the exact same state. This is part of the black-box aspect of an oracle: we don't know the internal details, and we are typically not interested in those. We want to investigate a specific property of the oracle, not its internal implementation.

The fourth function, *f4*, is a constant function that always returns the value 1, regardless of the input. As a consequence, the output of the second qubit after applying the oracle can be written as follows:

$$a \oplus f(x) = a \oplus 1 = \bar{a}$$

The horizontal bar above a variable indicates that this is the inverted variable, which in this case corresponds to a Pauli-X gate being applied to |a>. So, this oracle can be schematically presented as shown in figure 9.12.

Figure 9.12   Oracle circuit for *f4*

Exercise
Prove that the matrix corresponding to this oracle can be written as follows:

$$\begin{pmatrix} 0 & 0 & 1 & 0 \\ 0 & 0 & 0 & 1 \\ 1 & 0 & 0 & 0 \\ 0 & 1 & 0 & 0 \end{pmatrix}$$

9.5.2   *Balanced functions*

Let's have a look at the second classical function, *f2*. This function is defined as follows:

$$f(0) = 0$$
$$f(1) = 1$$

This can also simply be written as $f(x) = x$.

Using this in the general description of the oracle, as shown in figure 9.9, the scheme simplifies to figure 9.13.

Figure 9.13 **Oracle used in the Deutsch algorithm for f2**

This is exactly the state that would be obtained if the oracle had a CNot gate. Hence, a possible circuit for the oracle corresponding to the *f2* function is shown in figure 9.14.

Figure 9.14 Oracle circuit for f2

The matrix representation of this oracle is, thus, also the matrix representation of the CNot gate:

$$\begin{pmatrix} 1 & 0 & 0 & 0 \\ 0 & 0 & 0 & 1 \\ 0 & 0 & 1 & 0 \\ 0 & 1 & 0 & 0 \end{pmatrix}$$

Exercise

Calculate the matrix representation of the oracle corresponding to the *f3* function. The result you should obtain is this:

$$\begin{pmatrix} 0 & 0 & 1 & 0 \\ 0 & 0 & 0 & 1 \\ 1 & 0 & 0 & 0 \\ 0 & 1 & 0 & 0 \end{pmatrix}$$

9.6 *Deutsch algorithm*

The Deutsch algorithm requires only a single evaluation of the oracle to know whether the function under consideration is constant or balanced. Let's start with a naive approach and assume that all we need to do is apply the oracle and measure the result.

The code for this is in ch9/applyoracle. Before we explain the algorithm, we first point to the part of the code where the different oracles are created. As we stated before, the creation of an oracle is *not* part of the algorithm that tries to find out whether a function is balanced. Although for practical reasons, we create the oracle in the same Java class file as the algorithm, it should be stressed that the creator of the oracle (who might know the outcome of the problem) and the creator of the algorithm are not the same.

From the previous section, it should be clear that there are four different types of oracles. An infinite number of oracles can be used to represent the simple functions we discussed at the beginning of this chapter, but they all corresponds to one of the four gate matrices that we showed in the previous section. The algorithm will ask to pick a random oracle, and the code that constructs this random oracle is as follows.

Listing 9.4   Creating an oracle

When this function is called, an integer needs to be provided indicating what oracle type to return.

In all cases, the result is a 4 × 4 matrix of complex numbers.

```java
static Oracle createOracle(int f) {
    Complex[][] matrix = new Complex[4][4];

    switch (f) {
        case 0:
            matrix[0][0] = Complex.ONE;
            matrix[1][1] = Complex.ONE;
            matrix[2][2] = Complex.ONE;
            matrix[3][3] = Complex.ONE;
            return new Oracle(matrix);
        case 1:
            matrix[0][0] = Complex.ONE;
            matrix[1][3] = Complex.ONE;
            matrix[2][2] = Complex.ONE;
            matrix[3][1] = Complex.ONE;
            return new Oracle(matrix);
        case 2:
            matrix[0][2] = Complex.ONE;
            matrix[1][1] = Complex.ONE;
            matrix[2][0] = Complex.ONE;
            matrix[3][3] = Complex.ONE;
            return new Oracle(matrix);
        case 3:
            matrix[0][2] = Complex.ONE;
            matrix[1][3] = Complex.ONE;
            matrix[2][0] = Complex.ONE;
            matrix[3][1] = Complex.ONE;
            return new Oracle(matrix);
        default:
            throw new IllegalArgumentException("Wrong
                                    index in oracle");
    }
}
```

If the caller provides 0, an oracle with the matrix corresponding to *f1* will be returned.

If the caller provides 1, an oracle with the matrix corresponding to *f2* will be returned.

If the caller provides 2, an oracle with the matrix corresponding to *f3* will be returned.

If the caller provides 3, an oracle with the matrix corresponding to *f4* will be returned.

If we reach here, the caller provided a wrong value, and we throw an exception.

Now that we have the code that returns an oracle corresponding to a value we provide, we can focus on the algorithm that should detect whether the oracle is linked with a constant function or a balanced function.

We start with the naive approach where we just apply the oracle to two qubits that are initially 0. We hope the result will tell us with 100% confidence whether the underlying function is balanced.

Listing 9.5   Applying the oracle

```
static void try00() {
    QuantumExecutionEnvironment simulator =
            new SimpleQuantumExecutionEnvironment();
    Program program = null;
    for (int choice = 0; choice < 4; choice++) {
        program = new Program(2);

        Step oracleStep = new Step();
        Oracle oracle = createOracle(choice);
        oracleStep.addGate(oracle);
        program.addStep(oracleStep);

        Result result = simulator.runProgram(program);
        Qubit[] qubits = result.getQubits();

        boolean constant =
                (choice == 0) || (choice == 3);

        System.err.println((constant ? "C" : "B") +
            ", measured = |" + qubits[1].measure() +
            " , " + qubits[0].measure()+">");
    }
}
```

This function is called **try00** as it applies the oracles to two qubits that are in their initial state of |0>.

Iterates over the four possible oracle types

Creates a quantum program that contains two qubits

Creates the oracle corresponding to the loop index "choice" and adds it to the program

Executes the program and obtains the results

Based on the loop index "choice," we know if the oracle corresponds to a balanced or constant function. We print that information together with the measurements of the two qubits.

The results of this application are as follows:

```
C, measured = |00>
B, measured = |00>
B, measured = |10>
C, measured = |10>
```

Note that since we didn't use superposition, these results are always the same.

Let's investigate these results. There are two possible outcomes we can measure: the result is either |00> or |10>. Unfortunately, a single result doesn't tell us whether the function was constant (as indicated by the C) or balanced (as indicated by the B). For example, if we measure |00>, the function is either *f1* or *f2*; but since the first is constant and the second is balanced, we don't have an answer to our question.

We can be clever and try to run the application again, but this time we first flip one of the qubits, or both, to the |1> state using a Pauli-X gate. This is shown in the code in the same file; it is a good exercise to create this code yourself before looking at the example.

Doing so, we run four versions of our simple program, each corresponding to a different initial state of the two qubits. The results are shown here:

```
Use |00> as input
C, measured = |00>
B, measured = |00>
B, measured = |10>
C, measured = |10>

Use |01> as input
C, measured = |01>
B, measured = |11>
B, measured = |01>
C, measured = |11>

Use |10> as input
C, measured = |10>
B, measured = |10>
B, measured = |00>
C, measured = |00>

Use |11> as input
C, measured = |11>
B, measured = |01>
B, measured = |11>
C, measured = |01>
```

If you analyze this result, you will conclude that none of those versions is sufficient to detect whether the oracle corresponds to a constant or a balanced function by doing a single evaluation.

But so far, we didn't use the powerful superposition. We will do that now. Before we write the code for the algorithm, figure 9.15 shows the quantum circuit that leads to the result.

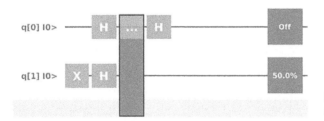

Figure 9.15   Quantum circuit of the Deutsch algorithm

We start with two qubits. The first qubit, q[0], will be evaluated. But instead of evaluating twice, the first time in the state |0> and the second time in the state |1>, we apply a Hadamard transform to it to bring it into a superposition. You can think of this as allowing us to evaluate both possible values in a single quantum step.

The second qubit, q[1], which is initially |0> as well, is first flipped into |1> by applying a Pauli-X gate. Next, a Hadamard gate is applied to this qubit. Both qubits are then used as input to the oracle we discussed in the previous section. After the oracle has been applied, we discard the second qubit. On the first qubit, a Hadamard gate is applied, and the qubit is measured.

Now we arrive at the great thing about this algorithm. The following statement can be mathematically proven: *If the measurement is 0, we are guaranteed that the function represented by the oracle is balanced. If the measurement is 1, we know the considered function is constant.*

If you are interested in the mathematics behind this, it can be proven mathematically that the probability of measuring 0 for the first qubit after the circuit is applied is given by

$$\left(\frac{1}{2} \left((-1)^{f(0)} + (-1)^{f(1)} \right) \right)^2$$

If f is a constant function, this will always result in 1. If f is a balanced function, this will always result in 0.

Instead of proving this, we will create code that runs the circuit for the four different functions and measure the output to see if our statement is correct. The interesting part of this algorithm is that we managed to make the first qubits dependent on the evaluation of all values. We don't have the measurements for all these evaluations, but that was not the original question. The original goal was to determine whether a given function is constant or balanced.

The following code implements the algorithm. It is taken from the ch09/deutsch example:

```
QuantumExecutionEnvironment simulator =
            new SimpleQuantumExecutionEnvironment();
    Random random = new Random();
    Program program = null;
    for (int i = 0; i < 10; i++) {          ◁   The loop will be executed
        program = new Program(2);               10 times, each time with
        Step step0 = new Step();                a random oracle.
        step0.addGate(new X(1));            ◁   The first step applies a Pauli-X
                                                gate to the second qubit.

        Step step1 = new Step();            ◁   The second step applies Hadamard
        step1.addGate(new Hadamard(0));         gates to both qubits.
        step1.addGate(new Hadamard(1));

        Step step2 = new Step();
        int choice = random.nextInt(4);         Chooses a random oracle
        Oracle oracle = createOracle(choice);   (from a predefined list)
        step2.addGate(oracle);              ◁

        Step step3 = new Step();
        step3.addGate(new Hadamard(0));     ◁   Applies another Hadamard
                                                gate to the first qubit

        program.addStep(step0);             ◁   Adds the steps to the
        program.addStep(step1);                 quantum program
```

Creates a program with two qubits — (annotation for `program = new Program(2);`)

Adds the oracle to the quantum circuit — (annotation for `step2.addGate(oracle);`)

**Executes the
quantum
program**

```
        program.addStep(step2);
        program.addStep(step3);
 ┌─⯈   Result result = simulator.runProgram(program);
        Qubit[] qubits = result.getQubits();              ⯇─┐
        System.err.println("f = " + (choice+1) +
            ", val = " + qubits[0].measure());
    }
```

**The first qubit is measured,
and, based on its value, we
know whether the oracle
corresponded with a constant
or balanced function.**

If you run this application, you will see the circuit, and the console will show output similar to the following:

```
f = 3, val = 1
f = 3, val = 1
f = 3, val = 1
f = 1, val = 0
f = 4, val = 0
f = 4, val = 0
f = 2, val = 1
f = 1, val = 0
f = 2, val = 1
f = 4, val = 0
```

For every line in this output, the type of function is printed (*f1*, *f2*, *f3*, or *f4*) followed by the measured value of the first qubit. As you can see, this value is always 1 for *f2* and *f3* (the balanced functions), and it is 0 for *f1* and *f4* (the constant functions).

9.7   *Deutsch-Jozsa algorithm*

The Deutsch algorithm shows that a specific problem that requires two evaluations in a classical approach can be solved by a single evaluation using a quantum algorithm. While this may sound a bit disappointing, the principle is very promising. The Deutsch algorithm can easily be extended to the Deutsch-Jozsa algorithm, in which the input function is operating not on a single Boolean value but on *n* Boolean values. In this case, the function can be represented as

$$f(x_0, x_1, ..., x_{n-1})$$

which indicates that the function uses as input *n* bits that are either 0 or 1. We are given such a function, and we are told that again the function is either constant (which means it always returns 0 or it always returns 1) or balanced (in half the cases it returns 0, and in the other half it returns 1).

The Deutsch algorithm is a special case of this situation, where $n = 1$. In that case, there are only two possible input scenarios. If $n = 2$, there are four possible input scenarios. In general, there are 2^n scenarios when there are *n* input bits.

How many classical evaluations do we need to do before we are 100% certain that the function is either constant or balanced? Suppose that we evaluate half of the possible scenarios ($2^n/2$, which is 2^{n-1}). If at least one of the results is 0 and at least one of the results is 1, we know that the function is not constant, so it must be balanced. But what can we conclude if all evaluations result in the value 1? In that case, it looks like the function is constant. But we still need one additional evaluation, as there is a probability that all the other evaluations will result in 0. To be 100% certain, a function with n bits as input requires $2^{n-1} + 1$ evaluations before we can conclude that the function is either balanced or constant.

However, using a quantum circuit similar to the one in the Deutsch algorithm, only a single evaluation is required. The importance of this is that it shows that quantum algorithms are great for problems that require exponential complexity using a classical approach.

The Deutsch-Jozsa algorithm is very similar to the Deutsch algorithm. It is shown in ch09/deutschjozsa, and the relevant snippet is as follows:

```
static final int N = 3;          ⟵───┐ Defines how many input bits
                                      │ we use (in this case, three)
...

    QuantumExecutionEnvironment simulator =
            new SimpleQuantumExecutionEnvironment();
    Random random = new Random();
    Program program = null;                    Creates a program with N + 1 qubits.
    for (int i = 0; i < 10; i++) {             We need N qubits for the input bits
        program = new Program(N+1);   ⟵──┘     and an additional ancilla qubit.
        Step step0 = new Step();
        step0.addGate(new X(N));      ⟵──┤ Applies a Pauli-X gate
                                           to the ancilla qubit

        Step step1 = new Step();
        for (int j = 0; j < N+1; j++) {  ⟵── Applies a Hadamard gate to
            step1.addGate(new Hadamard(j));   all qubits, bringing them
        }                                      into superposition

        Step step2 = new Step();
        int choice = random.nextInt(2);
        Oracle oracle = createOracle(choice);
        step2.addGate(oracle);

        Step step3 = new Step();                   Applies a Hadamard gate
        for (int j = 0; j < N; j++) {              to all input qubits (not
            step3.addGate(new Hadamard(j));  ⟵──   to the ancilla qubit)
        }

        program.addStep(step0);                  Executes the program
        program.addStep(step1);             and measures the result
        program.addStep(step2);                   of the first qubit
        program.addStep(step3);
        Result result = simulator.runProgram(program);  ⟵──
        Qubit[] qubits = result.getQubits();
        System.err.println("f = " + choice + ", val = "
            + qubits[0].measure());
    }
```

Adds a random oracle to the circuit ──→ (step2)

Exercise
Prove that the Deutsch-Jozsa algorithm is exactly the same as the Deutsch algorithm if $N = 1$.

The circuit for this algorithm, when we have three input qubits, is shown in figure 9.16. If we apply this circuit, it can again be proven that the probability of measuring 0 in the first qubit is given by the following equation:

$$\left(\frac{1}{2^n} \sum_{x=0}^{2^n-1} (-1)^{f(x)} \right)^2$$

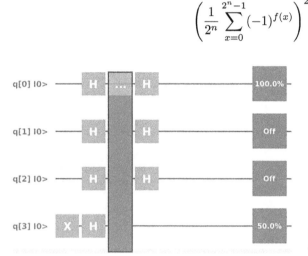

Figure 9.16   Quantum circuit of the Deutsch-Jozsa algorithm

Similar to the Deutsch algorithm, when $f(x)$ is a constant function, this equation shows that the probability of measuring 0 on the first qubit is 100%. When $f(x)$ is a balanced function, the first qubit will always be measured as 1 (as the probability of measuring 0 is null).

The code in the example randomly picks one of two predefined oracles. The first oracle corresponds to the Identity gate, and that corresponds to a constant function that always returns 0. The second oracle corresponds to a CNot gate, where the ancilla qubit is swapped when the last input qubit is 1.

Again, our goal is not to create those oracles. You can assume that the oracles are somehow provided to you, and you have to find out if they correspond to either constant or balanced functions.

9.8   *Conclusion*

In this chapter, you created the Deutsch-Jozsa algorithm. While there is no direct practical usage of this algorithm, you achieved a major milestone. For the first time in this book, you created a quantum algorithm that can execute a task much faster than a corresponding classical algorithm. The real speedup can only be seen if you use a real quantum computer; but the algorithms you created clearly show that a single evaluation is required to fix a specific problem, whereas in classical computing an exponential number of evaluations is required.

Two very important but challenging parts of quantum computing are

- Coming up with quantum algorithms like this that are proven to be faster than corresponding classical algorithms
- Finding practical use cases for such algorithms

In the next chapters, we discuss two algorithms that satisfy these requirements.

Summary

- Some problems can be solved without calculating the end results.
- There is a difference between function evaluation and function properties.
- Classical algorithms can distinguish between balanced and constant functions, but they require many function evaluations to do so.
- A quantum oracle is a black box related to a classical black box function.
- Using the Deutsch-Jozsa algorithm, you can detect whether a supplied oracle corresponds to a balanced or constant function.

Grover's search algorithm

This chapter covers

- Understanding Grover's search algorithm
- Grover's search algorithm relative to existing data storage systems
- Using Grover's search from classical Java code

In this chapter, we answer two important questions posed by developers:

- When is it a good idea to use Grover's search algorithm?
- How does the algorithm work?

Grover's search algorithm is one of the most popular and well-known quantum algorithms. Despite its name, this algorithm is not really a replacement for the search algorithms used today in classical software projects. In this chapter, we explain what kind of problems can benefit from Grover's search algorithm. After reading this chapter, you will be able to determine whether a particular application you are dealing with can use Grover's search algorithm. If so, you can immediately use the classical API in Strange to use Grover's algorithm.

182

10.1 *Do we need yet another search architecture?*

Many excellent libraries, protocols, and techniques are available for searching structured and unstructured data systems. Grover's search algorithm doesn't compete with those technologies.

10.1.1 *Traditional search architecture*

Searching a database is one of the most popular tasks delegated to computers. Many IT applications are architected in a three-tier approach, as shown in figure 10.1.

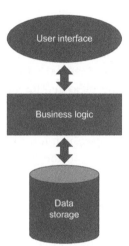

Figure 10.1 Typical three-layered architecture for classical applications

The three layers that are involved in this approach are as follows:

- A user interface (or presentation layer) allows interaction, requests input, and renders output. This is typically a standalone desktop application, a mobile app, or a website, but it can also be an API.
- A middle tier deals with business logic, rules, and processes. This tier handles requests from the presentation layer and may require access to data to process incoming requests.
- The data layer makes sure all data is stored and retrieved in data storage. Very often, the data is made available via a developer-friendly API that lets us search or modify data based on different criteria in a performant way.

In many cases, the middle tier needs to query the data layer to find specific data based on specific requirements. The quality and performance of many applications strongly depend on how flexibly, reliably, and performantly these queries are handled. Therefore, the area of data storage and retrieval is very important in today's IT industry.

There are many different approaches to storing and retrieving data, and this domain is constantly evolving. There are relational and non-relational databases and SQL versus NoSQL approaches. Quantum computing, and Grover's search algorithm in particular, do not provide a new architecture for storing and retrieving data.

> **WARNING**   Although the name *Grover's search algorithm* implies that it deals with search techniques, it does not cover the aspects that are typically discussed when talking about search architecture.

As a consequence, Grover's search algorithm is not a replacement for existing search software. It can be useful, however, in existing or new software libraries and projects that implement search functionality. The algorithm can thus be used in different database techniques.

10.1.2   *What is Grover's search algorithm?*

Now that we have discussed what Grover's search algorithm is *not* about, it is relevant to explain what it *is* about. We will briefly look at this here, and the link between search applications and Grover's algorithms will become clear in the subsequent sections.

Suppose we are given a black box that requires an integer number as input and returns an output. The output is always 0, except for one specific input value (often noted as w), in which case the output is 1. Grover's search algorithm lets us retrieve this specific input value in a performant way.

The concept of a black box is shown in figure 10.2. Somehow, the black box checks whether the provided input equals w. If so, the output is 1. Otherwise, the output is 0. It is important to realize that we don't know how the black box works internally. It might contain a very simple or a very complex algorithm. We have to assume someone created the black box and handed it over to us—we were not involved in how it was created. Indeed, if we were the creator of the black box, there would be no point in writing algorithms to retrieve the value of w, as we would have used that value to create the black box.

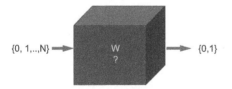

$\{0, 1,..,N\}$ → W ? → $\{0,1\}$

Figure 10.2   Black box returning either 0 or 1 based on an integer number

Somehow, the black box contains information about the value w, and by querying it in a smart way, Grover's algorithm can retrieve that value. The input for Grover's search algorithm is not a number, a search query, or an SQL string—but it is the black box that we just discussed. This is explained in figure 10.3.

Next, we explain how Grover's algorithm can help with traditional search problems. We start with a classical search problem and refine it until we are at the point where we can introduce Grover's search.

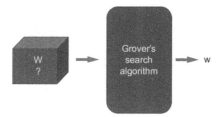

Figure 10.3 Grover's search algorithm takes a black box as input and returns the value *w* that causes the black box to evaluate to 1.

10.2 *Classical search problems*

Most enterprise IT cases use multiple databases with tables and rows. For demo purposes, we will create a simple data storage containing people with their age and country; see table 10.1.

Table 10.1 Table data used in our examples

	age	country
Alice	42	Nigeria
Bob	36	Australia
Eve	85	USA
Niels	18	Greece
Albert	29	Mexico
Roger	29	Belgium
Marie	15	Russia
Janice	52	China

Search applications can use this data to provide answers to questions like these:

- Who is 36 years old and lives in Australia?
- How many of the people live in Russia?
- Is there someone named "Joe" who lives in Greece?
- Give me the names of all people older than 34 years.

We will create an application that answers one specific question: "Find the person who is 29 years old and lives in Mexico." From table 10.1, you can see that the answer is "Albert."

> **NOTE** The SQL query to match this question would be something like `SELECT * FROM PERSON WHERE PERSON.AGE=29 AND PERSON.COUNTRY=MEXICO`. We will work with Java code instead of SQL queries, as this approach allows us to gradually introduce the ideas behind Grover's search algorithm.

We first address our question using the classical approach. Next, we reformulate the question so we can deal with it using a more functional approach that comes closer to

Grover's algorithm. Finally, we use Grover's algorithm to implement the functionality for this search. This process corresponds to the mental model shown in figure 10.4.

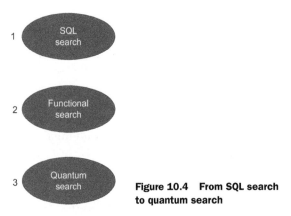

Figure 10.4   From SQL search to quantum search

10.2.1 General preparations

The upcoming examples share common code, and we will not repeat it in each example. In this section, we discuss this common code so that in the remainder of the chapter, we can focus on the search algorithm itself.

THE PERSON CLASS

Before we start writing the search functionality, we define the data we are talking about. Each row in the table represents a person, so we create a Java class named `Person`. The following code can be found in the ch10/classicsearch example.

Listing 10.1   Definition of a `Person`

```java
public class Person {

    private final String name;
    private final int age;
    private final String country;

    public Person(String name, int age, String cntry) {
        this.name = name;
        this.age = age;
        this.country = cntry;
    }

    public String getName() {
        return this.name;
    }

    public int getAge() {
        return this.age;
    }
```

A person has a name.

A person has an age.

A person lives in a country.

When a Person object is created, the three properties need to be defined.

Method to return the name of the person

Method to return the age of the person

```
public String getCountry() {        ◁────  Method to return
    return this.country;                     the country of
}                                            the person
}
```

We use this `Person` class in all of the upcoming examples.

CREATING THE DATABASE

While many high-quality database libraries are available in Java, we stick to a very simple database representation in this example. All instances of the `Person` class are stored in a simple Java `List` object, since this is a standard class in the Java platform and we want to avoid introducing dependencies that are not essential to understanding quantum computing. As we mentioned before, the goal of Grover's search algorithm is not to create another classical database library. On the contrary—we explain the algorithm without depending on a particular type of database.

The following code populates our database: we simply add a number of `Person` instances to the `List` that is then our data store. You can find this code in the Main.java file in ch10/classicsearch.

Listing 10.2 Creating the database

```
List<Person> prepareDatabase() {
    List<Person> persons = new LinkedList<>();
    persons.add(new Person("Alice", 42, "Nigeria"));
    persons.add(new Person("Bob", 36, "Australia"));
    persons.add(new Person("Eve", 85, "USA"));
    persons.add(new Person("Niels", 18, "Greece"));
    persons.add(new Person("Albert", 29, "Mexico"));
    persons.add(new Person("Roger", 29, "Belgium"));
    persons.add(new Person("Marie", 15, "Russia"));
    persons.add(new Person("Janice", 52, "China"));
    return persons;
}
```

We use this method in all of our examples. When you invoke this method, you will receive a `List` of `Person` items that match the predefined table 10.1.

10.2.2 Searching the list

We now write the code for the typical approach for searching our data store for an answer to the original question: "Find the person who is 29 years old and lives in Mexico." Given a list of people who might be the answer to this question, the following approach, which can also be found in the Main.java file in ch10/classicsearch, iterates over all the people until the one satisfying the criteria is detected:

```
Person findPersonByAgeAndCountry(List<Person> persons,
                      int age, String country) {

    boolean found = false;        ◁───  Boolean variable that indicates
                                        if we already got the result
```

```
int idx = 0;          ⟵── Index that tells us the position of
                          the element we are investigating

while (!found && (idx<persons.size())) {    ⟵──

    Person target = persons.get(idx++);

        if ((target.getAge() == age) &&          ⟵──
            (target.getCountry().equals(country))) {
            found = true;                         ⟵──
        }
    }

System.out.println("Got result in "+idx+" tries");    ⟵──

    return persons.get(idx-1);    ⟵──
}
```

Index that tells us the position of the element we are investigating

As long as we don't have a result and the index is still lower than the total number of elements, we execute the following loop.

Obtains the element under consideration from the list

Checks the properties (age and country) of that element

If the properties match, we flip the boolean variable to true, so the loop is not executed needlessly.

Prints the number of evaluations

Returns the result to the caller

NOTE If you are familiar with the Java Stream API, you might notice that the same thing could be achieved using it. Keep reading; we will come back to that in the next section. In this case, the procedural approach is easier to explain, and it lets us count how many evaluations are required.

If the list of people contains the answer, we are guaranteed that this function returns the correct result. If we are lucky and the correct person is the first one in the list, we get the answer after a single execution inside the `while` loop. If we have bad luck and the correct person is the last one in the list, the function requires n evaluations, with n being the number of elements in the list. On average, the algorithm will require $n/2$ evaluations before returning the correct result.

The `main` method of the `classicsearch` application runs the search function 10 times, and each time the number of required evaluations is printed. The function that invokes the `findPersonByAgeAndCountry` method is shown in the following code snippet:

```
void complexSearch() {
    for (int i = 0; i < 10; i++) {
        List<Person> persons = prepareDatabase();
        Collections.shuffle(persons);
        Person target = findPersonByAgeAndCountry(persons, 29, "Mexico");
        System.out.println("Result of complex search= " + target.getName());
    }
}
```

Note that before we do a find operation, we shuffle the list of people, so the result is truly random. Running the application therefore results in output similar to this:

```
Got result after 8 tries
Result of complex search = Albert
Got result after 1 tries
Result of complex search = Albert
```

```
Got result after 2 tries
Result of complex search = Albert
Got result after 3 tries
Result of complex search = Albert
Got result after 5 tries
Result of complex search = Albert
Got result after 7 tries
Result of complex search = Albert
Got result after 2 tries
Result of complex search = Albert
Got result after 1 tries
Result of complex search = Albert
Got result after 2 tries
Result of complex search = Albert
Got result after 5 tries
Result of complex search = Albert
```

10.2.3 Searching using a function

The example code from the previous section is very flexible: we can easily modify the search criteria by providing a different age or a different country to the findPerson-ByAgeAndCountry method. Unfortunately, this is not how Grover's search algorithm works. With Grover's algorithm, we don't provide search parameters, but we have to provide a single function that evaluates to 1 for exactly one input case and evaluates to 0 in all other cases.

In this chapter, we often use the variable w to indicate the input case that results in a function evaluation of 1—in other words, w is the value we are looking for. We can define this as follows:

$$f(w) = \qquad 1$$
$$f(x) = \quad 0, x \neq w$$

In this section, we modify the previous classical example so that it is using a functional approach, which can then be mapped conceptually to the quantum algorithm in the next section.

We perform the same search query, but instead of checking the entries by examining their properties one by one, we apply a function to each entry. When the function evaluates to 1, we know we have the correct entry.

We use the Java Function API to achieve this. Since the functions will always evaluate to an integer (0 or 1), we use the ToIntFunction. First we need to create the function.

Listing 10.3 Creating the function

If the age of the supplied person is 29 and the country is Mexico, the function returns 1. In all other cases, the function returns 0.

Creates a ToIntFunction that takes a Person as input and returns an integer as output

```
ToIntFunction<Person> f29Mexico
    = (Person p) ->
        ((p.getAge() == 29) &&
        (p.getCountry().equals("Mexico"))) ? 1 : 0;
```

When the function is applied, the parameter p contains the supplied person.

NOTE   This is a fixed function for a particular problem. If we want to retrieve a person whose age is 36, we need to create a new function.

Now that we have this function, we can write some Java code that iterates over the list of people and applies the function over each entry until the function returns 1—which means the correct answer has been found. The code is shown next:

```
Person findPersonByFunction(List<Person> persons,
            ToIntFunction<Person> function) {
    boolean found = false;
    int idx = 0;
    while (!found && (idx<persons.size())) {
        Person target = persons.get(idx++);
        if (function.applyAsInt(target) == 1) {
            found = true;
        }
    }
    System.out.println("Got result in "+idx+" tries");
    return persons.get(idx-1);
}
```

Instead of checking the properties of the target, as we did in the previous example, we apply our function to it. When the function returns 1, we know the target is the correct result.

While the approach is different, the amount of time required is similar to the previous algorithm. We still iterate over every person in the list and check whether the age and country of the considered person satisfy our criteria.

The second approach is closer to the quantum approach we discuss in the following section. Instead of providing several parameters, we provide a function. The search algorithm does not have to *create* that function, but it has to *evaluate* it. The differences between the two approaches are highlighted in figure 10.5.

Note that the function search implementation, as we call it in the figure, is still using classical code. However, it brings us closer to how Grover's search algorithm works on a quantum computer.

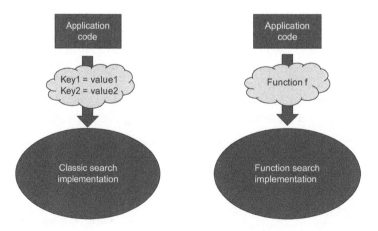

Figure 10.5 Searching using a classic approach versus using functions

NOTE As hinted in the previous section, we can rewrite the search method using the Java Stream API to make it even more functional. The end result will be the same as that shown earlier.

Rather than explicitly looping over all candidates (or at least until a matching one is found), we can use the Java Stream API, as shown in the following snippet:

Filters all person instances in the stream one by one and retains only those that return 1 when applying the provided function

Uses the Java Stream API to create a stream of all people that we evaluate in the following lines

```
Person findPersonByAgeAndCountry(List<Person> persons,
            Function<Person> function) {
    return persons.stream()
            .filter(p -> function.applyAsInt(p) ==1 )
            .findFirst().get();
}
```

If more candidates satisfy the condition, we pick the first one and return that person.

In this snippet, we use the Stream API introduced in Java 8 to filter all possible options so that only the ones with the requested age and country are returned. There are plenty of resources online that discuss the Java Stream API, but that discussion is not in scope for this book.

10.3 *Quantum search: Using Grover's search algorithm*

Grover's algorithm has some similarities with the function-based search discussed in the previous section. When a black box (or a quantum oracle) is provided that is linked to a function like the one described earlier, Grover's algorithm can return the unique input w that would result in a function evaluation of 1 in about $\sqrt{n}$ steps, where each step requires a single oracle evaluation.

NOTE In other words, while the classical search algorithm requires on average $n/2$ function evaluations, Grover's algorithm achieves the same goal in $\sqrt{n}$ function evaluations.

For small lists, this is not impressive. A list with eight elements requires on average four function evaluations for the classical case and about three evaluations for the quantum case. However, for large lists, the advantage becomes clear. A list with 1 million elements requires on average 500,000 evaluations, and in the worst case, it might require 1 million classical evaluations. The same result can be obtained with only 1,000 quantum evaluations.

NOTE Grover's search algorithm requires a predefined number of function evaluations, and we show later that this is number is $\sqrt{n}$. Contrary to the classical approach, there is no best case of one evaluation or worst case of, for example, *n* evaluations. We can only do a single measurement for a quantum application. If we tried to peek before the optimal number of steps was performed, we would have no way to resume the quantum calculation when it turned out that the number we measured was wrong. Therefore, the required number of evaluations is fixed.

The difference between the required evaluations for a classical search versus quantum search using Grover's algorithm is visualized in figure 10.6. We show only the difference between the classical search and Grover's search algorithm for lists of up to 100 elements. As you can see, the larger the size of the list, the more remarkable the differences become. So, it is clear that Grover's algorithm is particularly useful for lists with a huge number of elements.

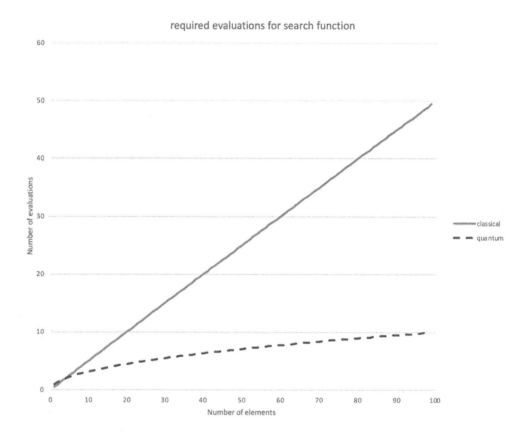

Figure 10.6   Required number of function evaluations as a function of the number of items

Quadratic speedup

It is often said that Grover's algorithm provides a quadratic speedup compared to classical search algorithms. This is true, since for a given number of evaluations (e.g., N), Grover's algorithm can deal with a list of N^2 elements, while a classical algorithm can only deal with lists of N elements.

At the end of this chapter, we explain how Grover's algorithm works. For developers, it is often more important to realize when an algorithm is applicable rather than how it works. Therefore, we first explain how to use the built-in Grover functionality in Strange, which hides the underlying implementation.

The Strange quantum library contains a classical method that under the hood uses Grover's search algorithm to implement a search operation. The signature of the classical method resembles the signature of the example we discussed earlier in this chapter:

```
public static<T> T search(List<T> list, Function<T, Integer> function);
```

This method takes two parameters as input:

- A list with elements of type T, where T can be a Person or any other Java class
- A function that takes as input an element of type T and returns either 1 (if the provided input is the one we are looking for) or 0 (in all other cases)

The following code snippet, from the example in ch10/quantumsearch, shows how we can use this method:

```
void quantumSearch() {
    Function<Person, Integer> f29Mexico
        = (Person p) -> ((p.getAge() == 29) &&
            (p.getCountry().equals("Mexico"))) ? 1 : 0;
    List<Person> persons = prepareDatabase();
    Collections.shuffle(persons);
    Person target = Classic.search(persons, f29Mexico);
    System.out.println("Result of function Search = "
        + target.getName());
}
```

Creates a function similar to the function in the previous example

Creates the initial database again

Randomly shuffles the elements in the database

Calls the search method that is under the hood invoking Grover's search

Prints the result

It is important to emphasize that the provided function is created outside the algorithm. In this case, the function is called f29Mexico, and the Classic.search method does not need to know anything about the internals of that function. The function is evaluated, but to the algorithm, this evaluation is a black box.

10.4 *Probabilities and amplitudes*

Before we can explain why Grover's search algorithm is capable of detecting the expected result, we need to discuss how probabilities are related to the actual state of a quantum system. We will explain the difference between the *state vector*, which describes the status of a quantum system at every moment, and the *probability vector*, which contains the probability of measuring a specific outcome.

10.4.1 *Probabilities*

Throughout this book, we have emphasized the importance of *probabilities*. After applying a quantum circuit, we are left with a number of qubits that can be in different states. The probability vector describes how likely we are to measure a specific value. The goal of many quantum algorithms is to manipulate the probability vector in such a way that the measured outcome is likely to be very relevant to the original question.

In Grover's search algorithm, we need n qubits if we want to search in a list of $2n$ elements. For example, if our list has 128 elements, we need 7 qubits. If we have to deal with 130 elements, we need 8 qubits, and so on. After applying Grover's algorithm, we hopefully obtain a set of qubits that, when measured, return the index of the element we are searching for in the list. This is explained in figure 10.7 for a list with up to 64 elements.

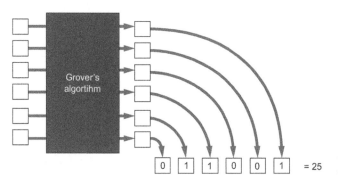

Figure 10.7 **High-level overview of what Grover's search algorithm achieves**

Suppose the element we are searching for has index 25. Initially, all qubits have the value 0. After applying Grover's algorithm, we measure the qubits, and we hope there is a very high probability of measuring the values 0, 1, 1, 0, 0, and 1, which is the binary representation of 25.

With 6 qubits, there are $2^6 = 64$ possible outcomes, so we have a probability vector with 64 elements. The goal of Grover's algorithm is to maximize the value of element 25 and minimize the value of all other elements. We will show that in most cases, the resulting probability for the correct value is very high, but not 100%.

Grover's search algorithm requires several steps. We will show that with each step, the probability of finding the correct answer increases.

Probabilities can be indicated by numbers or by corresponding horizontal bars. A probability of 1 indicates that this specific outcome is guaranteed to be measured, and it corresponds with a filled horizontal bar. A probability of 0 means there is no chance that this specific outcome can be measured, and it corresponds with an empty horizontal bar. Numbers between 0 and 1 correspond with partially filled horizontal bars.

If we have a system with three qubits, we have eight possible outcomes. Figure 10.8 shows two different probability sets for this system, both with a vector with numbers and a notation with bars. Note that the sum of all probabilities should equal 1.

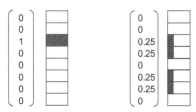

Figure 10.8 **Probabilities in a vector and bar notation**

10.4.2 *Amplitudes*

The probabilities in the probability vector are real, non-negative numbers. So far, we have managed to hide the internal details of the relationship between a qubit and its probability vector. To understand what Grover's search algorithm is exploiting, it helps to shine a bit of light on what is below those probabilities. Again, we will not go deep into the mathematics or physics, but we will explain why it is important to understand that just the probability is not the entire story.

The values in the state vector are actually complex numbers. A complex number c contains a real part and an imaginary part, such as $c = a + ib$ with i being the imaginary unit defined by $i = \sqrt{-1}$.

In this equation, both a and b are real numbers. (For more information about complex numbers, see https://en.wikipedia.org/wiki/Complex_number.)

The probability vector contains real, non-negative numbers only. How do we convert the values from the state vector to the probability vector? This is done by taking the square of the modulus of the value in the state vector.

The modulus of a complex number is defined as follows:

$$mod(s) = \sqrt{a^2 + b^2}$$

This is equivalent to the Pythagorean theorem (see https://en.wikipedia.org/wiki/Pythagorean_theorem), where the length of the hypotenuse in a right triangle is calculated as the square root of the sum of the squares of the lengths of the other sides, as shown in figure 10.9. This theorem is described by the famous equation $c^2 = a^2 + b^2$ and can also be visualized by stating that c is the vector sum of the orthogonal vectors a and b.

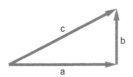

Figure 10.9   Pythagorean theorem and its relationship to the modulus of a complex number

Hence, if we denote the probability by p, we can square the previous equation and obtain $p = a^2 + b^2$.

In this equation, both a and b are real numbers. So, the probability p will always be a positive number as well. When we know a and b, it is easy to calculate p. However, given the probability p, many combinations of a and b result in the same value of p. Even in the simple case where the state only contains a real part (e.g., $b = 0$), two different values of a will lead to the same p; both a and -a give the same probability:

$$a * a = a^2 = p$$
$$(-a) * (-a) = a^2 = p$$

The difference between a state vector and a probability vector is shown in figure 10.10 for a simple case where the state vector contains real values only. There are four entries in the state vector with a value of 0, three entries with a value of 0.5, and one entry with the value –0.5. By taking the square of these values, we arrive at the probability vector in the same figure. By simply looking at the probability vector, we can no longer distinguish between the states with value 0.5 and the state with value –0.5.

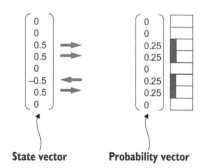

State vector   Probability vector   **Figure 10.10   From state vector to probability vector**

NOTE   The probability vector contains information about the likelihood of a particular outcome being measured. It is based on the state vector, but the latter contains even more information about the internal state of the quantum system. That internal state is important for a number of quantum algorithms.

We now discuss the different steps in Grover's search algorithm.

10.5   *The algorithm behind Grover's search*

The `Classic.search` method available in Strange lets us use Grover's search algorithm using classical computing only. One of its main benefits is that it allows developers to understand what type of problems could benefit from Grover's search.

The internal workings of the quantum algorithm are less relevant to most developers, but here are some reasons a basic understanding is beneficial:

- Grover's search algorithm doesn't require a classical function as input; rather, it uses a quantum oracle that corresponds to a classical function. We discuss this oracle in the upcoming sections.
- Understanding how Grover's search algorithm uses quantum computing characteristics can help us create or understand other quantum algorithms.

In the following sections, we explain the parts of Grover's search algorithm. The mathematical evidence is omitted, though.

10.5.1 Running the example code

The code in ch10/grover allows you to run Grover's search algorithm step by step. We use this code to explain the algorithm. The implementation of the algorithm is done in a method called doGrover that has the following signature:

```
private static void doGrover(int dim, int solution)
```

The first argument to this method, dim, specifies how many qubits should be involved. The second argument, solution, specifies the index of the element we are searching for. Again, note that in a real scenario, it doesn't make sense to provide the answer we are looking for (the solution). Someone should provide us with a black-box function. In this case, though, the code uses the solution to construct the black box.

The main method of this example is very short:

```
public static void main (String[] args) {
        doGrover(6,10);
    }
```

We simply call the doGrover method and specify that we have a system with 6 qubits (so we can accommodate a list with $2^6 = 64$ elements) and the target element is at index 10. When we run the example, the quantum circuit is shown, demonstrating the steps of the algorithm, along with the probability vectors after each step. The image looks similar to figure 10.11.

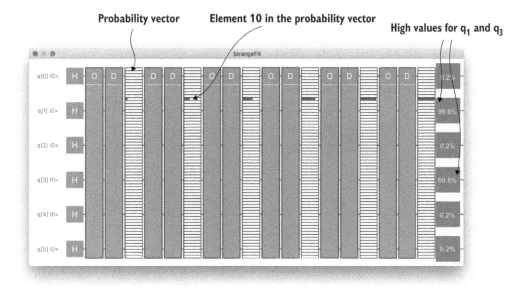

Figure 10.11 Running the Grover example

Shortly, we explain the circuit and its visualization, but first we take a quick look at the end results. The right side of the figure shows the qubits after the algorithm has been applied. Qubits 1 and 3 (denoted as q[1] and q[3]) have a very high probability of being measured as 1 (99.8%), while all other qubits have a very low probability of being measured as 1 (0.2%). As a result, there is a very high probability that the following sequence will be obtained when the qubits are measured:

```
0 0 1 0 1 0
```

Note that this sequence shows the highest-order qubit (q[5]) on the left side and the lowest-order qubit (q[0]) on the right side. Converting this binary sequence to a decimal number is done by adding powers of two when the corresponding qubit is 1:

$$001010$$
$$0{\times}2^5 + 0{\times}2^4 + 1{\times}2^3 + 0{\times}2^0 + 1{\times}2^1 + 0{\times}2^0 = 8 + 2 = 10$$

This is the binary representation of the number 10. Hence, Grover's search algorithm resulted in returning the index of the element we are searching for.

From figure 10.11, it is also clear that the algorithm contains a step that is repeated several times. The flow is shown in figure 10.12.

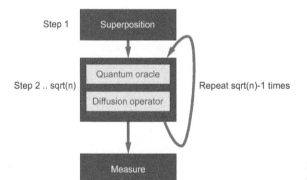

Figure 10.12   Flow of Grover's search algorithm

Each invocation of the step applies a quantum oracle denoted by an O and a diffusion operator denoted by a D. The quantum oracle is related to the function we have been given, and it will be explained later in this chapter, as will the diffusion operator.

After every invocation of this step, the probability vector is rendered. After the first step, which applies a Hadamard gate to each qubit, all options have the same probability. After the second step, all options have a rather low probability. The element at index 10 has a higher probability than the others, but it is still low. So, if we measure the system after this first step, there would be a fair chance of measuring the correct answer, 10, but an even bigger chance of measuring something else.

With each step, however, the probability of measuring 10 increases. At the last step, the probability of measuring 10 is 99.8%.

The example in `stepbystepgrover` is very similar to the example discussed earlier, but it deals with a list of only four items and thus can be handled by two qubits. This makes it easier to explain, and we use that example in the following subsections. Note that we also added more probability visualizations in this example. After every step, the probability vector is rendered; the result is shown in figure 10.13.

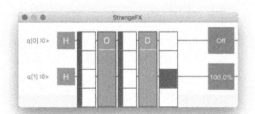

Figure 10.13 Running the Grover example with only two qubits

10.5.2 Superposition

The first step in Grover's algorithm brings all qubits into a superposition state. This approach is often used in quantum algorithms, as it allows the processing to be applied to different cases simultaneously.

In our two-qubit example, the two qubits initially have the state $|0\rangle$. Hence, the initial state vector is described by

$$\begin{bmatrix} 1 \\ 0 \\ 0 \\ 0 \end{bmatrix}$$

The probability vector, which is obtained by each element taking the square of the corresponding element in the state vector, looks exactly the same. The square of 1 is 1, and the square of 0 is 0. The first element in this vector corresponds with the probability of measuring the two qubits in the $|00\rangle$ state, which is exactly the initial state.

After applying a Hadamard gate to both qubits, the state vector becomes

$$\begin{bmatrix} \frac{1}{2} \\ \frac{1}{2} \\ \frac{1}{2} \\ \frac{1}{2} \end{bmatrix}$$

Each element in this vector has an amplitude of 1/2 or 0.5. In the corresponding probability vector, each element equals 1/4 or 0.25, which is the square of 1/2. Therefore, the probability vector after applying the Hadamard gates is written as

$$\begin{bmatrix} \frac{1}{4} \\ \frac{1}{4} \\ \frac{1}{4} \\ \frac{1}{4} \end{bmatrix}$$

TIP   The state vector shows *amplitudes*, while the probability vector shows *probabilities*. For real numbers, the probability is the square of the amplitude. This is also shown in the probability infogate in figure 10.14.

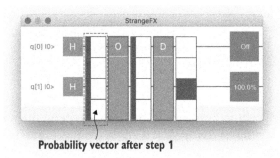

Probability vector after step 1

Figure 10.14   After step 1, all probabilities are equal.

10.5.3 *Quantum oracle*

The main requirement for the classical variant of Grover's search algorithm is that we are given a function that for a single specific value returns 1 and for all other values returns 0. You learned that Grover's search algorithm considers this function a black box and does not have any knowledge about the internals of this function. However, that is a classical function. If we want to really use the quantum algorithm, we need a quantum oracle that is linked to this classical function.

> **Remember the quantum oracle from the Deutsch algorithm**
> This is very similar to what you learned in the previous chapter about the Deutsch algorithm. In the case of the Deutsch algorithm, we were dealing with a function that was either constant or balanced. You created an oracle that operated on two qubits, where the first qubit was left intact and the second qubit was transferred via an operation that depended on the function evaluation.

Figure 10.15 schematically shows the difference between the classical version of Grover's search algorithm and the quantum version: in the classical version, the black box is realized by a classical function, while in the quantum version, the black box is realized by a quantum oracle. Obviously, there is a relationship between the classical function representing the black box and the quantum oracle representing the same black box.

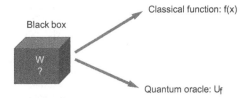

Black box

Classical function: f(x)

Quantum oracle: U_f

Figure 10.15 Black box in a classical versus quantum context

The quantum oracle related to a classical function *f(x)* does the following: for any value of |x> that is not the specific value *w*, *f(x)* is 0, so the original value |x> is returned. If the value *w* is passed through the oracle, the result is –|x>.

Let's give a concrete example. Suppose we have a list with four elements. In that case, we require two qubits (as $2^2 = 4$). The element that we hope to find has index 2. Hence, the function we would pass to a classical algorithm is the following:

$$f(0) = 0$$
$$f(1) = 0$$
$$f(2) = 1$$
$$f(3) = 0$$

This corresponds to the oracle defined by the following matrix:

$$\begin{pmatrix} 1 & 0 & 0 & 0 \\ 0 & 1 & 0 & 0 \\ 0 & 0 & -1 & 0 \\ 0 & 0 & 0 & 1 \end{pmatrix}$$

The code to create this quantum oracle in the example is as follows:

This method creates the oracle (which is a special gate) and it is invoked with a dimension parameter (the number of qubits) and the correct solution (the value that, when the classical function is applied, would return a result of 1).

The oracle is represented by a matrix with dimension N: e.g., with three qubits, we need an 8 × 8 matrix.

```
static Oracle createOracle(int dim, int solution) {
    int N = 1<<dim;
    System.err.println("dim = "+dim+" hence N = "+N);
    Complex[][] matrix = new Complex[N][N];
    for (int i = 0; i < N;i++) {
        for (int j = 0 ; j < N; j++) {
            if (i != j) {
                matrix[i][j] = Complex.ZERO;
            } else {
                if (i == solution) {
```

Loops over all rows (via the index i) and all columns (via the index j) of the matrix

If the considered element is not a diagonal element, its value is 0.

```
            matrix[i][j] = Complex.ONE.mul(-1);
        } else {
            matrix[i][j] = Complex.ONE;
        }
      }
    }
  }
  Oracle answer = new Oracle(matrix);
  return answer;
}
```

If the considered element is a diagonal element and its row (and thus also column) matches the correct solution, the matrix element should be -1.

Returns the oracle

Creates the oracle by passing the matrix to its constructor

If the considered element is a diagonal element but its row (and thus also column) does not match the correct solution, the matrix element should be 1.

When this function is applied to the example where we have two qubits (dim = 2) and where the correct solution is 2 (solution = 2), you can verify that the 4 × 4 matrix created by this function matches the matrix shown previously.

Before we apply this gate to the probability vector we obtained before, we apply it to a state vector containing a wrong value and to a state vector containing the correct value. Since the correct value is 2, the state vector representing 1 is a wrong state vector. As stated previously, applying the classical function $f(1)$ results in 0; and due to the definition of the oracle, we expect that applying the oracle to |01> will not change the input value. Let's double-check by doing the following matrix multiplication:

$$\begin{pmatrix} 1 & 0 & 0 & 0 \\ 0 & 1 & 0 & 0 \\ 0 & 0 & -1 & 0 \\ 0 & 0 & 0 & 1 \end{pmatrix} \begin{bmatrix} 0 \\ 1 \\ 0 \\ 0 \end{bmatrix} = \begin{bmatrix} 0 \\ 1 \\ 0 \\ 0 \end{bmatrix}$$

As you can observe, the state did not change. Next, we apply this oracle to the state vector representing 2 since the classical function $f(2)$ returns 1. The state vector 2 corresponds to the qubit sequence |10>, so let's apply the quantum oracle to this vector:

$$\begin{pmatrix} 1 & 0 & 0 & 0 \\ 0 & 1 & 0 & 0 \\ 0 & 0 & -1 & 0 \\ 0 & 0 & 0 & 1 \end{pmatrix} \begin{bmatrix} 0 \\ 0 \\ 1 \\ 0 \end{bmatrix} = \begin{bmatrix} 0 \\ 0 \\ -1 \\ 0 \end{bmatrix}$$

Doing the matrix multiplication shows that the state vector is inverted.

> **TIP** From this simple example, you can see that while the state vector has changed, the probability vector is still the same as the original input. The square of 1 is equal to the square of –1, so we won't notice a difference when just looking at the probability vector.

In theory, we could apply this oracle to every single state vector representing a possible index. In all cases except one, the result would be identical to the input. When we applied the oracle to the correct value, the result would be inverted. However, this would mean we would again need on average $N/2$ evaluations before finding the correct value. Using the superposition state we created earlier, we can apply the oracle to a combination of all possible input states.

Multiplying this matrix and the state vector obtained after applying the Hadamard gates results in the following:

$$\begin{pmatrix} 1 & 0 & 0 & 0 \\ 0 & 1 & 0 & 0 \\ 0 & 0 & -1 & 0 \\ 0 & 0 & 0 & 1 \end{pmatrix} \begin{bmatrix} \frac{1}{2} \\ \frac{1}{2} \\ \frac{1}{2} \\ \frac{1}{2} \end{bmatrix} = \begin{bmatrix} \frac{1}{2} \\ \frac{1}{2} \\ -\frac{1}{2} \\ \frac{1}{2} \end{bmatrix}$$

Note that the third element in this vector, corresponding to the state |10> (which is the value 2), is now negative. If we look at the probability vector, though, all elements in this vector are still equal to $1/4$, as shown in figure 10.16.

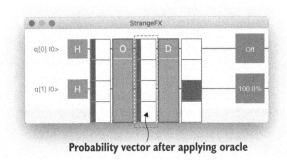

Probability vector after applying oracle

Figure 10.16   After applying the quantum oracle, all steps still have an equal probability.

The quantum oracle does not change the probabilities. If we measured the system now, we would have an equal chance of measuring any value. However, the quantum circuit itself works with the amplitudes, which are modified. In the next step, we take advantage of this.

This situation shows a very important difference between the state vector, which contains amplitudes, and the probability vector, which contains probabilities. We typically talk about probabilities, but in this case, let's take a deeper look at the amplitudes.

Figure 10.17 shows the state vector after applying the quantum oracle, with the four different amplitudes as horizontal lines. A line to the right indicates a positive amplitude, and a line to the left indicates a negative amplitude.

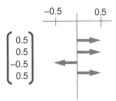

Figure 10.17   Visualization of the state vector after applying the quantum oracle

The probability is the squared modulus of the amplitude. So, if the amplitude is 0.5, the probability is 0.25. If the amplitude is –0.5, the probability is 0.25 as well, as shown in figure 10.16.

> **NOTE** By applying the quantum oracle to a superposition of all possible states, we put the quantum system into a state where the desired result is different from all other possible outcomes. However, we are not able to measure this yet.

10.5.4 *Grover diffusion operator: Increasing the probability*

The next step of Grover's search algorithm applies a diffusion operator to the state of the system. This operator somehow makes the implicit information of the quantum system more explicit. Remember from the previous step that the system already contains the information we need (the entry at the desired outcome has a negative amplitude), but we can't measure it yet (all probabilities are equal). This diffusion operator can be constructed by applying quantum gates or creating its matrix. (You can see the implementation in the code either in Strange or in the ch10/grover example.)

This code can be found in the `createDiffMatrix(int dim)` method in the `Main` class in the ch10/grover example. The resulting diffusion operator is a mathematical construct that is needed to ultimately increase the probability of receiving the correct result while decreasing all other probabilities. The mathematical concepts behind this operator are less relevant for developers, so we don't go into detail about them. Instead, we explain at a high level what this operator is achieving. You can find the proof online; for example, in this article about Grover's algorithm on the website of Carnegie Mellon University: https://www.cs.cmu.edu/~odonnell/quantum15/lecture04.pdf.

The diffusion operator does an *inversion about the mean*, which is as follows:

1 All values in the state vector are summed.
2 The average is calculated.
3 All values are replaced with the value that would be obtained by mirroring the value about the mean.

Let's calculate what that does with our current state vector. The four elements in the state vector are 1/2, 1/2, –1/2, 1/2. The sum of those elements is thus 1:

$$\frac{1}{2} + \frac{1}{2} - \frac{1}{2} + \frac{1}{2} = 1$$

So, the average is $\frac{1}{4}$.

We now need to "mirror" the elements (which are either 1/2 or –1/2) around this value of 1/4. As shown in figure 10.18, mirroring 1/2 results in 0. Interestingly, mirroring –1/2 results in 1!

> **NOTE** The diffusion operator is the part of Grover's search algorithm that allows us to retrieve higher probabilities for negative amplitudes.

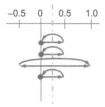

-0.5   0   0.5   1.0

Figure 10.18   Visualization of the state vector after applying the diffusion operator

The real power of Grover's search algorithm comes from the combination of the quantum oracle, which flips the sign of the amplitude of the target value, and the diffusion operator, which inverts all amplitudes over their mean, thereby amplifying the negative amplitude into the largest element. In this particular case, with only two qubits, a single step is sufficient to find the correct answer to the original problem. We were provided with an oracle, and a single evaluation of that oracle was enough to determine that the element at index 2 was given the correct answer to the original function.

If there are more than two qubits, the probability of measuring the correct answer is larger than the probability of measuring any of the other options, but it is not 100%. In that case, the quantum oracle and the diffusion operator have to be applied multiple times.

It can be proven mathematically that the number of steps that provides the optimal result is the value closest to $\sqrt{N} * \Pi/4$. In the doGrover method in the Main class of ch10/grover, this is done by the following construct:

```
private static void doGrover(int dim, int solution) {
        int N = 1 << dim;
        double cnt = Math.PI*Math.sqrt(N)/4;
...
        for (int i = 1; i < cnt; i++) {
// apply a step
        }
...
    }
```

Looking back at figure 10.11, where $N = 64$, we saw a good result after six steps. Indeed, according to the algorithm just shown, the optimal number of steps is 6.28.

NOTE   When we apply more steps than are optimal, the quality of the result will decrease. Therefore, it is highly recommended to follow the algorithm we have shown.

10.6   *Conclusion*

Grover's search algorithm is one of the most popular quantum algorithms. In this chapter, you learned that while the algorithm itself is not related to searching a database, it can be used in applications that require searching through unstructured lists.

As is often the case with quantum algorithms, Grover's search algorithm increases the probability of measuring the correct response and reduces the probability of measuring the wrong response.

Without any upfront knowledge, all possible answers have the same probability. After applying one step of the algorithm, the correct answer already has a higher probability than the other possible outcomes. After applying the optimal number of steps (the number closest to $\sqrt{N} * \Pi/4$), the correct answer will have the highest probability.

Summary

- Classical algorithms to search for a specific element in an unstructured list can be written in Java using a Java function.
- Using the quantum equivalent of a classical Java function, you can use a quantum algorithm to do the same search.
- The time it takes a classical algorithm to find the desired element is linearly proportional to the number of elements in the list. In the quantum approach, using Grover's search algorithm, the time to find this element is proportional to the square root of the number of elements.
- Grover's search algorithm can be implemented using Strange.

Shor's algorithm

This chapter covers

- Understanding Shor's algorithm and why it is relevant
- Solving integer factorization with classical and quantum computing techniques

In this chapter, we discuss one of the most famous quantum algorithms currently known. More important than the results of this algorithm is the approach taken to reach the algorithm. The mental model shown in figure 11.1 outlines the chapter.

11.1 A quick example

Before we explain and discuss Shor's algorithm, let's look at some real Java code that invokes Shor's algorithm on a quantum computer simulator. The example in ch11/quantumfactor has everything you need. We discuss the example later; for now, it is important to know that we use Strange to simulate the behavior of a real quantum computer. If you run the example, you will see the following output:

```
Factored 15 in 3 and 5
```

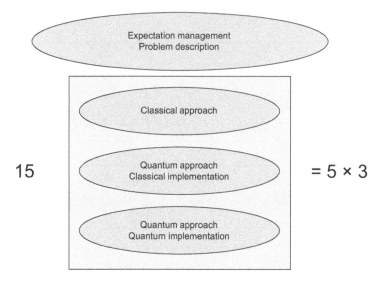

Figure 11.1   Mental model for this chapter. We gradually develop a Java application that uses quantum computing to factor 15 into 5 and 3.

That's it. The main application in the last chapter of this book factors 15 into 3 and 5. While that is something you could easily do with a classical computer, or even in your head, it is a great example of where quantum computers can make a real difference, and why. As we said before, the results of the code in this chapter are not impressive. But there are two important reasons we put so much emphasis on this algorithm:

- Once there are quantum computers with enough high-quality qubits, the results of Shor's algorithm will be very impressive and actually very threatening to many current encryption techniques.
- The approach taken by Shor to implement this problem on a quantum computer might help others to find similar approaches to various problems.

NOTE   You don't need a quantum computer or a quantum computer simulator to find out that $15 = 3 \times 5$. However, by understanding how a quantum computer can do integer factorization, you can work on similar problems that will benefit from quantum advantages once quantum computers are really powerful. For example, optimization algorithms and some machine learning algorithms might use the same quantum techniques as described in this chapter.

11.2   *The marketing hype*

In talks about quantum computing, the question is often raised about what areas are expected to change considerably because of quantum computing. One of the most common answers is encryption. Often, when people are asked what they know about quantum computing, the answer is, "It will break encryption." While that is not necessarily a wrong answer, it should be placed in the right context. Clearly, it is an answer that sparks discussion and therefore often increases interest in quantum computing. But there are a few caveats:

- There are many impressive targets for quantum computing other than breaking encryption.
- It is expected to be several years before quantum computers are powerful enough to break the most common encryption techniques used today.

The second caveat should again be taken with a grain of salt. Current quantum computers are by no means capable of decrypting messages sent with a 2048-bit RSA key. However, those encrypted messages can be stored on disk today, and once quantum computers are powerful enough, they can be decrypted. It's possible that in the 2030s, some secrets from today will be unveiled.

The basic idea behind the statement that "quantum computing will break current encryption" is that many encryption techniques used today rely on the assumption that it is extremely hard to factor a large integer. Until now, the largest number that has been factored had 829 bits, and the process required about 2,700 core-years using Intel Xeon Gold 6130 CPUs. Since the current best-performing algorithms are still in the sub-exponential time complexity class, adding a single bit makes it almost exponentially harder for classical computers to factor the target. It is therefore assumed that, for example, a 2048 bit key is very secure.

However, in 1994, Peter Shor wrote a paper titled "Algorithms for Quantum Computation: Discrete Logarithms and Factoring" (https://ieeexplore.ieee.org/document/365700) in which he explained how a quantum computer would be able to factor integers in a much faster and (especially) more scalable way than the best possible classical computers. The algorithm, which was coined *Shor's algorithm* after its inventor, has been implemented on quantum computer simulators (e.g., Strange) and on real quantum computers. The results might look unimpressive, but since the algorithm has polynomial time complexity, the real benefits will become visible only once the problem is more challenging and there are more stable qubits in a quantum computer.

> **NOTE** We want to be sure you don't have unrealistic expectations. There is no consensus among physicists that we will ever be able to create a quantum computer with sufficient stable qubits to factor a 2048-bit key. Regardless of this discussion, the approach of Shor's algorithm is very interesting, and it can serve as the basis for other algorithms and ideas. Therefore, it deserves some explanation.

11.3 Classic factorization vs. quantum factorization

Many encryption algorithms rely on the assumption that it is very hard for computers to factor large numbers. But is it really that difficult?

Since breaking encryption is a rewarding exercise, considerable research has been done to find the best possible algorithm to factor large numbers. Currently, the best-known algorithm for doing this is of the sub-exponential time complexity class.

NOTE   We discussed time complexity in chapter 1. It might be good to reread that information, as we talk about polynomial and exponential time complexity throughout this chapter.

Shor's algorithm solves the problem in polynomial time. The absolute numbers depend on many factors, but the general idea should be clear from figure 11.2, where we compare the sub-exponential curve and the polynomial curve. (The values on the axes are not relevant—they are just indications.)

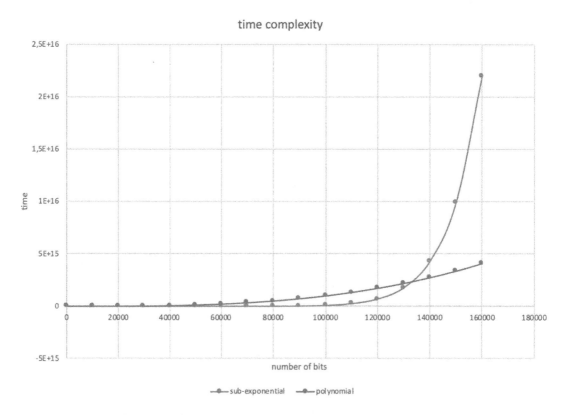

Figure 11.2   Required computing time for sub-exponential versus polynomial algorithms as a function of a number of bits

The main observations of this comparison are as follows:

- For small numbers of bits, the sub-exponential approach (e.g., the classic algorithm) work very well and maybe even better than the polynomial approach (quantum algorithm).
- Once the number of bits becomes large enough, adding a single bit makes the problem much harder using the classic algorithm compared to using the quantum algorithm.

In conclusion, Shor's algorithm really shows its power when we have to factor large numbers, which is typically the case when dealing with encryption. This requires more qubits than are available on today's quantum computers, so we don't see the real benefit *yet.*

11.4 A multidisciplinary problem

There are several ways that you can look at Shor's algorithm. Obviously, it uses properties specific to quantum physics; otherwise, it wouldn't benefit from quantum computing. The algorithm itself is based on linear algebra and mathematical equations. Finally, to be of practical use, it should be written in a programming language and integrated with other software components. This multidisciplinary approach is shown in figure 11.3.

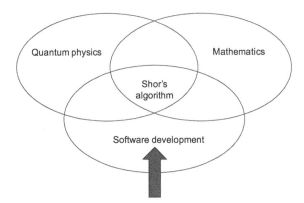

Figure 11.3 Fields with different expertise are required for Shor's algorithm. In this chapter, we focus on the field of software development, but that does not mean the other fields are less important!

The success of Shor's algorithm is mainly related to its promising performance. The ultimate performance combines the properties in the three fields shown in figure 11.3. Lots of research has been done to find the best approach, taking into account a number of characteristics:

- How many qubits are required?
- How many elementary gates are required?
- What is the depth of the algorithm (related to how many gate operations can be executed in parallel)?

The answers to these questions are related to the number of bits in the integer that we need to factor. It can be proven that both the number of qubits and the number of gates required are polynomial with the number of bits.

In this chapter, we focus on the software development parts of Shor's algorithm. The mathematical and physical backgrounds of the algorithm are complex; you can find more information in the following paper from Stephane Beauregard: "Circuit for Shor's Algorithm using 2n+3 qubits" (https://arxiv.org/abs/quant-ph/0205095).

11.5 *Problem description*

The core concept of many encryption techniques is prime numbers. An integer is a prime number if it can only be divided by 1 or itself. For example, 7 is a prime number, but 6 is not—as 6 can be divided by 1, 2, 3, and 6.

Suppose that you know two prime numbers, 7 and 11. Calculating the product of those two prime numbers is easy:

$$7 \times 11 = 77$$

The reverse operation is more complex: given a number that is the product of two unknown prime numbers, come up with those two prime numbers. In the previous simple case, it is still easy:

$$77 = 7 \times 11$$

We say that 77 can be *factored* into 7 and 11. You don't even need a calculator for this.

However, once the prime numbers become bigger, the problem becomes more complex. A slightly more difficult number is 64,507. Can you quickly say whether this number can be factored into two prime numbers? That is already more difficult to answer than factoring 77. The opposite question is much easier: what is the product of 251 and 257?

$$251 \times 257 = 64,507$$

This is one of the basic rules for encryption: it is easy to go from A to B (from factors to numbers) but very hard to go from B to A (number to factors). Hence, the core problem we try to solve in this chapter is the following: given an integer N, find two integers a and b so that $N = a * b$, with both a and $b > 1$.

We first solve this problem in a purely classical way. This corresponds to the first approach shown in the mental model, as highlighted in figure 11.4.

In general, the classical way of doing integer factorization is straightforward, as shown in figure 11.5. This approach immediately tries to find the factors for the given integer and return them. While this may sound very obvious, we show later that the quantum approach takes a different path.

A naive approach for doing this is provided in the example ch11/classicfactor. The `main` method is as follows.

Listing 11.1   Source code for the classic `main` method

Picks a random integer between 0 and 10000

```
public static void main (String[] args) {
        int target = (int)(10000 * Math.random());
        int f = factor (target);
        System.out.println("Factored "+target+" in "
            + f + " and "+target/f);
}
```

Invokes the factor method to obtain one factor of the picked integer

Prints the obtained factor and the corresponding one that, when multiplied, return the originally picked integer

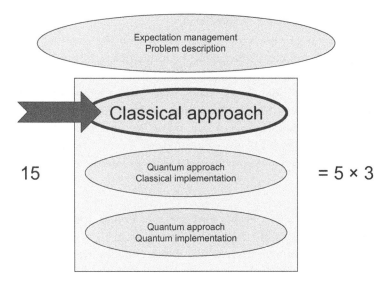

Figure 11.4   Referring to the mental model, we will now explain the classic approach.

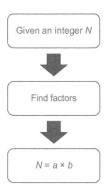

Figure 11.5   Classic flow for factoring integers. A classic algorithm focuses on finding the factors for a given number and returning those factors.

The main method delegates the work to the factor method, which looks like this:

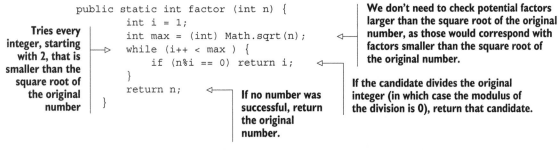

Clearly, this is a very naive approach, and more performant approaches exist.

11.6 *The rationale behind Shor's algorithm*

The mathematical details of Shor's algorithm are beyond the scope of this book. If you're interested, see the paper by Stephane Beauregard mentioned earlier; it contains the detailed instructions for creating the circuit that implements the algorithm.

However, the rationale behind those details is very important, as it applies to many potential quantum algorithms. Shor's algorithm translates the original problem into another problem: finding the *periodicity* of a function. We now look into this problem, and next, we explain how those problems are related. We show how finding the periodicity of a special function (modular exponentiation) helps us find the factors of an integer.

11.6.1 *Periodic functions*

A function is called *periodic* if its evaluations are repeated at regular intervals. The length of this interval is called the *periodicity* of the function.

An interesting periodic function is modular exponentiation, which is defined as

$$f(x) = a^x \mod N$$

where a and N are parameters with $a < N$. Because of the modular operator, the outcome of this function is always smaller than N.

To give you a more tangible idea of what this function looks like, consider the case where $a = 7$ and $N = 15$. In that case, figure 11.6 shows the value for

$$y = 7^x \mod 15$$

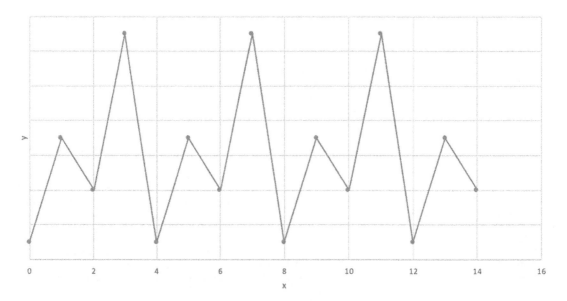

Figure 11.6 Example of a periodic function. The periodicity of this function is 4: the same pattern in the y values comes back after every four evaluations. For example, the peaks in the function occur at x values of 3, 7, and 11.

There is a pattern in this function that repeats itself. Whenever we increase x by 4, the value of the function is the same as the original value. This is illustrated in the following table, where we show the values of y for x ranging from 0 to 8.

x	0	1	2	3	4	5	6	7	8
y	1	7	4	13	1	7	4	13	1

From these observations, it turns out that the periodicity of this function is 4.

11.6.2 Solving a different problem

Finding the periodicity of a function is a problem that can be solved by a quantum computer in polynomial time. After the quantum computing part, the result needs to be translated to the original problem again. This flow is shown in figure 11.7.

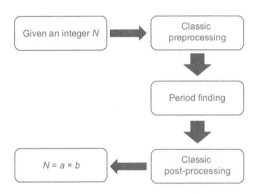

Figure 11.7 Solving a different problem. Instead of directly finding the factors for the number *N*, we translate the original problem to a different problem, solve that, and translate the result back to the original question, which can then be answered.

> **NOTE** Quantum computers can provide a huge speedup for some algorithms, but not all. Therefore, the key to creating quantum applications is often in finding a way to translate the original problem into a problem that can be solved easily by a quantum computer (e.g., in polynomial time instead of exponential time) and then transforming it back to the original domain.

The original problem is to find two integers that, when multiplied together, yield the integer N that we want to factor. The problem that we actually solve using a quantum computer looks very different and is formulated as follows: given an integer A and an integer N, find the periodicity of the function

$$a^x \mod N$$

While that problem looks very different from the original problem, it can be proven mathematically that they are related. Once we find the periodicity of this function, we can find the factors for N easily.

We are not going to provide the mathematical proof, but we will show the relationship between periodicity and factors by looking at some Java code. The flow that we follow in this code is illustrated in figure 11.8.

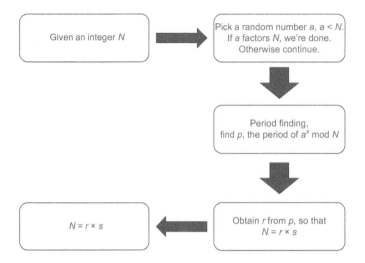

Figure 11.8   Detailed flow for both classic and quantum implementations. The preprocessing and post-processing, which transform the original problem into the problem of period finding, are similar for the classic and quantum implementations. The period finding can be implemented in a classic way or a quantum way.

In the next section, we explain how the critical part—finding the periodicity of the modular exponentiation—is achieved using a quantum algorithm. Before we do that, we will write out the complete algorithm using classical computing. This is the second approach in our mental model, as shown in figure 11.9.

The code example in the ch11/semiclassicfactor directory contains a classical implementation of Shor's algorithm. Before looking at the code, let's run the example:

```
mvn compile javafx:run
```

The result will be something like this:

```
We need to factor 493
Pick a random number a, a < N: 6
calculate gcd(a, N):1
period of f = 112
Factored 493 in 17 and 29
```

This means the algorithm discovered that 493 could be written as the product of 17 and 29.

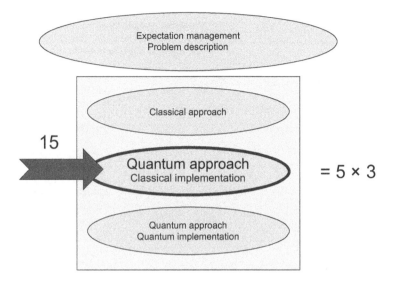

Figure 11.9 Mental model: classic implementation of the quantum approach. We don't use direct factorization techniques as we did in the classic approach. We use the technique of period finding, which is part of the quantum approach, but we first develop that in a classic way.

Let's have a look at the main method for this example:

```
public static void main (String[] args) {
        int target = (int)(10000 * Math.random());
        int f = factor (target);
        System.out.println("Factored "+target+" in "+f+ " and "+target/f);
    }
```

This code is straightforward and exactly the same as the main method shown in listing 11.1. A random integer between 0 and 10,000 is generated, and then the factor method is called to find a divider of this integer. Finally, the divider and the other divider are printed.

This method delegates the bulk of the work to the factor method, so let's look at that method. It is worth keeping an eye on figure 11.8 while looking at the code.

Listing 11.2 Factor method: classical implementation of the quantum approach

```
public static int factor (int N) {
    // PREPROCESSING
    System.out.println("We need to factor "+N);
    int a = 1+ (int)((N-1) * Math.random());
    System.out.println("Pick a random
                      number a, a < N: "+a);
    int gcdan = gcd(N,a);
    System.out.println("calculate gcd(a, N):"+ gcdan);
    if (gcdan != 1) return gcdan;
```

Preprocessing part begins

Picks a random number a between 1 and N

Calculates the greatest common denominator (GCD) between a and N

If the GCD is not 1, we are done, since that means the GCD is a factor of N.

```
// PERIOD FINDING
int p = findPeriod (a, N);
```

Finds the periodicity of the modular exponentiation function. This is the bulk of the work, and it is detailed in the next listing.

```
// POSTPROCESSING
System.out.println("period of f = "+p);
 if (p%2 == 1) {
    System.out.println("odd period, restart.");
    return -1;
}
int md = (int)(Math.pow(a, p/2) +1);
int m2 = md%N;
if (m2 == 0) {
    System.out.println("m^p/2 + 1 = 0 mod N,
                                       restart");
    return -1;
}
int f2 = (int)Math.pow(a, p/2) -1;
return gcd(N, f2);

}
```

If the period turns out to be an odd number, we can't use it and have to repeat the process. We return -1 to inform the caller that the operation failed.

Performs minor mathematical operations on the period to obtain a factor of N. This may still fail, in which case we return -1 to the caller.

The `factor` method calls the `findPeriod` method to obtain the periodicity of the function $a^x \bmod N$. This function can be executed *fast* on a quantum computer.

NOTE When we say the function can be executed *fast*, we mean it is done in polynomial time.

11.6.3 *Classic period finding*

We can, of course, achieve this on a classical computer as well, but for large numbers, doing so will take a very long time. However, for small numbers (e.g., smaller than 10,000, as we have in our code), this approach works very well on classical computers.

Remember from figure 11.6 that a modular exponential function has a clear period. The first evaluation of that function, evaluating $x = 0$, leads to a value of 1. Increasing x by 1 returns a new value, and a pattern begins. At a given moment, the function evaluates to 1 again, and the pattern repeats. Hence, once we determine the value of x that results in the value 1 when applying the function, we know the period. A naive approach for a classical Java function that does this is shown next.

Listing 11.3   Classic implementation for finding the period of a function

The periodicity of a function is at least 1. Note that for r = 0, the value of any ar mod N is always 1.

```
public static int findPeriod(int a, int N) {
        int r = 1;
        long mp = (long) (Math.pow(a,r)) % N;
        BigInteger bn = BigInteger.valueOf(N);
        BigInteger bi = BigInteger.valueOf(a);
        while (mp != 1) {
            r++;
```

Calculates the first result of a1 mod N

As long as the result is not 1 (which is the result of a 0 mod N), we need to keep increasing r and continue.

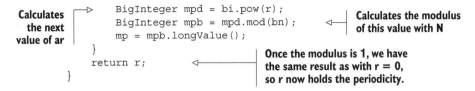

Calculates the next value of ar

```
        BigInteger mpd = bi.pow(r);
        BigInteger mpb = mpd.mod(bn);
        mp = mpb.longValue();
    }
    return r;
}
```

Calculates the modulus of this value with **N**

Once the modulus is 1, we have the same result as with r = 0, so r now holds the periodicity.

This function (finding the periodicity of a modular exponentiation) can also be implemented on a quantum computer, using a quantum algorithm with quantum properties. It is the core of Shor's algorithm, and we discuss it in the next section.

11.6.4 *The post-processing step*

While the most critical part of the algorithm is to find the period of a function, it is still important that we can convert this periodicity into a factor. This is done in the post-processing steps. We won't give a rigorous mathematical proof for the algorithm but rather will show the different steps together with some values so that you can follow what is happening.

Let's first recap the parameters we are dealing with:

- N is the number we want to factor: e.g., $N = 493$.
- a is the random number, smaller than N, that we use to initiate the period finding part. The random number used in our example was $a = 6$.
- p is the period of the function $a^x \bmod N$, which we obtained from the period-finding part of the algorithm. It turned out that in our case, $p = 112$.

Because of the definition of a period function, we know that

$$f = a^x \mod N = a^{x+p} \mod N$$

For $x = 0$, this means

$$a^0 \mod N = a^p \mod N$$

or

$$1 = a^p \mod N$$

With the numbers we have, this comes down to

$$6^{112} \mod 493 = 1$$

Before we use this to find the factors of 493, we first check if this is correct. While it is possible to create a Java application to do this in such cases, it is often easier to simply use `jshell`, which is distributed with the Java SDK—so you have it on your system. JShell is the Java REPL tool that is part of the Java SDK, and you can find more information about it at http://mng.bz/raYy.

The example repository contains a script named `checkperiod` in the ch11/jshell directory that can be loaded into `jshell`. The contents of this script are as follows:

Prints the result, which we hope is equal to 1.

Initializes the values to the ones we use in our example

Initializes variable u with the value 1. It will hold the result of the calculations.

Inside this loop, the modular exponentiation is executed as a number of modular multiplications. This allows the result to stay below N, as otherwise, the result would soon be too large to fit in an Integer value.

```
int N = 493;
int a = 6;
int p = 112;
int u = 1;
for (int i = 0; i < p; i++) {
    u = (u * p) % N;
}
System.out.println("This should be 1: " + u);
```

You can either type the entries in the script or use the /open command in `jshell` to load the script. In both cases, the result will be printed. Following is the result of this operation in `shell`. Note that we added a /list command at the end to show the list of commands that were executed:

```
|  Welcome to JShell -- Version 17
|  For an introduction type: /help intro

jshell> /open jshell/checkperiod
This should be 1: 1

jshell> /list

   1 : int N = 493;
   2 : int a = 6;
   3 : int p = 112;
   4 : int u = 1;
   5 : for (int i = 0; i < p; i++) {
           u = (u * p) % N;
       }
   6 : System.out.println("This should be 1: " + u);

jshell>
```

Clearly, we are on the right track. From

$$a^p \mod N = 1$$

it follows that

$$a^p - 1 = kN$$

with k an integer as well. We now use the equation

$$x^2 - 1 = (x + 1)(x - 1)$$

and we can write the previous equation as

$$(a^{p/2} + 1)(a^{p/2} - 1) = kN$$

Let's simplify this as follows:

$$(u+1)(u-1) = kN$$

with

$$u = a^{p/2}$$

By expanding both the left and right terms to their factors, it follows that the factors of *N* (if there are factors, which is not the case if *N* is prime) should also be on the left-hand side of the equation. Therefore, the greatest common denominator (*gcd*) of *N* and u + 1 should be a factor of *N*.

Let's verify this with the values from our example. The same directory containing the checkperiodjshell script also has the script calculatef, which has does exactly what we described:

```
int gcd(int a, int b) {                    Defines a function that calculates the
        int x = a > b ? a : b;             greatest common denominator of two
        int y = x == a ? b : a;            integers. We don't go into the details of this
        int z = 0;                         function, but you can check that it works by
        while (y != 0) {                   invoking it with numbers you know.
            z = x % y;
            x = y;
            y = z;
        }
        return x;
}                            Again, defined the
                             values we use in
int N = 493;                 this example
int a = 6;
int p = 112;                                 Calculates the u
int u = 1;                                   value as described
for (int i = 0; i < p/2; i++) {              previously
        u = (u * p) % N;
}                                                            Calculates the gcd
System.out.println("This is u mod N: " + u);                of u + 1 and N to
System.out.println("This is gcd: " + gcd(u + 1, N));        find a factor of N,
                                                            and prints it
```

Prints the value of u

Running this in jshell by invoking /load jshell/calculatef shows the following result:

```
|  Welcome to JShell -- Version 16-ea
|  For an introduction type: /help intro

jshell> /open jshell/calculatef
This is u mod N: 407
This is gcd: 17
```

And indeed, 17 is a factor of the original value of N = 493:

$$493 = 17 * 29$$

In this section, you succeeded in calculating a factor for *N*, assuming that you could calculate the period of a function $a^x \bmod N$. For now, that period calculation was still done in a classic way, but in the next section, we present the quantum implementation. The post-processing, explained in this step, stays the same.

11.7 *The quantum-based implementation*

Let's go back to the original example in this chapter, which is in the ch11/quantum-factor directory. That example has a very simple `main` method:

```
public static void main (String[] args) {
        int target = 15;
        int f = Classic.qfactor (target);
        System.out.println("QFactored "+target+" in "+f+ " and "+target/f);
    }
```

The only real work in this method is the invocation of the `Classic.qfactor` API. The `qfactor` method in Strange returns a factor of the supplied integer. This single factor allows us to calculate the other factor as well. For example, if we ask for a factor of the integer 15 and the value 3 is returned, we know that 5 is another factor, as it equals 15/3.

The `qfactor` method uses classical computing for the preprocessing and post-processing steps, similar to what we did in the previous section. But the `findPeriod` method is implemented very differently in this approach. In our mental model, we are about to discuss the third approach, as shown in figure 11.10.

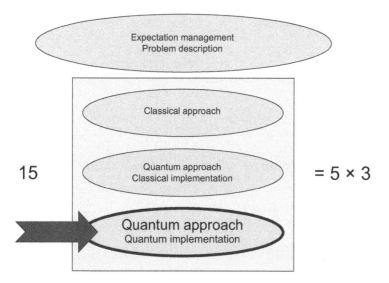

Figure 11.10   Mental model: quantum implementation of the quantum approach. In this approach, the preprocessing and post-processing are done in a classic way, but the period finding is done using a quantum algorithm.

The implementation of `Classic.qfactor` can be found in the source code of Strange, but it is extremely similar to the code snippet shown in listing 11.2. The only difference is the implementation of the `findPeriod` method. In the following, we explain how this method is implemented in Strange using a quantum algorithm.

From the code snippet in listing 11.2, the challenge we are facing is to find the periodicity of the following function:

$$f = a^x \mod N$$

Instead of calling the classical function `findPeriod` shown in listing 11.3, we now use the quantum implementation, which can be found in `Classic.findPeriod (int a, int mod)`. Note that the signature of this method is exactly the same as the one containing the classical implementation.

The general trick that we apply again here is the following: we try to evaluate the function for all integers between 0 and *N* at once by creating a superposition state and then manipulate the system so that when we measure the result, a useful value is obtained.

We split that challenge into two issues:

- Create a periodic function, and perform a measurement.
- Calculate the periodicity based on a measurement.

Schematically, the flow for this is shown in figure 11.11.

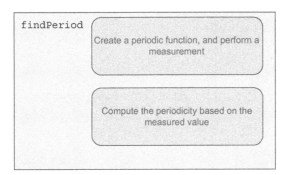

Figure 11.11 High-level flow for period finding in Shor's algorithm

The first part (creating the periodic function and performing a measurement) is done with quantum code, and the second part is done using classic code only. The implementation of the `findPeriod` function illustrates this approach:

```
public static int findPeriod(int a, int mod) {
       int p = 0;
       while (p == 0) {
           p = measurePeriod(a, mod);
       }
       int period = Computations.fraction(p, mod);
       return period;
   }
```

Prepares the periodic function and does a measurement

Uses the measured value to compute the periodicity

Note that the first part may not return a useful result. In that case, the `measurePeriod` function returns 0, and the function is invoked again.

The heavy lifting of Shor's algorithm is done in the first part. We discuss it now, combining almost everything we have learned previously.

11.8 Creating a periodic function using quantum gates

As we said before, we won't go into the mathematical details that prove the correctness of Shor's algorithm. In this section, we give an intuitive approach that explains why the approach works.

11.8.1 The flow and circuit

This part of the algorithm also contains various steps. We highlight those steps by showing the flow of the algorithm, the quantum circuit that realizes each step, and the code, and we discuss the different steps in a bit more detail.

The flow for creating the periodic function is shown in figure 11.12. Since this part is done using a quantum algorithm, a quantum circuit is involved; see figure 11.13.

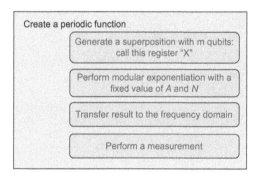

Figure 11.12   Flow for creating a periodic function

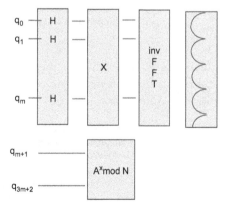

Figure 11.13   Quantum circuit that creates a periodic function

The qubits involved in this schema are divided into two *registers*, where a register is just a set of qubits that together have a conceptual meaning. The top register is called the *input register*, and the bottom register is called the *ancilla register*. The code for creating the periodic function and making a measurement is shown next. Keep in mind that Strange is under active development, and the implementation is subject to change. Hence, the code you see here in the book might be different from the code you will find in Strange, or in the samples.

```
private static int measurePeriod(int a, int mod) {        ◁──┐  Creates a periodic
    int length = (int) Math.ceil                                function a^x % mod and
                    (Math.log(mod) / Math.log(2));              returns a measurement
    int offset = length + 1;
    Program p = new Program(2 * length + 3 + offset);
    Step prep = new Step();
    for (int i = 0; i < offset; i++) {                          This step creates a
        prep.addGate(new Hadamard(i));        ◁──────────────  superposition over the
    }                                                           first qubit register.
    Step prepAnc = new Step(new X(length +1 + offset));
    p.addStep(prep);
    p.addStep(prepAnc);
    for (int i = length - 1;                                    This step adds to the
            i > length - 1 - offset; i--) {    ◁──             ancilla register the gates
        int m = 1;                                              for performing modular
        for (int j = 0; j < 1 << i; j++) {                      exponentiation.
            m = m * a % mod;
        }
        MulModulus mul =
            new MulModulus(length, 2 * length, m, mod);
        ControlledBlockGate cbg =
            new ControlledBlockGate(mul, offset, i);
        p.addStep(new Step(cbg));                               Transforms the first
    }                                                           register into the
    p.addStep(new Step(new InvFourier(offset, 0)));   ◁──      frequency domain
    System.err.println("Calculate periodicity");
    Result result = qee.runProgram(p);
    Qubit[] q = result.getQubits();
    int answer = 0;
    for (int i = 0; i < offset; i++) {                          Measures the
        answer = answer + q[i].measure()*(1<< i);  ◁──        first register
    }
    return answer;
}
```

11.8.2 The steps

In this section, we briefly discuss the steps that are executed in the measurePeriod function.

CREATING A SUPERPOSITION

We first apply a Hadamard gate to each qubit in the input register. This brings the input register into a superposition, and the upcoming calculations can thus be done with a combination of all possible values that the input register can contain.

This can't be done on a classical computer, and it is an intuitive indication of why a quantum computer can handle this problem much faster. However, keep in mind that even though we can create a superposition of all possible values, we can only make a single measurement on the system. Hence, we need to apply some smart steps so the single measurement we obtain is actually useful.

PERFORMING MODULAR EXPONENTIATION

Next, the input register is used to calculate the modular exponentiation $a^x \mod N$, and that result is computed and stored in the ancilla register. As a consequence of this operation, the input register is now a periodic function with periodicity r, where r is the periodicity of $a^x \mod N$.

This is interesting, as we now have a periodic function. However, we can only make a single measurement, and regardless of what we measured, we would not get much information about the periodicity of the function.

APPLYING AN INVERSE QUANTUM FOURIER TRANSFORM

By applying an inverse quantum Fourier transform, the periodic function is transformed into a function with peaks at specific "frequencies." It can be proven that the probability vector has exactly r peaks, where the first peak occurs at the value $|0\rangle$ and the other peaks are evenly spread. After this, the probability matrix has several peaks, as shown in figure 11.14.

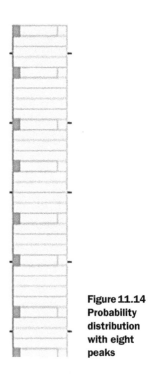

> **NOTE** It can be proven that the period of the function we created equals the number of peaks after applying an inverse quantum Fourier transform. This is a key element in Shor's algorithm.

Since we are interested in finding the period of the function, we need to be able to count the number of peaks. But how do we do that? We can only make a single measurement. Does that allow us to determine the number of peaks (hence the periodicity of the function)? As we explain in the next section, there is a reasonable chance that a single measurement will indeed lead to this.

**Figure 11.14
Probability
distribution
with eight
peaks**

11.9 *Calculating the periodicity*

If we could measure the probability vector, we would be able to count how many peaks it has. Unfortunately, we can't do that. We can only measure the qubits, and a single measurement corresponds to a single entry in the probability vector. The previous step, creating the periodic function and making a measurement, resulted in a single value only. That value is not the periodicity of the function, but it reveals enough information that we can hopefully deduce the periodicity.

By looking at the probability distribution in figure 11.14, we know that there is a very high chance that the entry we measure is in one of the peaks of the probability vector. Based on that information, it is possible to determine the number of peaks with a high probability.

We use the continued fraction expansion algorithm to do this. The algorithm takes the measured value as input, along with the maximum value of the answer, and returns the periodicity. This algorithm is implemented in `Computations`, and its signature is

```
public static int fraction (double d, int max);
```

In this algorithm, `d` is the measured value divided by the maximum value, so it is a value between 0 and 1, and `max` is the maximum number that can be returned. Based on the knowledge that the measured value is on or near a peak in the probability distribution, the result of this algorithm returns the number of peaks in the probability distribution.

We may have bad luck, for example, if the measured value is on the first peak, which is at the value 0. In that case, we cannot find any information about the periodicity, and we have to redo the experiment. That means we have to execute the quantum algorithm again. But even if we have to redo this experiment several times, the algorithm's complexity doesn't change. It would be worse if the chances of measuring 0 increased with the number of qubits, but that is not the case.

Now that we know the periodicity, the factors of the original number can be computed in the exact same way as in the semi-quantum approach, as illustrated in listing 11.2. We can now continue the algorithm from the POSTPROCESSING step to calculate and print the factors.

> **NOTE** Congratulations—you managed to apply Shor's algorithm to factor an integer! It is important to keep in mind that only a portion of the algorithm is done with a quantum algorithm, but it is precisely that part that drastically speeds up the total computation time.

11.10 *Implementation challenges*

Shor's algorithm relies heavily on modular exponentiation. While this may look like just an implementation detail, it is actually a significant challenge.

Mathematical operations on a quantum computer are not trivial to implement, since all gates need to be reversible, as we explained previously. For example, an addition operation in a classical circuit could be implemented as shown in figure 11.15. The inputs to this gate are two values x and y, which are probably bits, and the output is a single value, $x + y$.

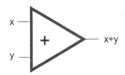

Figure 11.15 Classic addition operation

This won't work in the quantum world, as there is no way to go from $x + y$ back to x and y. For example, if $x + y = 1$, we don't know if x was 0 and y was 1 or if, on the other hand, y was 0 and x was 1. Therefore, a quantum adder gate is implemented, as shown in figure 11.16.

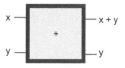

Figure 11.16   Quantum addition operation

The result of this gate keeps the original y value, so based on $x + y$ and y, it is possible to obtain the original x value. Hence, this gate has an inverse gate that brings back the original state. We discussed the quantum adder gate in Chapter 7, so if you want a refresher on the details of how it works, you can read it there.

The addition gate is the basis for the multiplication gate, which in turn is the basis for the exponential gate. Adding to the complexity is the modular aspect of the arithmetic operations. If we want to create a circuit for modular exponentiation, we need to be able to perform modular multiplication, which means we must be able to perform modular addition.

While there is no direct advantage in doing basic arithmetic operations on a quantum computer, it is important to realize that those operations are available. For example, as you just learned, Shor's algorithm depends heavily on modular exponentiation. Modular exponentiation requires modular multiplication, which requires modular addition, which in turn requires regular addition, which is what we showed here.

So, if you need those operations in your own algorithms, you can use the arithmetic operations in the `org.redfx.strange.gate` package. That way, your algorithms can use quantum arithmetic operations using the Strange simulator, but the same algorithm will also work on a real quantum computer, when and if one is available.

Summary

- Finding the factors of an integer is a very popular challenge in a number of IT domains.
- Using a classical approach requires an exponential amount of time when the target (the integer that needs to be factored) becomes larger.
- The goal of Shor's algorithm is to find the factors of an integer.
- Shor's algorithm shows that it can be beneficial to transform a specific problem into another problem: one that can be solved more easily (faster) by a quantum computer. In particular, Shor's algorithm transforms the problem of factorization into the problem of finding the periodicity of a periodic function.

appendix A
Getting started
with Strange

A.1   Requirements

Strange is a modular Java library that uses the module concepts introduced in Java 11. To run applications using Strange, you need the Java 11 runtime or higher. Developing applications requires the Java 11 or higher SDK to be installed, which also includes the Java 11 runtime. You can download the Java SDK from http://jdk.java.net. We recommend selecting the latest "ready for use" version (e.g., JDK 17).

> **NOTE**   The Java release cycle is very predictable. Every six months, a new major version is released. In September 2021, JDK 17 was released. In March 2022, JDK 18 will be released. Depending on the current date, it is easy to detect what the latest Java release version is.

If you want to know what version of Java you are using, you can pass the -version parameter to the java command. You will see something similar to the following:

```
java -version
openjdk version "15" 2020-09-15
OpenJDK Runtime Environment (build 15+36-1562)
OpenJDK 64-Bit Server VM (build 15+36-1562, mixed mode, sharing)
```

This shows that we are currently using Java 15.

> **TIP**   Be sure to download the version that matches your platform (e.g. Linux, macOS, or Windows).

Most Java developers use an integrated development environment (IDE) to create Java applications. The most common IDEs for Java development are Eclipse, Apache

NetBeans, and IntelliJ IDEA. Strange is a modular Java library that follows the same rules and conventions as any other Java library, so it can be used out of the box on those IDEs, since they provide support for the Java modular system.

> **NOTE** If there are different versions of your favorite IDE available, be sure to select a version that uses Java 11 at minimum.

Instead of an IDE, some developers prefer to use command-line tools to create, maintain, and execute applications. Those applications typically use a build tool like Maven or Gradle, and dependencies are declared in specific files: e.g., a pom.xml file for Maven or a build.gradle file for Gradle.

All IDEs provide support for Maven and Gradle. We assume that you are familiar with how your IDE supports Maven or Gradle, and we use command-line-driven Maven or Gradle projects for our examples. You have the choice to run the examples either using the command-line approach or in your favorite IDE, using the IDE-specific Maven and Gradle integration.

A.2   *Obtaining and installing the demo code*

The examples and demos in this book are available in a Git repository located at https://github.com/johanvos/quantumjava. You can get a local copy of the examples by cloning the repository via command-line `git` commands, such as

```
git clone https://github.com/johanvos/quantumjava.git
```

or via the Git support offered by your favorite IDE.

Cloning the repository creates a directory called quantumjava on your local filesystem. You will notice that this directory contains subdirectories that correspond to the chapters of this book. Please note that the code in those samples is subject to changes and improvements. Also, when there are changes in the Strange library, this might require changes in the demo code as well. However, the code at the time of writing this will still be available if you want to check that out. The README instructions in the GitHub repository explain what to do if this is the case.

A.3   *The HelloStrange program*

The ch02 directory contains the examples used in chapter 2. The first example we run is in hellostrange. Like all the other examples, this one can be opened in your favorite IDE. As discussed earlier, we use the Maven and Gradle command-line approach in this book. However, if you prefer to run the examples from your IDE, that should work equally well.

Running the program

All the examples in this book can be executed using Maven or using Gradle. A build tool like Maven or Gradle makes it easier to compile and run applications and also takes care of any dependencies your code has. This happens in a transitive approach:

if your code depends on other code that depends on still other code, all the required code will be downloaded and processed by the build tools.

USING MAVEN

Maven is a very stable build tool. With the latest version of Maven, you can compile and run all the examples in this book, and we expect that future versions of Java will keep working with the current versions of Maven. Therefore, it is recommended that you install Maven. The instructions at https://maven.apache.org are self-explanatory.

Once Maven is installed, you can use the mvn command on the command line. If you are using an IDE, it is very likely to have built-in integration for Maven. In that case, you can simply open every example as a project in your IDE and follow the typical flow.

You can run the examples from the command line by going to the directory that contains the example you want to run and entering

```
mvn clean javafx:run
```

For example, if you do this in the directory ch02/hellostrange, you will see the following output:

```
[INFO] Scanning for projects...
[INFO]
[INFO] ------------------------------------------------------------------
[INFO] Building hellostrange 1.0-SNAPSHOT
[INFO] ------------------------------------------------------------------
[INFO]
[INFO] --- maven-clean-plugin:2.5:clean (default-clean) @ helloquantum ---
[INFO] Deleting /home/johan/quantumcomputing/manning/public/quantumjava/ch02
    /hellostrange/target
[INFO]
[INFO] >>> javafx-maven-plugin:0.0.7:run (default-cli) > process-classes @
    helloquantum >>>
[INFO]
[INFO] --- maven-resources-plugin:2.6:resources (default-resources) @
    helloquantum ---
[INFO] Using 'UTF-8' encoding to copy filtered resources.
[INFO]
[INFO] --- maven-compiler-plugin:3.1:compile (default-compile)@helloquantum
[INFO] Changes detected - recompiling the module!
[INFO] Compiling 1 source file ...
[INFO]
[INFO] <<< javafx-maven-plugin:0.0.4:run (default-cli) < process-classes @
    helloquantum <<<
[INFO]
[INFO] --- javafx-maven-plugin:0.0.4:run (default-cli) @ helloquantum ---
Using high-level Strange API to generate random bits
----------------------------------------------------
Generate one random bit, which can be 0 or 1. Result = 1
Generated 10000 random bits, 5085 of them were 0, and 4915 were 1.
[INFO] ------------------------------------------------------------------
[INFO] BUILD SUCCESS
```

```
[INFO] ------------------------------------------------------------------------
[INFO] Total time: 2.389 s
[INFO] Finished at: 2020-10-11T17:02:58+02:00
[INFO] Final Memory: 14M/54M
[INFO] ------------------------------------------------------------------------
```

As you can see, the output from our application is surrounded by informational messages from Maven. If you don't want to see them, you can add the -q option to the mvn command, which tells Maven to be quiet about its own operations. For example, the command

```
mvn -q clean javafx:run
```

returns the following output:

```
Using high-level Strange API to generate random bits
---------------------------------------------------
Generate one random bit, which can be 0 or 1. Result = 1
Generated 10000 random bits, 4983 of them were 0, and 5017 were 1.
```

USING GRADLE

All the examples contain wrapper scripts that first check whether the correct Gradle version is already installed on the system. If this is not the case, the wrapper script will automatically download and install the required version of Gradle.

If you are using Linux or macOS, the Gradle wrapper script is invoked using

```
./gradlew
```

If you are using Windows, the Gradle wrapper script should be invoked via

```
gradlew.bat
```

Running the hellostrange demo application is very simple and straightforward. The only thing you have to do is invoke the gradle run task. To avoid duplicating Gradle binaries, there is a single Gradle build file in the root directory of the examples (which contains all the chapters as subdirectories). You can run any example by specifying the chapter and the example name to the Gradle command. On Linux and macOS, this is done by calling

```
./gradlew ch2:hellostrange:run
```

And on Windows, this is achieved using

```
gradlew.bat ch2:hellostrange:run
```

The result of this action depends on whether you already have the required Gradle version. If you do, the output will look similar to this:

```
To honour the JVM settings for this build a new JVM will be forked. Please
    consider using the daemon: https://docs.gradle.org/6.5/userguide/
    gradle_daemon.html.
Daemon will be stopped at the end of the build stopping after processing

> Task :run
Using high-level Strange API to generate random bits
--------------------------------------------------
Generate one random bit, which can be 0 or 1. Result = 1
Generated 10000 random bits, 4960 of them were 0, and 5040 were 1.

Deprecated Gradle features were used in this build, making it incompatible
    with Gradle 7.0.
Use '--warning-mode all' to show the individual deprecation warnings.
See https://docs.gradle.org/6.5/userguide/
    command_line_interface.html#sec:command_line_warnings
```

Similar to with the Maven case, you can suppress the output about Gradle by specifying the -q parameter

```
./gradlew -q run
```

in which case the output will look as follows:

```
Using high-level Strange API to generate random bits
--------------------------------------------------
Generate one random bit, which can be 0 or 1. Result = 1
Generated 10000 random bits, 5039 of them were 0, and 4961 were 1.
```

Developers using the Strange APIs can benefit from quantum computing without having to deal with linear algebra. If you want to understand what is going on under the hood, some basic knowledge of linear algebra is required. Throughout this book, we try to minimize the dependencies on linear algebra. The computations we use fall into three categories: matrix-vector multiplication, matrix-matrix multiplication, and tensor multiplication. By no means should this appendix be considered an introduction to linear algebra; we simply explain matrix-vector multiplication, matrix-matrix multiplication, and tensor multiplication, as you may be interested in validating the results of your quantum circuits.

B.1   *Matrix-vector multiplication*

A quantum gate can be represented as a matrix that is acting on the input quantum state, represented as a vector. The resulting quantum state is a vector, defined as the product of the gate matrix and the input state vector. This is written as $y = Ax$, where x is the input state vector, A is the matrix representing the gate, and y is the resulting vector.

In the following explanation, we do not take quantum restrictions into account. As you learn in the book, the quantum state vectors need to follow some rules (e.g., the sum of the square of the individual elements should equal 1); but to explain matrix-vector multiplication, we ignore this restriction.

A simple example is the following situation:

$$x = \begin{bmatrix} 1 \\ 2 \end{bmatrix}$$

$$A = \begin{pmatrix} 1 & 0 \\ -3 & 4 \end{pmatrix}$$

The resulting vector *y* is obtained as follows: vector *y* contains *n* elements, where *n* is the size of vector *x*. We denote y_i to be the *i*th element of vector *y*. The value of y_i is calculated by multiplying each element of row *i* of matrix *A* by the corresponding element in vector *x* and summing the results. This is shown in figure B.1.

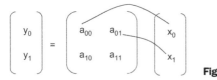

Figure B.1   Matrix-vector multiplication

This leads to the following result:

$$y_0 = a_{00}x_0 + a_{01}x_1 = 1 * 1 + 0 * 2 = 1$$

$$y_1 = a_{10}x_0 + a_{11}x_1 = -3 * 1 + 4 * 2 = 5$$

Hence,

$$y = \begin{bmatrix} 1 \\ 5 \end{bmatrix}$$

B.2   *Matrix-matrix multiplication*

The principle of matrix-vector multiplication can be expanded to matrix-matrix multiplication. We limit ourselves here to square matrices with an equal number of rows and columns.

The multiplication of two matrices *A* and *B*, each with *m* rows and *m* columns, results in a new matrix *C*, with *m* rows and *m* columns. Each element c_{ij} of matrix *C* is obtained by multiplying each element in row *i* of matrix *A* with the corresponding element in row *j* of matrix *B* and summing the results. This is shown in figure B.2.

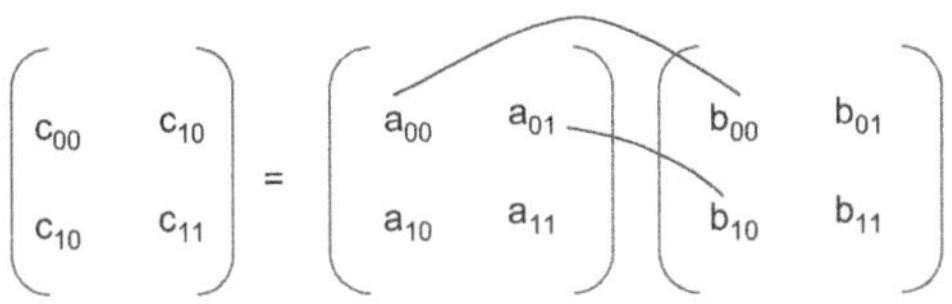

$$\begin{pmatrix} c_{00} & c_{10} \\ c_{10} & c_{11} \end{pmatrix} = \begin{pmatrix} a_{00} & a_{01} \\ a_{10} & a_{11} \end{pmatrix} \begin{pmatrix} b_{00} & b_{01} \\ b_{10} & b_{11} \end{pmatrix}$$

Figure B.2   Matrix-matrix multiplication

Let's create a simple example. Suppose we have the following two-by-two matrices *A* and *B*:

$$A = \begin{pmatrix} 1 & 2 \\ 0 & -3 \end{pmatrix}$$

$$B = \begin{pmatrix} -2 & 2 \\ 1 & -2 \end{pmatrix}$$

The top-left element of the resulting matrix C, which is c_{00}, is obtained by multiplying each element of the first row of matrix A (row 0) with the corresponding element in the first column of matrix B (column 0). This results in the following:

$$c_{00} = a_{00}b_{00} + a_{01}b_{10} = 1 * (-2) + 2 * 1 = 0$$

A good exercise is to compute the other elements of the matrix. If you do this correctly, you will find the following matrix C:

$$y = \begin{pmatrix} 0 & -2 \\ -3 & 6 \end{pmatrix}$$

B.3   *Tensor product*

The tensor product of two matrices combines both matrices. Suppose we have a matrix A with k rows and l columns and a matrix B with m rows and n columns. The tensor product of A and B is a new matrix C with $k \times m$ rows and $l \times n$ columns.

Every element in matrix A is replaced in a matrix where the given element in A is multiplied with the matrix in B. This explains why the dimensions of the new matrix are the product of the dimensions of the original matrices. Schematically, this is shown in figure B.3 for two 2×2 matrices.

$$\begin{pmatrix} a_{00} & a_{01} \\ a_{10} & a_{11} \end{pmatrix} \otimes \begin{pmatrix} b_{00} & b_{01} \\ b_{10} & b_{11} \end{pmatrix} = \begin{pmatrix} a_{00}[B] & a_{01}[B] \\ a_{10}[B] & a_{11}[B] \end{pmatrix}$$

$$= \begin{pmatrix} a_{00}b_{00} & a_{00}b_{01} & a_{01}b_{00} & a_{01}b_{01} \\ a_{00}b_{10} & a_{00}b_{11} & a_{01}b_{10} & a_{01}b_{11} \\ a_{10}b_{00} & a_{10}b_{01} & a_{11}b_{00} & a_{11}b_{01} \\ a_{10}b_{10} & a_{10}b_{11} & a_{11}b_{10} & a_{11}b_{11} \end{pmatrix}$$

Figure B.3   Matrix-matrix tensor multiplication

As an example, we will calculate the tensor product of two vectors. The first vector has three elements, and the second vector has two elements. Hence, the result will be another vector (as both source vectors have one column and the product of $1 \times 1 = 1$) with six elements (as $3 \times 2 = 6$).

The original vectors are

$$a = \begin{bmatrix} 2 \\ 3 \end{bmatrix}$$

and

$$b = \begin{bmatrix} -1 \\ 0 \\ 2 \end{bmatrix}$$

The tensor product is thus

$$a \otimes b = \begin{bmatrix} 2 \begin{bmatrix} -1 \\ 0 \\ 2 \end{bmatrix} \\ 3 \begin{bmatrix} -1 \\ 0 \\ 2 \end{bmatrix} \end{bmatrix} = \begin{bmatrix} -2 \\ 0 \\ 4 \\ -3 \\ 0 \\ 6 \end{bmatrix}$$

index